Laslo

FIELD BOOK OF
COMMON MUSHROOMS

PLATE I. M

38

1 inch

Mary E. Eaton

FIELD BOOK OF
COMMON MUSHROOMS

*With a Key to Identification of the Gilled
Mushrooms and Directions for
Cooking Those that are
Edible*

By

WILLIAM STURGIS THOMAS, M.D.

LATE PRESIDENT, NEW YORK MYCOLOGICAL SOCIETY

MEMBER, NEW YORK BOTANICAL GARDEN,
TORREY BOTANICAL CLUB

FELLOW, NEW YORK ACADEMY OF MEDICINE

New and enlarged Third Edition

*With 93 species in Color and numerous
Black and White illustrations*

G. P. PUTNAM'S SONS
NEW YORK—LONDON

FIELD BOOK OF COMMON MUSHROOMS

⌣

TO MY SON

WILLIAM STEPHEN THOMAS

PREFACE TO THIRD EDITION

For twenty years this book has met an otherwise unfilled need in the realm of popular natural history. There is no other handy-sized volume which presents such a comprehensive group of descriptions of common mushrooms. A great many of these the layman is apt to find within easy range of his trips afield in the northern hemisphere. The simple, non-technical key for ready identification and the high quality of the colored reproductions of Miss Mary E. Eaton's illustrations are important features of the volume.

The text of this Third Edition has been scrutinized for accuracy in the light of new scientific knowledge. In addition, Dr. Donald P. Rogers, Curator of the New York Botanical Garden has kindly checked the scientific nomenclature and his valuable aid is gratefully acknowledged. Other persons who have assisted in preparing this new edition either by giving advice or in lending encouragement include: Dr. Carroll W. Dodge, mycologist of the Missouri Botanical Garden, Dr. Fred. B. Seaver, N. Y. Botanical Garden, Dr. Alexander H. Smith of the University Herbarium, University of Michigan, Dr. Gertrude S. Burlingham of Winter Park, Florida, Mr. John A. Stevenson, mycologist in charge, Mycology and Disease Survey, Bureau of Plant Industry, Beltsville, Maryland, Dr. Leo Tanghe of Rochester, N. Y., and my wife, Katharine Cornish Thomas.

Dr. William Sturgis Thomas (1871-1941), the author of this *Field Book,* was a busy physician who practiced in New York City for almost fifty years and made the study of wild mushrooms a consuming hobby though he balanced it with other diversions arising from his many skills and deep curiosity about man and the world of nature. After a few years of surgical and general practice, Dr. Thomas became a specialist in the field of allergy and director of the Department of Allergy of St. Luke's Hospital, New York. During both the Spanish-American War and World War I he saw active service at sea as a naval medical officer. Five books and fifty articles in such diverse fields as botany, camping, fly-fishing, medicine and American history bear witness to his industry as an author and his range of interests. His self-acquired knowledge of Greek and Latin was supplemented by conversational ability in German and a fair fluency in French which he acquired after he was fifty. He was an excellent carpenter and mechanic and at various times indulged spare moments in fine wood-carving. He played the flute avidly and practiced an hour or more daily the last twenty years of his life. At the age of seventy he was a participating member of two amateur orchestras.

Doctor Thomas began to take active interest in mushrooms in 1909 and it was not long before he became remarkably well versed in the fungus flora in and around New York City. His zest for collecting trips was a natural outgrowth of his love of nature which he also manifested as an ardent hiker, camper and fisherman. He inquired thoroughly into the edibility of fungi and tested personally all the recipes for cooking them which are included in the ensuing pages. In pursuing his hobby of mushrooms he saw that there were exceedingly few popular books on the subject. He compiled the present guide as a labor of love, not because he felt he had knowledge which needed to be imparted but because he wished others to share his interest and to be helped and not frustrated by scientific technicalities. While studying fungi for his own pleasure my father devised the non-technical key of this book (see Chapter VI) which enables the user to identify gilled mushrooms by any one or a combination of several of nineteen characteristics. The author of the *Field Book* had an infectuous enthusiasm which he imparted to others and it was natural he should be popular as leader for

PREFACE

many field trips such as those sponsored by the Torrey Botanical Club. Around him grew a coterie of amateur naturalists who founded the New York Mycological Society in the early thirties and chose him as their first president.

W. STEPHEN THOMAS

Rochester Museum of Arts and Sciences,
Rochester, N. Y.
June 30, 1948

PREFACE TO SECOND EDITION

The first edition of this book dealt solely with common gilled mushrooms because they constitute the greater portion of all fungi encountered in woods and fields. In this second edition attention is given also to some of the common mushrooms other than those with gills. One or more representatives of several kinds are described and are accompanied by illustrations. It is thought that the usefulness of the book will thus be enhanced.

The illustrations of the non-agaric mushrooms were made by Mr. Robert Snedigar of the staff of the American Museum of Natural History.

PREFACE TO FIRST EDITION

This book is designed to assist persons who are interested in mushrooms in identifying some of the species of gilled fungi found growing in fields, woods and dooryards. It aims to supply the need for a means of ascertaining the names of common kinds that are new to the collector. The name of a fungus is not the vital thing but it is the first thing to be learned if one would wish to talk about it with other persons and read about it.

The method of the key is new, I believe, and its preparation has occupied some of an amateur mycologist's spare time during the past ten years or more. The reader is advised to read the introduction to the key before using it.

One portion of the book comprises descriptions of the mushrooms and they are arranged and numbered alphabetically according to their botanical names. The numbers agree with those of the illustrations of species. The one hundred and twenty-eight species keyed, described and illustrated include nearly all of the agarics called common in the writings of the late Professor Charles H. Peck, State Botanist of New York.

The directions for cooking mushrooms have been derived from the writings of many authorities and from my own experience during the past eighteen years.

In an article on the poisonous properties of fungi by William W. Ford and Ernest D. Clark of Johns Hopkins University and published in *Mycologia*, the following warning appears: "Unfortunately there are mushroom 'handbooks' in this country which are unfailing sources of misinformation and they have evidently been written by people of no training and poor judgment." I desire to state in this connection that the descriptions and statements herein contained adhere strictly to the authoritative writings of Professor Peck, Dr. W. A. Murrill, the late Professor C. F. Atkinson of Cornell University and Professor C. H. Kauffman of the University of Michigan.

I consider myself fortunate in being able to offer to readers the original colored plates which were painted by Miss Mary E. Eaton, Artist to the New York Botanical Garden.

Dr. N. L. Britton, Director of the New York Botanical Garden, has given encouragement and co-operation which is gratefully acknowledged. Thanks are also due to Dr. M. A. Howe, Assistant Director of the Garden, for his kind assistance in paving the way for the preparation of this little book. Acknowledgment is also made to George S. Godard, State Librarian of Connecticut and to C. J. Calpin, Ph.D., of the U. S. Department of Agriculture, for their courtesy in permitting me to use some of the half-tones in this book. Dr. Howard A. Kelly of Baltimore has favored me with his interest and valuable suggestions.

FOREWORD

Here is a handbook which, as the name indicates, treats of the common gilled mushrooms, and one would have to tramp the fields and woods many a day throughout the season to find all the species figured and described herein. It is of pocket size and therefore truly a field book.

Doctor Thomas has brought together in condensed and usable form descriptions of 128 species, compiled from Peck, Murrill, Atkinson, Kauffman, and other recognized authorities, in many cases from publications now out of print. Although the author makes no statements not to be found in authoritative works, it was only possible for this material to be gathered and stated clearly and concisely, because of the many years of first-hand experience he has had with these fascinating plants in their native haunts.

The analytical and yet non-technical key, based upon the striking, easily observed features of the mushrooms, is original and one of the most valuable features of the book. The seasonal key is also unique, and of especial value in the early and late months of the season. The key to genera is an extension of a good plan introduced by McIlvaine.

The beautiful colored plates by Miss Mary E. Eaton, the well known artist of the New York Botanical Garden, are most helpful, and to find an illustration of every species treated in the book is a feature that will win the hearty gratitude of all students.

CLYDE FISHER.

American Museum of Natural History,
New York.

CONTENTS

ILLUSTRATIONS IN COLOR

The above color plates depict 96 species of mushrooms.

ILLUSTRATIONS IN BLACK AND WHITE

xvii

ILLUSTRATIONS

ILLUSTRATIONS

ILLUSTRATIONS

FIELD BOOK OF
COMMON GILLED MUSHROOMS

————

CHAPTER I

HOW TO COLLECT AND EXAMINE MUSHROOMS

CHAPTER I

HOW TO COLLECT AND EXAMINE MUSHROOMS

Mushrooms of one kind or another are to be found at almost every season but they occur in greatest abundance after showery weather in the months of July, August and September.

The collector will find a basket to be a good receptacle for them and different species may be kept separate from each other and uncrushed by having leaves or leafy twigs among them, or better yet, by being carried in paper bags. Folding paper boxes, such as are used for holding crackers are also good for this purpose.

The mushroom is plucked entire from the ground or wood upon which it grows and especial care must be taken not to cut or break the stem. Unless the whole plant is obtained it will be difficult or impossible to know whether the stem is provided with a volva or cup at the base, or whether its base is bulbous or hairy or attached to other stems. The dirt adhering to the stem, if there is any, is removed before the specimen is put with others into the receptacle. In collecting mushrooms for the table, the stems are cut off close to the cap.

The beginner is warned against attempting to identify a new species with but one or two specimens at hand. It is desirable to have for this purpose several specimens of varied stages of development, so that one or more of them may be cut across in order that the form of the gills and interior of the stem may be noted, while yet other caps may be needed for spore prints. It is important to keep separate from each other the specimens of the various species collected.

FIELD BOOK OF COMMON GILLED MUSHROOMS

On arriving at home with the collected fungi, they should be spread out on a convenient surface, the collector remembering the liability of many species to decay quickly.

No single feature of any mushroom is sufficient to determine its identity or its edibility. It cannot be too often emphasized that the only certain way in which a mushroom may be identified is to know it thoroughly. Once its personality is established in the collector's mind, he will recognize it as he would the face of a friend.

There are other characters than general shape and color which distinguish mushrooms from each other. These other characters need careful scrutiny in determining the species to which a specimen belongs as is the case among many things met with in our everyday affairs. Careful attention to the especial characters and parts of mushrooms will soon familiarize one with their peculiarities and will enable him to use this guide or any text book on mushrooms intelligently. To this end the student of mushrooms will do well to make written notes of the features of gilled fungi collected by him, using as a guide the form for field notes which will be found on page 24.

Spore prints of mushrooms show the color of the spores and are sometimes indispensable before a specimen can be unmistakably identified. In many instances however, specimens can be identified by means of this key in the field or at home without waiting for the making of spore prints.

Spore prints are made by laying the mature cap from which the stem has been cut and gills downward upon a piece of paper. It is protected from draughts of air by being covered with a glass tumbler. In order to get satisfactory prints, care should be taken to have the gills in a vertical position. After a few hours a print of the gills, radiating from the center like the spokes of a wheel, will be found upon the paper.(Fig 1.) The color of the spore print assists in determining to what family of mushrooms the specimen belongs. There are five of these

FIG. I.

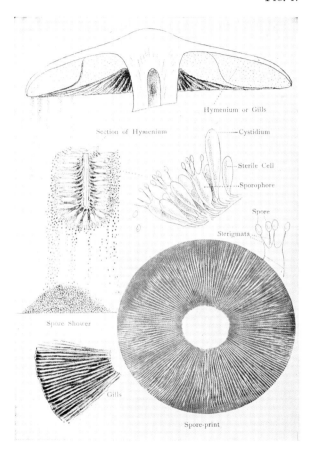

Hymenium or Gills

Section of Hymenium

Cystidium

Sterile Cell

Sporophore

Spore

Sterigmata

Spore Shower

Gills

Spore-print

FIG. I.—Spore print and magnified representation of the parts of a gilled mushroom concerned in spore formation.

From W. Hamilton Gibson's *Our Edible Mushrooms*, by permission of Messrs. Harper and Bros.

families, each of whose spores are respectively either white, some shade of pink, rusty-brown, purple or black. Odd species vary from these standard spore colors in having lilac and green hues.

CHAPTER II

GILLED MUSHROOMS, THEIR PROPAGATION AND STRUCTURE

CHAPTER II

Gilled mushrooms, or agarics as they are called, are plants that belong to the botanical group known as fungi. No leaves, flowers, pollen or seeds are to be found on any fungi and that is, perhaps, why they are regarded as belonging to a lower order of vegetation.

These plants, although rather unfamiliar to many persons, occur in profusion in one form or another, throughout the natural world. Among them are included germs or bacteria which cause fevers and contagious diseases in man and in the lower animals. Other fungi that grow upon the higher plants, occur in endless numbers and constitute pests that damage or destroy food crops and trees. Some of them are known as rusts, others as smuts, rots, scabs and bunts. Mildews and molds also belong among the fungi as do all the yeasts with their mysterious power of bringing about the process of fermentation.

Among the fungi commonly known as mushrooms are the puffballs, club fungi, coral fungi, hedgehog fungi, truffles, trembling fungi, morels, stinkhorns, tube-bearing fungi and lastly, the gilled fungi or agarics to which attention is directed in this book. All fungi, whether bacteria, yeasts or agarics, have in common an important characteristic feature that distinguishes them from the higher plants, and that is their lack of chlorophyl. This remarkable substance that makes green the leaves of trees and herbs, also enables them to utilize for their nutrition the simple elements of air, water and earth. Fungi, on the other hand, possessing no chlorophyl, must, like animals, depend for their nourishment upon living or dead organic matter. Loam, decaying wood and dead leaves support the majority of mushrooms.

Propagation of gilled fungi

Herbs, trees and grasses—in fact all of the higher plants are propagated from seeds that have been fertilized by contact with dust-like particles of pollen shed by a parent plant of the same species. This fertilizing contact requires for its accomplishment the union of two elements,—male and female, pollen and ovum. Since mushrooms are apparently devoid of these sexual elements, so far as cross fertilization of seeds is concerned, the question arises, how are they propagated. In the case of mushrooms, the method of propagation, though more simple than it is in the case of seed bearing plants is no less wonderful. Each species of mushroom reproduces its own kind by means of very minute spores that are dropped from mature fruiting plants and that are seemingly, in many cases formed without the intervention of any sexual process.

Single spores consist of a tiny bit of living matter or protoplasm enclosed within a wall or membrane, as an egg is contained in its shell. They are so small that one of them alone cannot be seen without the aid of a microscope but in mass they appear as dust that may have any one of several colors. Spore color affords an important means of classifying gilled fungi into groups or genera. The manner of collecting spores is described on page 4. They are exceedingly light and may be carried by the wind for long distances. They are dropped from the surfaces of the gills in vast numbers. A single mushroom of the cultivated variety commonly sold in the markets, may produce as many as one billion, eight hundred thousand spores. The shaggy-mane mushroom has been estimated to cast off five billion or more spores from a single mature plant. The proportion of spores that reach places suitable to their

FIG. 2.

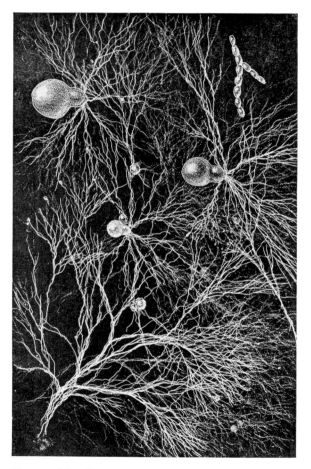

FIG. 2.—Mycelium and early vegetation of a gilled mushroom.

From W. Hamilton Gibson's *Our Edible Mushrooms*, by permission of Messrs. Harper and Bros.

development is very small; the vast majority of them are wasted. This fact illustrates the saying that Nature is careless of the individual, but careful of the species.

When a cast-off spore alights upon ground or decayed wood or on some other spot where conditions are favorable to its growth, it begins to germinate.

First, a tiny thread grows from it and penetrates the wood or loam upon which it rests. This thread, absorbing nourishment from organic matter in contact with it grows longer and sends out branches until a network of threads or fibres, now easily visible, is formed. This matted network of fibres or hyphæ, as they are called, is known to botanists as the mycelium or plant body. Those who cultivate mushrooms for the market speak of it as spawn. Weeks, months or even years, in some cases, must pass before the mycelium will grow and mature sufficiently for it to be ready to develop fruit that will in turn produce fresh spores.

When the proper time has arrived, little knots or enlargements appear at one or many places on the mycelial threads. These swellings increase in size until they project outside of the soil or wood in which they started to grow. Each one of these knobs is destined to develop into a full-grown mushroom or spore-bearing structure.

The Structure and Parts of Gilled Mushrooms

A fully developed, typical gilled mushroom is rather simple in its gross structure. It is formed somewhat after the manner of an umbrella and consists of three main parts corresponding to the cover, ribs and handle. In the mushroom, these parts are known as the cap, the gills and the stem, or as botanists designate them, pileus, lamellæ and stipe.

If a gilled mushroom in the button stage of its development be cut through in the middle from top to bottom, there will be seen, in embryo, cap gills and stem, all enclosed in an outer membrane or veil. The cap is folded and its gills lie close along the stem, giving somewhat the appearance of a closed umbrella. The outer or universal veil usually disappears as the plant grows larger and as the cap expands, but in some species part of it persists throughout the life of the plant in

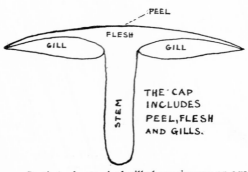

FIG. 3.—Section of a typical gilled mushroom or agaric.

the form of a sheath or cup enclosing the base of the stem. In other cases, part of the wrapper may be seen in the form of patches or flakes adhering to the upper surface of the mature cap. Both of these features may be seen in the fly mushroom or Amanita muscaria and they afford marks that help to identify that species.

Agarics, during the button stage of their existence are provided with another veil or membrane that extends from the stem to the margin of the cap. In some kinds of mushrooms this inner or secondary veil persists, at least in part, and by its presence aids in identification of the species possessing it. When this inner veil remains after the rupture or disappearance of the outer cover, it hides the gills from sight. (Pl. II, species 3). Sooner or later, during the growth of the plant, it breaks away from the edge of the cap as this expands or spreads open. In the case of most of the agarics, it disappears

PROPAGATION AND STRUCTURE

In addition to the foregoing general characters of gilled fungi that aid in their identification are the character, color and form of their separate parts. Each of these receives especial notice in the key.

Cap or pileus—The cap is the part of a gilled mushroom that first attracts the collector's attention. It is covered with a skin or peel beneath which is the flesh. This flesh or trama is composed of interwoven fibres called hyphæ that can be separately seen only under the microscope.

Amongst the characters of the caps of mushrooms, there is one possessed by some varieties that is apt to confuse the inexperienced collector. When moist, these particular caps have a water-soaked or soggy appearance. When dry they lose this look and become opaque and they often become lighter in shade. Such caps are said to be hygrophanous and this feature may aid in identifying them. The rind or peel, of many species, when moist from rain or humidity, is gelatinous or sticky to the touch. These are described as being viscid.

Color—While the color of mushrooms is one of their most striking characteristics, it is not so useful a clue in all cases as the beginner in their study is apt to believe. Certain species exhibit great variability of color in different individuals. Many kinds of mushrooms resemble each other in hue so closely that they must be identified by other qualities.

Form of Cap—There is the greatest variety in the shape of the cap of gilled mushrooms. Some species have conical caps (59[1]), some are bell-shaped (86), others flat (116) and yet others funnel-shaped (26). The cap of the majority of species is convex when it is young. As the plant matures the cap usually expands and becomes flat or even depressed at the center. The edge may be regular, lobed (10) or wavy (11).

---

[1] Figures in parentheses refer to numbers given to species in this book. They direct the reader to illustrations of the various characteristics mentioned.

The surface may be smooth, dry, sticky or perhaps covered with scales (38 Frontispiece).

If the cap has a knob protruding from its center it is said to be umbonate (15) (umbo—a knob). The opposite form, that of a little pit, sometimes occurs (93), in which case the cap is said to be umbilicate (provided with a navel).

Where no mention in this book is made of a mushroom's form, it is assumed that the cap is of a convex form when young and is plane or nearly so when mature. When reference is made to the cap of a mushroom, a mature specimen is meant unless otherwise specified.

Other features of caps are mentioned in the key under the heading, "Cap, Form of."

Gills—The gills (lamellæ) are thin, knife-like blades attached by their upper edge to the under surface of the cap and extending like the spokes of a wheel (or ribs of an umbrella) from the stem to the margin. They always grow with their flat surfaces vertical. Upon these gill-surfaces are formed the spores that are cast off for the purpose of propagation.

In form gills may be broad or narrow, varying with different species. An important distinction is made between gills that extend to the stem (116, 118) (adnexed), those that are attached broadly to it (adnate) (95, 96) and others that do not reach it but are said to be free (85). Gills that run down the stem are termed decurrent (15); those that are notched in their edge near the stem (123), are known as sinuate or emarginate.

Not always are gills thin; mushrooms of the type of Cantharellus have blunt narrow gills resembling coarse leaf-veins. Again, the free edge of the gills, instead of being knife-edged, as is usually the case, may be notched like a saw (81) (serrate) or wavy.

The spore-bearing surface of the gills is called the hymenium, which, in some cases, extends also across the under surface of the cap between them. The hymenium is composed of microscopic elongated cells sticking out at right angles to the surface. (Fig. 1.) From the free end of many of these protrude little prongs, usually 4 in number, each bearing a spore at its tip. The main cell is called a basidium; the prongs, sterigmata. Those pavement cells that are sterile and bear no spores are called paraphyses.

The spores may possess any one of several colors according to the genus to which the specimen belongs. Their color often determines the hue of the gills in mature plants and it affords an important clue in ascertaining to what genus the mushroom belongs. See Pl. 1A and figs. 5–8.

The spores vary in size and shape in different species. They are so light that when they are cast off from the sterigmata, and they fall in obedience to the law of gravity, it is so slowly that any breath of air propels them for a long distance.

The stem is usually attached to the under surface of the cap at its center, but some kinds of mushrooms have the stem attached to their margins and others between margin and center while still others have no stems.

Stems may be long or short, thick or thin, hollow, pithy or solid. When the inner veil remains attached in part to the stem, it is called the annulus.

CHAPTER III

HOW TO USE THE KEY.—TABLE OF FEATURES
OF GILLED MUSHROOMS USED IN
THEIR IDENTIFICATION

CHAPTER III

HOW TO USE THE KEY

1. Have at hand a number of specimens of the species whose name is desired.

2. Select some feature of these plants which attracts attention and which may be used as a clue to their identification. Such characteristic features are mentioned in this key under the order followed in the subjoined table.

Mushroom
- Character of the whole plant
- Manner of its growth
- Odor
- Place of growth
- Season of its appearance
- Taste

Cap
- Character
- Color
- Form
- Size

Gills
- Character
- Color
- Form

Stem
- Character
- Form
- Size

Spores
- Color

N. B.—A full enumeration of the features possessed by gilled mushrooms as they are mentioned in this book will be found on pages 24 to 26.

Let us suppose that the mushrooms we desire to identify have a milky juice.

3. With milky juice as a character in mind, turn to those pages of the key headed "Character of the Mushroom" (page 31) where will be found in the first column the words Milky Juice.

The mushrooms in hand will be named somewhere in this group unless they belong to some uncommon species not included in this book.

4. Next, observe the color of the caps of the specimens and find in the second column of the key, headed "Color of Cap," the description which fits them.

5. When it appears likely that the correct color description has been found, look next at the accompanying "Remarks" in the third column of the key where will be found mentioned further distinguishing characteristics which will aid in identifying the specimens.

Names of species are placed in column number four, farthest to the left of each page of the key. Coming as they do in answer to the inquiry "What is the name of the plant?" the names will be the last things to be read.

Complete descriptions of the species will be found in Chapter V following the key.

Let us take another example of the use of the key. On a winter walk in the woods, clusters of a small reddish-yellow mushroom are found growing upon a stump. Their caps are moist and sticky, their gills lighter in color but their stems are darker than the surface of the cap and are rather velvety. How shall their name be found in the key?

Looking in the key under "Time of Growth" and where the first column says "December," we find that a cap in the Color of Cap Column is described as being reddish-yellow or tawny and (in the third column) that its size is $\frac{1}{2}$ to 2 inches broad and that in all other respects its description corresponds with our specimen. In the last column its name is given as Collybia velutipes. Turning to the full description of Collybia velutipes in Chapter V (page 163) the identification is further corroborated.

Another example of the use of the key might be in the case of Lepiota americana. We have collected specimens of a gilled mushroom having a prominent knob protruding from the center of the cap. Looking in the key under "Form of Cap," we find eight species mentioned. Reading their condensed tabulated descriptions, it is quickly found that only one of them is said to be colored white with reddish scales upon its surface. It is probable therefore that our specimens are either Lepiota americana or else that they are some uncommon variety not mentioned in this book.

Turning the pages next to the full description of Lepiota americana, it is seen to tally in every respect with the specimen before us and on the next occasion when this mushroom is found, it is probable that it will be at once recognized as would be the face of an acquaintance.

It is the aim of the key, so far as it may be possible, to assist the reader in identifying specimens of gilled fungi without the necessity of ascertaining the color of their spores. The reason for this aim is that it often requires many hours to learn the color of spores by taking a spore print (see page 4). Nevertheless, a knowledge of the spore color of a mushroom is one of the greatest of all helps in determining its identity, and such knowledge is often indispensable.[1] Spore prints, however, are furnished by Nature and may be ready and waiting for the collector's recognition. It is not uncommon to find the colored spore-dust about growing mushrooms—rusty, pink, white, purplish-brown or black dust, shed by mature plants on their stems, on the caps of neighboring fellows or upon the wood or ground that harbors them. These indications of spore color should always be sought by the collector and their presence should be noted.

[1] Figs. 5 to 8 and Pl. 1A.

The color of a mushroom's gills is by no means a certain in-dication of the color of the spores that are shed by them. Colored gills may produce white spores and, on the other hand, many white-gilled species drop colored spores. Once the color of the spores of a mushroom is known, the unravelling of its identity is facilitated.

In order to see clearly the form of the gills of a mushroom, its cap and stem should be cut through vertically in the center. This cut will also reveal the interior of the stem and will show whether it is solid, stuffed or hollow.

The beginner in mycology may be aided in the study of gilled mushrooms by referring to the subjoined table.

Table of Features of Gilled Mushrooms Used in Their Identification

(Figures in parenthesis refer to numbers of those species illustrating the feature mentioned).

Mushroom

Mushroom, Character of—Glows in the dark (phosphores-cent); with milky juice; waxy in appearance.

Manner of Growth—Solitary (single); in groups; in clusters or tufts; in curved lines on the ground (87).

Place of Growth—On ground; on wood; in open places; in woods; in special places.

Odor—Of bitter almonds (peach pits or wild cherry bark); of anise; branny (mealy or farinaceous); disagreeable; gar-licky; of radishes; spicy; fungous.

Season of Growth—Note the month in which the specimen was collected.

Taste—Acrid (biting, peppery); astringent (puckery, bitter); disagreeable but not acrid; mild; sweetish.

Cap

Cap, Character of—Brittle, coriaceous (leathery); downy or hairy (floccose, tomentose) (78); fragile; sticky when moist (viscid); tough; scaly, i.e., with scales or warts on the surface (81); water-soaked in appearance when moist, changing to opaque and often of different color when dry (hygrophanous); silky.

Cap, Color of—While some shade of tan or brown is the commonest color of gilled mushrooms, there is scarcely any color that does not occur among them.

Cap, form of—Attached to wood by its top (resupinate) (48, at right); bell-shaped (campanulate even when mature) (95); cone-shaped or conic (59); inverted cone-shaped (obconic) (22); cylindrical (38, Frontispiece); with edge turned up (revolute) (32); funnel-shaped (infundibuliform) (26); with edge turned downward and inward (involute) (100); fleshy (flesh is the portion between the upper surface of the cap and its lower surface to which the gills are attached) (2); thin (111); membranous (with little or no flesh; kidney-shaped (reniform) (47); with a knob protruding from the center (umbonate) (15); lobed at the edge (13); nippled (a nipple-like elevation at the center; notched at the edge (81); with a pit or small depression at the center (umbilicate) (93); with radiating marks or furrows near the edge (striatulate or striate) (116); split at the edge (5); with fragments of the veil attached to the edge of the cap (97); with a wavy edge (12); smooth; scaly (squamose or squamulose) (38, Frontispiece).

Cap, Size of—Large (four or more inches in diameter; medium (one to four inches in diameter); small (less than one inch in diameter).

Gills

Gills, Character of—Brittle; liquefying (deliquescing) when old (38, frontispiece); separable easily from the cap; with veins in the spaces between the gills; free from the stem (85); close together, crowded; far apart, distant (13).

Gills, Color of—Mentioned in the key only when the color is different from that of the cap.

Gills, Form of—Attached broadly to the stem (adnate) (56); extending as far as the stem but not attached broadly to it (adnexed) (2); extending down the stem (decurrent) (13); forked, branched or joined together (13); broad (34); narrow (32); notched near the stem end (emarginate, sinuate) (123); with a sawlike edge (serrate) (81); thick (12); blunt edged (17); equal in length to each other (113); of different lengths (29).

Stem

Stem, Character of—Absent (46); downy or hairy at the base (90); cartilaginous, like gristle; attached to the cap between its center and its edge (eccentric) (107); attached to the cap at the edge (marginal) (45); fragile; hollow (3); solid; stuffed; separable easily from the cap; tough.

Stem, Form of—Bulbous at base (44); rooted, extending deeply into the ground (35); with a ring or collar surrounding it (annular) (1); inserted into a cup (volva) at the base (8); with ring but without cup (1); with both cup and ring (6); thick (114); thin (86).

Stem, Size of—Long (i.e. longer than the breadth of the cap) (85); short (i.e. shorter than the breadth of the cap) (114).

Spores

Spores, Color of—Black; brown; brownish-black; rusty (ochraceous); pink (rosy, salmon or flesh-color); lilac; green; white; yellow or yellowish.

Beginners in the study of gilled fungi are advised to read the chapter about the propagation and structure of these plants so that they may the better understand the use of the key.

HOW TO USE THE KEY

The reader should bear in mind the fact that there exist hundreds—perhaps thousands—of species of mushrooms and that mistaken identification might result from superficial attention to descriptions of the comparatively few kinds of plants dealt with in this book.

No plant key can be perfect. There are species very difficult of identification even by expert specialists. Should the reader fail to identify a collected species after careful use of the key, his non-success will be probably due to the fact that his specimen is not one of our common mushrooms. Botanists able and willing to identify specimens sent to them, may be found in many of the larger universities, at State capitals and at the United States Department of Agriculture in Washington.

CHAPTER IV

KEY TO COMMON GILLED MUSHROOMS. PICTORIAL KEY TO GENERA

CHAPTER IV

KEY TO COMMON GILLED FUNGI

Figures attached to names of species refer to corresponding numbers in the illustrations and descriptions.

IDENTIFICATION BY CHARACTER OF THE MUSHROOM

Character	Color of Cap	Remarks	Name
Glows in the dark (Phosphorescent)	Orange-yellow or saffron	3 to 6 inches broad. On wood, in tufts. Stem often at side.	Clitocybe illudens (25)
	Tawny	¼ to ¾ inch broad. Tough; kidney-shaped; attached to wood; marginal stem.	Panus stypticus (99)
	Lactarius, all species, *e.g.*		
	Brownish red	½ to 1 ½ inches broad. Odor of sweet clover.	Lactarius camphoratus (71)
	Dark reddish brown	3 to 5 inches broad. Milk copious, white. Wrinkled surface.	Lactarius corrugis (72)
	Orange, with stripes	2 to 5 inches broad. Orange milk.	Lactarius deliciosus (73)
	Sooty brown	1 to 4 inches broad. Milk white; slightly acrid. Long stem.	Lactarius lignyotus (74)
Milky juice appears if plant is wounded	White	3 to 5 inches broad. Often covered with dirt. Milk very peppery.	Lactarius piperatus (75)
	Brownish-red	½ to 2 ½ inches broad. Milk white; slightly bitterish.	Lactarius subdulcis (76)
	Tawny-reddish	2 to 5 inches broad. Milk turns to a sulphur-yellow; bitterish.	Lactarius theiogalus (77)
	White or whitish	2 to 5 inches broad. Soft and wooly to the touch. Milk white; acrid.	Lactarius vellereus (78)
	Orange-brown	2 to 5 inches broad. Milk white; mild.	Lactarius volemus (79)

IDENTIFICATION BY CHARACTER OF THE MUSHROOM
(Continued)

Character	Color of Cap	Remarks	Name
Waxy appearance	**Hygrophorus, all species**		
Shriveling when dry; reviving when moist	Reddish-brown or grayish-red when moist; grayish-brown when dry	¾ to 1½ inches broad. Gills grayish-brown; free from stem. Stem slender; tough.	Collybia confluens (32)
	All species	of	Marasmius
	All species	of	Panus

IDENTIFICATION BY MANNER OF GROWTH

Manner of Growth	Color of Cap	Remarks	Name
Clustered (intufts) on wood (Cæspitose)	Honey-yellow to dark reddish brown	Ring on stem; cap 1 to 6 inches broad.	Armillaria mellea (10)
	Saffron or orange	Cap 3 to 6 inches broad.	Clitocybe illudens (25)
	Silky gray or grayish brown	Taste and odor slightly branny; gills salmon when old; commonly seen in abortive form.	Clitopilus abortivus (29) (seldom tufted)
	Pale tan or flesh-red when wet, whitish when dry	Cap 1 to 2 inches broad; in dense tufts; not sticky when wet.	Collybia acervata (31)
	Reddish-brown of grayish-red when wet; pallid when dry	Cap ¾ to 1½ inches broad; long, slender stem.	Collybia confluens (32)
	Tan, Yellowish or chestnut	Cap ½ to 2 inches broad Gills light. Stem brown; hollow. In groups.	Collybia dryophila (33)
	Yellow or tawny, darker at center	Cap 1 inch or more broad; sticky when moist; stem brown, hairy when mature. On wood.	Collybia velutipes (36)

KEY TO COMMON GILLED FUNGI

Manner of Growth	Color of Cap	Remarks	Name
	Pale yellow	1 to 2 inches broad; taste bitter; gills rusty when old.	Flammula flavida (52)
	Wine buff to wine purple or lavender	1 to 2 inches broad; sticky when wet; stem yellowish or purplish, and scaly.	Flammula polychroa (53)
	Bay or tawny brown when moist, brownish yellow when dry	Hygrophanus; fragments of veil at margin; 1 or 2 inches broad.	Hypholoma appendiculatum (63)
Clustered (in tufts) on wood	Brownish, red, yellowish at margin	1 to 3 inches broad; gills often eaten by insects, pale yellow becoming greenish or purplish when old.	Hypholoma perplexum (65)
	Dark brick red, often paler at edge	1 to 3 inches broad; gills like H. perplexum.	Hypholoma sublateritium (66)
	Brownish-flesh color when moist, paler when dry	½ to 2 inches broad; gills saw-like on edge; stem often off center of cap, furrowed.	Lentinus cochleatus (80)
	White or pale rusty; brownish scales	2 to 4 inches broad; edge of gills saw-like.	Lentinus lepideus (81)
	White with reddish-brown scales	1 to 4 inches broad; ring on stem.	Lepiota americana (82)
	(Variable) Some shade of brown or gray	Cap conical; radial marks on surface; ¼ to 1¼ inches broad; stem slender, hairy at base.	Mycena galericulata (90)
	Yellowish-rusty to dull yellow	¼ to 1 inch broad; stem very slender, hairy at base.	Omphalia campanella (94)

IDENTIFICATION BY MANNER OF GROWTH (*Continued*)

Manner of Growth	Color of Cap	Remarks	Name
Clustered (in tufts) on wood	White	Cap 8 inches or larger; stem marginal.	Panus strigosus (98)
	Yellow; scaly	Sticky when moist; 1 to 4 inches broad; often with flaky ring on stem.	Pholiota adiposa (101)
	Watery cinnamon when moist, pale yellow when dry	1 to 2 inches broad; sticky when moist; ring on stem.	Pholiota discolor (103)
	White or ashy gray, yellowish when old	2 to 5 inches broad; stem at margin; gills extend down the stem.	Pleurotus ostreatus (106)
	White, yellowish, ashy-gray, dull lilac or even brownish	2 to 5 inches broad. Like Pleurotus ostreatus except that spores have a lilac tint.	Pleurotus sapidus (107)
	White	3 to 5 inches broad; on elm wood; Sept. to Nov.	Pleurotus ulmarius (108)
	Whitish, grayish or grayish brown	Cap ¼ to 1 inch broad; thin, conic to bell-shaped, with radiating lines; spores black.	Psathyrella disseminata (111)
In Curved Lines or Circles on the Ground	White or yellowish	2 to 5 inches broad. Open places. Gills pink; blackish when old; ring on stem.	Agaricus arvensis (1)
	Egg-yolk	1 to 3 inches broad. funnel-shaped; gills narrow; forked.	Cantharellus cibarius (13)
	Pure white	2 to 3 inches broad. Soft texture.	Clitocybe albissima (20)
	Reddish-brown when moist; paler when dry	¾ to 1½ inches broad. Thin; tough; gills whitish or yellowish gray.	Collybia confluens (32)

KEY TO COMMON GILLED FUNGi

IDENTIFICATION BY **MANNER** OF **GROWTH** (*Continued*)

Manner of Growth	Color of Cap	Remarks	Name
In curved lines on Ground (Fairy rings)	White, with brown scales	4 to 12 inches broad. Gills white or green. Stem with large ring.	Lepiota molybdites (83)
	Buff or tawny	1 to 2 inches broad. Shrivels when dry. Gills broad; stem tough. In fields.	Marasmius oreades (87)
	Grayish-buff, rusty brown or yellowish	2 to 4 inches broad. Edge of cap turned down and in; gills forked; decurrent.	Paxillus involutus (100) (seldom in rings)

IDENTIFICATION BY **ODOR**

Odor	Color of Cap	Remarks	Name
Almonds (wild cherry bark)	Yellowish or dingy-rusty	2 to 4 inches broad. On ground. Sticky when moist. Radiating furrows at margin. Odor of bitter almonds.	Russula fœtens (116)
Anise	Grayish-brown or blackish-brown	3 to 5 inches broad. Edge often upturned and wavy when old. Gills broad. Stem white.	Collybia platyphylla (34)
	Green or dingy-green, fading when old	1 ½ to 3 inches broad. On ground. Gills white or pallid. Stem whitish or greenish.	Clitocybe odora (28)
Branny (farinaceous)	Whitish; brown-tinged when moist	½ to 1 ½ inches broad. Depressed at center when mature. On ground. Stem frosted.	Clitocybe albidula (19)
	White when moist; shiny silky white when dry	½ to 1 ½ inches broad. On ground. Pit at center. Stem waxy and polished; rooting; hairy at base.	Clitocybe candicans (21)
	Gray or grayish-brown	2 to 4 inches broad. Gills whitish, turning salmon when old. Spores salmon-pink. See description for abortive form.	Clitopilus abortivus (29) (slightly)

IDENTIFICATION BY ODOR (Continued)

Odor	Color of Cap	Remarks	Name
Branny	Whitish or grayish	2 to 3 inches broad. On ground in woods. Bloom on surface. Gills whitish, salmon when old.	Clitopilus prunulus (30)
	Hazel-nut or umber	1 to 2 inches broad. Taste, odor branny. Gills rosy pink; notched.	Entoloma commune (49)
	Whitish-gray or brownish-gray	1 to 3 inches broad. Taste branny. Gills pink. Stem silky; white or pallid.	Entoloma grayanum (50)
	Tawny-red, turning reddish-brown when old	2 to 4 inches broad. Sticky when moist. Gills notched; lighter than cap.	Tricholoma transmutans (127)
Sweet clover (Mellilot)	Bay-red or brownish-red	1 to 2 inches broad. Milky juice. Flesh tinged with color of cap.	Lactarius camphoratus (71)
Chlorine	White; warty	4 to 6 inches broad. Gills white; free from stem. Stem with ring and cup at base.	Amanita chlorinosma
Pleasant		See under Sweet Clover.	Lactarius camphoratus (71)
	Tawny-rusty	1½ to 2 inches broad. Slight knob at center. Edge curved in. Gills notched. Gills pallid to tawny. Stem cream-colored.	Hebeloma precox (56)
Radishes	Cinnamon	1 to 2 inches broad. Webby veil under gills when young. Gills yellow, turning rusty when old.	Cortinarius cinnamomeus (41) (when fresh)
Spicy	White or tinged with yellow or pink	2 to 5 inches broad. On ground in woods. Gills pink, turning black. Stem ringed.	Agaricus silvicola (3)
	Green or dingy green; fading when old	1½ to 3 inches broad. On ground in woods.	Clitocybe odora (28)

KEY TO COMMON GILLED FUNGI

IDENTIFICATION BY **ODOR** (*Continued*)

Odor	Color of Cap	Remarks	Name
Spicy	Grayish-brown or blackish brown	3 to 5 inches broad. Edge often upturned and wavy when old. Gills broad; notched near stem.	Collybia platyphylla (34) (at times, when fresh)
	Brownish-flesh color when moist; paler when dry	½ to 2 inches broad. In tufts. Gills saw-like on edge. Stem sometimes at side; grooved.	Lentinus cochleatus (80)
Strong	Saffron-yellow or orange yellow	3 to 6 inches broad. On wood; in tufts. Stem aside from center.	Clitocybe illudens (25)

IDENTIFICATION BY **PLACE OF GROWTH**

Place of Growth	Color of Cap	Remarks	Name
On bridge timbers, railroad ties or fence posts	White or pale rusty; brownish scales	2 to 4 inches broad; edge of gills saw-like; stem sometimes off center of cap.	Lentinus lepideus (81)
On compost heaps	White with reddish or reddish brown scales	1 to 4 inches broad; ring on stem; no cup at base.	Lepiota americana (82)
Damp places or swamps	Sooty-brown when moist; grayish, yellowish or brownish when dry	1 to 2 inches broad; funnel-shaped; gills narrow; far apart.	Cantharellus infundibuliformis (17)
	Yellowish or brownish	1 to 2 inches broad; webby veil at edge when young; gills attached to stem; close together.	Cortinarius cinnamomeus (41)

IDENTIFICATION BY **PLACE** OF **GROWTH** (*Continued*)

Place of Growth	Color of Cap	Remarks	Name
	Pale yellow; sometimesredtinged at center	¾ to 1¾ inches broad. Webby veil at edge when young. Gills attached to stem.	Hygrophorus chlorophanus (58)
	Red, vermilion or yellow	½ to 2 inches broad. Thin; fragile.	Hygrophorus miniatus (60)
	Bright red	1 to 3 inches broad. Sticky when moist. Gills yellow or red; thick; far apart.	Hygrophorus puniceus (62)
Damp places or swamps	Pale-red, buff-red or flesh-red when moist; pale rusty, grayish or buff when dry	½ to 2 inches broad. Gills thick; broad. Stem 1 to 3 inches. Gills often powdered white when old.	Laccaria laccata (69)
	Orange with bright mottled rings	2 to 5 inches broad. Yellowish milky juice. Gills white or cream.	Lactarius deliciosus (73)
	Sooty-brown	1 to 4 inches broad. Velvety. Milky juice. Spores yellowish.	Lactarius lignyotus (74)
	Yellow	2 to 4 inches broad. Cap often flaky, wrinkled. Stem ringed. Spores rusty.	Pholiota caperata (102)
	Rosy or blood red	2 to 4 inches broad. Sticky when moist. Gills chalk-white. Stem white or red-tinged.	Russula emetica (115)
On manure	Brownish, tinged with gray or lead	½ to 1 inch broad. Bell-shaped. Stem long, slender. Spores black.	Panæolus campanulatus (95)
	Tan, gray or brownish	½ to 1½ inches broad. Network of cracks, fragments of veil at edge.	Panæolus retirugis (97)

KEY TO COMMON GILLED FUNGI

Place of Growth	Color of Cap	Remarks	Name
	Yellowish orange	1 to 3 inches broad. Sometimes funnel-shaped. Gills narrow; forked.	Cantharellus aurantiacus (11)
	Variable. Grayish, brownish, yellowish or bluish-gray	½ to 1½ inches broad. Sometimes funnel-shaped. Gills narrow; repeatedly forked.	Cantharellus dichotomus (15)
Hilly and mountainous districts	Pale tan or flesh-red when moist; whitish when dry	1 to 2 inches broad. Gills whitish. Stem slender; brittle.	Collybia acervata (31)
	Dark violet	2 to 4 inches broad. Hairy-scaled. Gills rusty when old. Stem bulbous at base.	Cortinarius violaceus (44)
	Pale yellow or whitish	1 to 2 inches broad. Gills rusty when old. Stem downy at base.	Flammula flavida (52)
	Bay brown when moist; brownish-yellow when dry	1 to 2 inches broad. Fragments of veil at edge. In tufts. Spores purplish brown.	Hypholoma appendiculatum (63)
	White with reddish or reddish brown scales	1 to 4 inches broad. Ring on stem; no cup at base.	Lepiota americana (82)
Hot-houses	Whitish, grayish or grayish-brown	¼ to 1 inch broad. Conic or bell-shaped. In tufts. Spores black.	Psathyrella disseminata (111)
		Stem without ring; cup at base. Spores rosy.	Volvaria
Leaves (Among fallen)	Variable, Grayish, brownish, yellowish, or bluish-gray	½ to 2 inches broad. Sometimes funnel-shaped. Gills narrow; repeatedly forked.	Cantharellus umbonatus (15)

IDENTIFICATION BY **PLACE** OF **GROWTH** (*Continued*)

Place of Growth	Color of Cap	Remarks	Name
Leaves (Among fallen)	Shining white	½ to 1¼ inches broad. Stem waxy white; hairy at base; rooting.	Clitocybe candicans (21)
	Reddish or pale tan; fading when old	2 to 3 inches broad. Funnel-shaped when mature.	Clitocybe infundibuliformis (26)
	Pale tan or flesh-red when moist; whitish when dry	1 to 2 inches broad. Gills whitish. Stem slender; brittle.	Collybia acervata (31)
	Reddish, brownish, or grayish when moist; pallid, whitish or grayish when dry	¾ to 1½ inches broad. Stem long (2 to 5 inches); slender.	Collybia confluens (32)
	Dark violet	2 to 4 inches broad. Hairy-scaled. Gills rusty when old. Stem bulbous at base.	Cortinarius violaceus (44)
	Gray (whitish or brownish)	1 to 3 inches broad. Taste branny. Gills pink when mature.	Entoloma grayanum (50)
	Deep-red, vermilion or yellow	½ to 2 inches broad. Gills color of cap; waxy. Stem slender; 1 to 3 inches.	Hygrophorus miniatus (60)
	Rusty-red; a little darker at center	¼ to ½ inch broad. Bell-shaped with radiating furrows. Stem blackish.	Marasmius siccus (86)
	Brownish; black spot at center	¼ to ½ inch broad. Stem slender; black; shiny.	Marasmius rotula (89)
In moss	Variable, Grayish, brownish, yellowish or bluish-gray	½ to 1½ inches broad. Gills narrow; repeatedly forked; extending down the stem.	Cantharellus umbonatus (15)

IDENTIFICATION BY **PLACE** OF **GROWTH** (*Continued*)

Place of Growth	*Color of Cap*	*Remarks*	*Name*
In Moss	Pale-yellow; sometimes red at center	¾ to 1¾ inches broad. Sticky when moist; waxy. Stem 1½ to 3 inches.	Hygrophorus chlorophanus (58)
	Red, vermilion or yellow	½ to 2 inches broad. Thin; fragile; waxy. Stem long; slender.	Hygrophorus miniatus (60)
	Bright red; paler or yellow when old	1 to 3 inches broad. Conic or bell-shaped; thin; fragile; sticky when moist.	Hygrophorus puniceus (62)
	Pale-red, buff-red or flesh-red when moist; rusty, grayish or buff-red when dry	½ to 2 inches broad. Gills broad; thick; attached to stem.	Laccaria laccata (69)
	Orange with brighter zones	2 to 5 inches broad. Orange milky juice.	Lactarius deliciosus (73)
	Sooty-brown	1 to 4 inches broad. Milky juice.	Lactarius lignyotus (74)
	Tawny or brownish red	½ to 2½ inches broad. Milky juice.	Lactarius subdulcis (76)
	Yellow or pale orange	1 to 3 inches broad. Cap thin with pit at center. Stem long, slender.	Omphalia fibula (94)
On sawdust heaps	White, with reddish-brown scales and elevated center	1 to 4 inches broad. Marginal radiating lines. Stem ringed but no cup at base.	Lepiota americana (82)
	Dingy brown; rarely white, yellow, ashy or blackish	2 to 2½ inches broad. Gills pink when mature; free from stem.	Pluteus cervinus (110)

IDENTIFICATION BY **PLACE** OF **GROWTH** (*Continued*)

Place of Growth	Color of Cap	Remarks	Name
(In woods among special kinds of trees)	Egg yolk	1 to 3 inches broad; gills, stem and cap colored alike. Gills thick; far apart.	Cantharellus cibarius (12)
Hemlocks	Grayish-buff or rusty-brown or yellowish	2 to 4 inches broad; Margin curled downward and inward; gills forked.	Paxillus involutus (100)
	Reddish-white, reddish-brown or leaden-brown	2 to 4 inches broad; cup at base of stem; no ring on stem; gills free from stem.	Amanitopsis vaginata (8)
	Orange or red; paler at margin	3 to 6 inches broad; stem with ring; cup at base. No warts on cap.	Amanita cæsarea (4)
(Amongst special kinds of trees)	Egg yolk yellow	1 to 3 inches broad; gills, stem and cap same color. Gills thick and far apart.	Cantharellus cibarius (12)
Ever-greens	Whitish tinged with brown when moist; whitish when dry	½ to 1½ inches broad; gills thin; close together; attached to stem or extending down it.	Clitocybe albidula (19)
	Grayish-brown or sooty-brown	1 to 3 inches broad. Conic with apex down. Stem club shaped.	Clitocybe clavipes (22)
	Orange or grayish orange with brighter mottled zones	2 to 5 inches broad. Orange milky juice of mild taste.	Lactarius deliciosus (73)
	Tawny red, turning brownish red when old	2 to 4 inches broad; odor and taste branny; gills notched at stem.	Tricholoma transmutans (127)

KEY TO COMMON GILLED FUNGI

IDENTIFICATION BY **PLACE** OF **GROWTH** (*Continued*)

Place of Growth	Color of Cap	Remarks	Name
Pines	Whitish tinged with brown when moist; whitish when dry	½ to 1½ inches broad; pit in center when mature; taste and odor branny; in groups; stem short.	Clitocybe albidula (19)
	Orange or grayish orange with brighter mottled zones	2 to 5 inches broad. Orange milky juice.	Lactarius deliciosus (73)

IDENTIFICATION BY **TASTE**

Taste	Color of Cap	Remarks	Name
Acrid, biting, when raw	Pale honey-yellow to dark reddish-brown	1 to 6 inches broad. Stem with ring. Tough.	Armillaria mellea (10) (slightly acrid)
	Egg-yolk yellow	1 to 3 inches broad. Funnel-shaped. Gills narrow; far apart; forked. Plant all yellow.	Cantharellus cibarius (12) (slightly acrid)
	Lactarius, all species; some slightly, some extremely so.		
	White, with reddish or reddish-brown scales	1 to 4 inches broad. Gills white; free from stem. Stem usually with ring.	Lepiota americana (82)
	Light yellowish or pale brick-red; turning wood-color or tan when old	1 to 2 inches broad. In woods. Dries without putrifying. Stem downy at base.	Marasmius peronatus (88)
	Tawny	¼ to ¾ of an inch broad. Kidney or shell-shaped. On wood. Stem at edge.	Panus stypticus (99) (acrid and puckery)

43

IDENTIFICATION BY **TASTE** (*Continued*)

Taste	Color of Cap	Remarks	Name
Acrid, biting when raw	Yellow	2 to 4 inches broad. Wrinkled and often scaly. Stem with thick ring. Gills whitish; turning rusty when old.	Pholiota caperata (102)
	Rosy or blood-red	2 to 4 inches broad. Fragile. Sticky when moist. Gills pure white. Stem white or red-tinged.	Russula emetica (115)
	Yellowish	3 to 5 inches broad. Sticky when moist. Marginal radiating furrows. Odor of bitter almonds.	Russula foetens (116)
Bitter	Pale yellow	1 to 2 inches broad. In woods on wood. Gills yellow, turning rusty when old. White down at base of stem.	Flammula flavida (52)
	Dark brick-red often paler at margin	1 to 3 inches broad. On wood; in clusters. Gills yellowish or greenish, turning brown when old.	Hypholoma sublateritium (66)
	Tawny, or brownish-red	½ to 2½ inches broad. White milky juice.	Lactarius subdulcis (76)
	Tawny-reddish	2 to 5 inches broad. White milky juice, turning yellow when exposed.	Lactarius theiogalus (77)
	White, with reddish or reddish-brown scales	1 to 4 inches broad. Gills free from stem. Stem with ring especially when young.	Lepiota americana (82)
	Yellowish or dingy-rusty	3 to 5 inches broad. Odor of bitter almonds. Sticky when moist. Radial striations at margin.	Russula foetens (116)
	White; sometimes yellowish	2 to 4 inches broad. On ground in woods. Dry. Margin turned in when young. Gills notched.	Tricholoma album (122)

IDENTIFICATION BY **TASTE** (*Continued*)

Taste	Color of Cap	Remarks	Name
Bitter (cont.)	Whitish, yellowish or greenish-yellow; streaked with brown or blackish fibers	1 to 3 inches broad. Gills notched at stem. Stem solid; stout; white.	Tricholoma sejunctum (126)
Branny, farinaceous, mealy	Whitish, brown-tinged when moist; whitish when dry	½ to 1½ inches broad. On ground, in groups in woods. Gills thin; close together; attached to stem or extending down it.	Clitocybe albidula (19)
	White; shiny when dry	½ to 1¼ inches broad. On ground in groups, in woods. Gills very thin, close together. Stem waxy; polished; rooting and hairy at base.	Clitocybe candicans (21)
	Gray or grayish-brown	2 to 4 inches broad. Gills grayish, turning salmon when old.	Clitopilus abortivus (29)
	Hazel-nut or umber	1 to 2 inches broad. Gills pink; notched.	Entoloma commune (49)
	Whitish or brownish gray	1 to 3 inches broad. Gills whitish when young, pink when mature.	Entoloma grayanum (50)
	Tawny-red, turning reddish-brown when old	2 to 4 inches broad. In groups or clusters. Sticky when moist. Gills notched.	Tricholoma transmutans (127)
Disagreeable but not acrid	Saffron or orange	3 to 6 inches broad. In clusters on wood. Stem often eccentric. Gills decurrent (Poisonous).	Clitocybe illudens (25)
	Watery-white, grayish, yellowish or grayish-brown	1 to 3½ inches broad. In clusters on ground. Often irregular in shape from pressure by its fellows.	Clitocybe multiceps (27)

IDENTIFICATION BY **TASTE** (*Continued*)

Taste	Color of Cap	Remarks	Name
Sweet	Tawny-rusty	1 ½ to 2 inches broad. Slight knob at center. Edge turned in. Gills notched; pallid to tawny. Stem cream-colored.	Hebeloma precox (56)

IDENTIFICATION BY **TIME** (SEASON) OF **GROWTH**

Time (Season) of Growth	Color of Cap	Remarks	Name
January, February and March	Reddish yellow or tawny; sometimes darker at center	1 to 2 inches broad; in tufts on wood; gills whitish; stem brown.	Collybia velutipes (36)
	Tawny	¼ to ¾ of an inch broad; short stem at side; on wood; taste acrid.	Panus stypticus (99)
	White or whitish	½ to 1 ½ inches broad; cap attached by edges; dry; leathery; gills split at edge.	Schizophyllum commune (120)
April	Yellow or tawny; darker at center	1 to 1 ½ inches broad; in tufts; sticky when moist; stem brown; hairy when mature.	Collybia velutipes (36)
	Whitish, adorned with scattered yellowish scales. Turns black when old	Cap oblong or cylindric. 1 ½ to 3 inches long before spreading; liquefies black when old.	Coprinus comatus Frontispiece (38)
	Buff yellow; sometimes glistening with minute particles when young	1 to 2 inches broad; bell-shaped or expanded. In clusters. Gills liquefy black when old.	Coprinus micaceus (39)

46

KEY TO COMMON GILLED FUNGI

IDENTIFICATION BY **TIME** (SEASON) OF **GROWTH** (*Continued*)

Time (Season) of Growth	Color of Cap	Remarks	Name
April (continued)	Tawny or rusty-colored	1 to 2 inches broad. Hemispheric or convex. Sticky when moist.	Naucoria semi-orbicularis (92)
	Yellowish rusty to dull yellow. Darker when moist	¼ to 1 inch wide. Cap thin with pit at center. Stem slender, polished; hairy at base; on wood.	Omphalia campanella (93)
	Tawny	¼ to ¾ of an inch broad; cap tough; kidney-shaped. Stem at margin.	Panus stypticus (99)
	White or whitish	½ to 1½ inches wide; leathery; dry; downy. Stem at margin.	Schizophyllum commune (120)
May	Tan, yellowish or chestnut	½ to 2 inches broad. Gills light; stem brown; hollow. In groups.	Collybia dryophila (33)
	Grayish brown or blackish brown	3 to 5 inches broad. Gills broad, notched near stem; stem white.	Collybia platyphylla (34)
	Reddish yellow or tawny; darker at center	1 to 1½ inches broad. Sticky when moist. Gills whitish; stem brown; hairy when mature.	Collybia velutipes (36)
	Grayish brown; often yellowish tint; blackening when old	1 to 3 inches broad. Egg-shaped when young. Gills liquefy black when old.	Coprinus atramentarius (37)
	Whitish adorned with scattered yellowish scales, liquefying black whe old	Oblong or cylindric cap: 1½ to 3 inches long, before expansion. Split at edge when old.	Coprinus comatus (38) (Frontispiece)

Time (Season) of Growth	Color of Cap	Remarks	Name
	Buff-yellow, often brighter at center	1 to 2 inches broad; liquefying black when old. Radial marks at edge.	Coprinus micaceus (39)
	Whitish; yellow-tinged when moist	1 to 3 inches broad. On ground. Fragile. Fragments of veil at margin when young.	Hypholoma incertum (64)
	Pale red, buff-red or flesh-red when moist; grayish or buff when dry	½ to 2 inches broad. Gills attached to stem. pale flesh-red or violet and powdered white when old.	Laccaria laccata (69)
	Buff or tawny	½ to 2 inches broad; in grass; shrivelled when dry; reviving when moist. Stem slender, firm, tough.	Marasmius oreades (87)
May	Tawny or rusty	1 to 2 inches broad; Gills rusty; broad; near together. Stem yellowish or reddish-brown. Spores rusty.	Naucoria semiorbicularis (92)
	Yellowish rusty to dull yellow	¼ to 1 inch broad. Cap thin, convex, with pit at center. Gills yellow. Stem brown; slender.	Omphalia campanella (93)
	Whitish-gray, often yellow-tinged	½ to 1½ inches broad. In open places. Hemispheric. Gills broad, gray, turning black when old. Stem long, slender. Spores black.	Panæolus papilionaceus (96)
	Cinnamon or tanned leather	¼ to 1¾ inches broad. On wood. Leathery. Stem at edge.	Panus stypticus (99)
	Whitish or tinged with tan	1 to 2 inches broad. Stem with ring near top; easily separable from cap.	Pholiota praecox (104)
	Dingy brown; rarely white, yellow, ashy or blackish	2 to 2½ inches broad; gills pink when mature; free from stem.	Pluteus cervinus (110)

KEY TO COMMON GILLED FUNGI

IDENTIFICATION BY **TIME** (SEASON) OF GROWTH (*Continued*)

Time (Season) of Growth	Color of Cap	Remarks	Name
	Whitish, grayish or grayish-brown	½ to 1 inch broad. In clusters. Spores black.	Psathyrella disseminata (111)
	Smoky-brown or reddish brown	½ to 1 inch broad. In grass. Cap conic. Gills brown; broad. Stem slender; fragile.	Psilocybe fœnisecii (112)
May	White or whitish	½ to 1½ inches broad. Leathery; downy; stem at edge.	Schizophyllum commune (120)
	Light yellowish	½ to 1½ inches broad; Hemispheric. Sticky when moist. Stem long; slender. Gills yellow, turning black when old.	Stropharia semiglobata (121)
June		Amanitopsis vaginata (8) Cantharellus minor (18) Clitocybe multiceps (27) Collybia dryophila (33) Collybia platyphylla (34) Collybia radicata (35) Collybia velutipes (36) Coprinus comatus (38) Frontispiece Coprinus micaceus (39) Cortinarius corrugatus (43) **Crepidotus calolepis (46)** Crepidotus malachius (47) Crepidotus versutus (48) Galera hypnorum (54) Galera tenera (55) Hygrophorus cantharellus **(57)** Hygrophorus miniatus (60) Hypholoma incertum (64) Laccaria laccata (69) Lentinus lepideus (81) Lepiota molybdites (83) Marasmius oreades (87) Marasmius peronatus (88) Marasmius rotula (89) Mycena galericulata (90) **Naucoria semiorbicularis (92)** Omphalia campanella (93) Panæolus campanulatus (95) Panæolus papilionaceus (96) Panæolus retirugis (97) **Pholiota praecox (104)** Pleurotus ostreatus (106) Pleurotus sapidus (107) Pleutius cervinus (110) Psathyrella disseminata (111) Psilocybe fœnisecii (112) Stropharia semiglobata (121)	

Gilled mushrooms appearing during the months of July, August, September and October are not named in this section of this book. The majority of common species occur during these months.

Time (Season) of Growth	Color of Cap	Remarks	Name
November	Yellowish brown	4 to 8 inches broad. Cap thin, downy. Gills forked; grayish-green.	Cantharellus crispus (14)
	Yellow or tawny; darker at center	1 inch or more broad. On wood. In clusters. Sticky when moist.	Collybia velutipes (36)
	Grayish-brown, often yellow-tinged. Black when old	1 to 3 inches broad. On ground. Egg-shaped when young. Gills liquefy black when old.	Coprinus atramentarius (37)
	Wine-buff or orange-buff ground with marginal scales of buff, purple or lavender. Often purple when young	1 to 2 inches broad. Clusters on wood. Margin in-curved when young. Sticky when moist.	Flammula polychroa (53)
	Brownish-red; yellowish at margin	1 to 3 inches broad. Gills often eaten by insects, pale yellowish turning greenish and purplish when old.	Hypholoma perplexum (65)
	Dark brick-red; often paler at edge	1 to 3 inches broad. Gills like H. perplexum. In clusters on wood.	Hypholoma sublateritium (66)
	White; center rarely yellowish or smoky	2 to 4 inches broad. In grass. Gills free from stem. Stem with ring; bulbous a base.	Lepiota naucina (84)
	Cinnamon or tanned leather	1/4 to 1 3/4 inches broad. Stem at edge of cap or absent. On wood. Leathery. Taste puckery.	Panus stypticus (99)
	White, yellowish, ashy-gray, dull lilac or brownish	2 to 5 inches broad. In clusters on wood. Stem eccentric or at margin of cap. Spores of P. sapidus lilac.	Pleurotus ostreatus (106) sapidus (107)

KEY TO COMMON GILLED FUNGI

IDENTIFICATION BY **TIME** (SEASON) OF **GROWTH** (*Continued*)

Time (Season) of Growth	Color of Cap	Remarks	Name
November	Saffron-rust color	3 to 5 inches broad. In clusters on wood. Scaly surface. Ring on stem.	Pholiota squarrosa (105)
	Whitish, grayish, or gray-ish-brown	½ to 1 inch broad. In clusters on wood and ground. Cap fragile; bell-shaped.	Psathyrella dis-seminata (111)
	White or whitish	½ to 1½ inches broad. On dead wood. Downy; leathery. Stem at edge of cap.	Schizophyllum commune (120)
	Light-yellowish	½ to 1½ inches broad. Hemispheric. Stem long; slender. Gills yellow; turning black when old.	Stropharia semi-globata (121)
December	Reddish-yellow or tawny	½ to 2 inches broad. Gills lighter than stem or cap. Stem brown; velvety. In clusters on wood.	Collybia velutipes (36)
	Brownish-red, yellowish at margin	1 to 3 inches broad. Gills often eaten by insects (before frost); pale yellowish, turning purplish and greenish when old; In clusters on wood.	Hypholoma perplexum (65)
	Dark brick-red; often paler at margin	Like H. perplexum, next above.	Hypholoma sublateritium (66)
	Cinnamon or tanned leather	¼ to 1¾ inches broad. On wood. Leathery. Stem at edge of cap.	Panus stypticus (99)
	Saffron-rust-color	3 to 5 inches broad. In clusters on wood. Scales on surface. Ring on stem.	Pholiota squarrosa (105)
	White, yellowish, ashy-gray, dull lilac or brownish	2 to 5 inches broad. In clusters on wood. Stem eccentric or at edge of cap.	Pleurotus ostreatus (106) sapidus (107)
	White or whitish	½ to 1½ inches broad. On wood. Leathery; downy. Stem short; at edge of cap.	Schizophyllum commune (120)

IDENTIFICATION BY **CHARACTER** OF **CAP**

Character of Cap	Color of Cap	Remarks	Name
Coriaceous (see Leathery)			
Downy, hairy. (Fibrillose, floccose, tomentose).	Dull, white, yellowish or, rarely, reddish-brown	1 to 3 inches broad. On ground in or near woods. Gills free from stem. Stem with large cup or sheath at base.	Amanitopsis volvata (9)
	Pale honey yellow to dark reddish-brown	1 to 6 inches broad. In groups or clusters. Stem with ring.	Armillaria mellea (10)
	Yellowish-brown	4 to 8 inches broad. On wood; often in tufts. Cap thin. Gills narrow; wavy; grayish-green. Stem at edge or absent.	Cantharellus crispus (14)
	Yellowish, inclining to rusty	Cap 2 to 4 inches broad; funnel-shaped; 3 to 6 inches high (long). Gills thick; branched.	Cantharellus floccosus (16) (Hairy scales)
	Dark violet	2 to 4 inches broad. On ground in woods. Stem bulbous at base.	Cortinarius violaceus (44)
	Whitish, yellowish or pale rusty when dry	⅔ to 2 inches broad. Attached to wood at edge or by short, marginal stem.	Crepidotus calolepis (46)
	White	⅓ to 1 inch broad. Attached to wood by its upper surface.	Crepidotus versutus (48)
	White or whitish	2 to 5 inches broad. Milky juice.	Lactarius vellereus (78)
	White	8 inches or more broad. On stumps. Hairy stem at side of cap.	Panus strigosus (98)
	White or whitish	½ to 1½ inches broad. On dead branches. Cap tough; leathery; dry. No stem; attached at edge.	Schizophyllum commune(120)
Filbrillose See Downy			

IDENTIFICATION BY **CHARACTER** OF **CAP** (*Continued*)

Character of Cap	Color of Cap	Remarks	Name
Floccose See Downy			
	Reddish-white, reddish-brown or leaden	2 to 4 inches broad. Gills free from stem. Stem with cup but no ring.	Amanitopsis vaginata (8)
	Dull white, yellow-ish; rare-ly red-dish-brown	2 to 3 inches broad. Gills free from stem. Large cup at base of stem. No ring.	Amanitopsis volvata (9)
	Grayish-brown or blackish-brown	3 to 5 inches broad. Gills white; brittle; broad.	Collybia platy-phylla (34)
	Pale yel-low; some-times red-tinged at center	¾ to 1¾ inches broad. Thin cap; sticky when moist. Radiating lines at edge. Gills waxy.	Hygrophorus chlorophanus (58)
Fragile	Bright red or sul-phur yellow	½ to 1½ inches broad. Waxy. Cap conic. Gills and stem yellow.	Hygrophorus conicus (59)
	Deep-red, vermilion or yellow	½ to 2 inches broad. Waxy. Gills yellow. Stem slender; polish-ed; long.	Hygrophorus miniatus (60)
	Bright red; paler or yellow when old	1 to 3 inches broad. Sticky when moist. Gills broad; thick; far apart; yellow or red-dish. Stem long; vari-colored.	Hygrophorus puniceus (62)
	Whitish, yellow-tinged when moist	1 to 3 inches broad. Fragments of veil at edge. Gills whitish, turning brownish when old. On ground.	Hypholoma incertum (64)
	Whitish, grayish or grayish-brown	¼ to ½ inch broad. In crowded tufts. Cap thin; bell-shaped; with radiating lines. Gills never liquefy.	Psathyrella dis-seminata (111)

IDENTIFICATION BY **CHARACTER** OF **CAP** (*Continued*)

Character of Cap	Color of Cap	Remarks	Name
Fragile	Red, purple, olive or green	2 to 4 inches broad. Gills pale yellow, turning rusty when old. Stem thick; white or red.	Russula alutacea (113)
	Rosy or blood red	2 to 4 inches broad. Sticky when moist. Gills pure white. Taste acrid.	Russula emetica (115)
	Yellowish	2 to 5 inches broad. Odor of bitter almonds. Radiating furrows at edge. Sticky when moist.	Russula fœtens (116)
Glutinous See Sticky			
Hygrophanous See Watery			
Leathery (coriaceous)	Buff, tawny or *café au lait*	1 to 2 inches broad. In grass. Dries without putrifying; revives when moist. Gills far apart; whitish. In "fairy rings."	Marasmius oreades (87) (when dry)
	Light yellowish or pale brick-red	1 to 2½ inches broad. Taste acrid; in woods. Radial marks at edge when dry.	Marasmius peronatus (When dry) (88)
	White	8 inches or more broad. Hairy. Stem at side of cap. On wood.	Panus strigosus (98)
	Tawny	¼ to ¾ inch broad. Kidney-shaped; tough. Attached to wood by short stem at edge of cap.	Panus stypticus (99)
	White or whitish	½ to 1½ inches broad. On wood. Tough; dry; downy. Stem at edge.	Schizophyllum commune (120)
Phosphorescent (Glows in the darkness)	Saffron or orange	3 to 6 inches broad. In clusters on wood. Gills decurrent. Stem often eccentric.	Clitocybe illudens (25)

KEY TO COMMON GILLED FUNGI

Character of Cap	Color of Cap	Remarks	Name
Phospho-rescent (Glows in the dark-ness)	Tawny	¼ to ¾ inch broad. Leathery; kidney-shaped; Attached to wood by short stem at edge of cap.	Panus stypticus (99)
Scaly or Warty	Yellow or orange	3 to 6 inches broad. All yellow. Stem with ring; cup at base.	Amanita muscaria (5)
	Brownish-red or reddish	3 to 5 inches broad. Gills white. Stem with ring; bulbous.	Amanita rubescens (7)
	Reddish-white, reddish-brown or leaden-brown	2 to 4 inches broad. Striated. Stem long; sheath or cup at base.	Amanitopsis vaginata (8)
	Pale honey-yellow to dark red-dish-brown	1 to 6 inches broad. In clusters or singly. Stem with ring; usu-ally scaly.	Armillaria mellea (10)
	Yellowish, inclining to rusty	2 to 4 inches broad. Funnel-shaped. Gills blunt; forked; thick.	Cantharellus floccosus (16)
	Whitish with yel-lowish scales	1½ to 3 inches broad. Oblong or cylindric before expansion. Liquefies black when old.	Coprinus comatus Frontispiece (38)
	Dark violet with hairy scales	2 to 4 inches broad. Gills violet, turning rusty when old. Stem bulbous.	Cortinarius violaceous (44)
	Whitish, yellowish or pale rusty when dry. Small tawny scales	⅔ to 2 inches broad. Round or divided. Attached to wood at edge of cap.	Crepidotus calolepis (46)
	Wine-buff, orange-buff or greenish with wine-colored scales on margin	1 to 2 inches broad. Gills cream, to brown or purplish. Stem yellowish; tough.	Flammula polychroa (53)

IDENTIFICATION BY **CHARACTER** OF **CAP** (*Continued*)

Character of Cap	Color of Cap	Remarks	Name
	Tanned leather, rusty at center, brown lines radiating	½ to 1 inch broad. Gills adnate; whitish when young; rusty when old. Stem whitish above, brownish below.	Inocybe abundans (67)
	White or pale rusty with brownish scales	2 to 4 inches broad. On wood. Tough. Gills saw-edged.	Lentinus lepideus (81)
	White, with reddish or brownish scales	1 to 4 inches broad. Gills free from stem. Stem with ring when young.	Lepiota americana (82)
	White, with brown scales that merge at the center	4 to 12 inches broad. Gills white when young; green when mature. Stem with large ring.	Lepiota molybdites (83)
	Brownish, with darker scales.	3 to 5 inches broad. Gills far from stem. Stem long; with ring.	Lepiota procera (85)
Scaly or Warty	Whitish-gray, often yellow-tinged	½ to 1½ inches broad. Gills broad; gray; black when old. Stem long; whitish; sometimes stained black by spores.	Panæolus papilionaceus (96)
	Tawny, with small scales	¼ to ¾ inch broad. Kidney-shaped. Attached to wood by short stem at edge of cap.	Panus stypticus (99)
	Yellow	1 to 4 inches broad. Cap sticky. Gills yellow when young; rusty when old. Stem with slight flaky ring.	Pholiota adiposa (101)
	Yellow, often with whitish flakes or scales	2 to 4 inches broad. Surface wrinkled. Gills whitish to rusty. Stem white; stout; with thick ring.	Pholiota caperata (102)

KEY TO COMMON GILLED FUNGI

Character of Cap	Color of Cap	Remarks	Name
Scaly or Warty	Saffron-rusty	3 to 5 inches broad. Stem with ring and scaly.	Pholiota squarrosa (105)
	Green or grayish-green	2 to 4 inches broad. Gills white; some forked.	Russula virescens (119)
	Rosy red or flesh-color	2 to 5 inches broad. Sometimes small scales. Gills white; often red-spotted. Stem short; thick.	Tricholoma russula (125)
	Silky-white	2 to 8 inches broad. Gills flesh-colored; free from stem. Large cup at base.	Volvaria bombycina (128) (Scaly when old)
Silky	White or with dingy hues	1½ to 3 inches broad. Open places. Gills pink, turning brown and black when old. Ring on stem when young.	Agaricus campestris (2)
	White or tinged with yellow or pink	2 to 5 inches abroad. Gills pink, turning brown and black when old. Ring (sometimes double) on stem.	Agaricus silvicola (3) (Slightly silky)
	Shining white when dry	½ to 1¼ inches broad. Gills thin; close together. Stem polished; rooting; hairy at base.	Clitocybe candicans (21)
	Watery-white, grayish, yellowish gray or grayish brown	1 to 3½ inches broad. In clusters on ground.	Clitocybe multiceps (27) (Slightly silky)
	Yellowish-brown	1 to 2 inches broad. Radiating cracks. Stem slightly swollen at base.	Inocybe rimosa (68)
	White; center rarely yellowish	2 to 4 inches broad. Gills white; free from stem. Stem ringed.	Lepiota naucina (84)
	Brownish, with spotlike scales	3 to 5 inches broad. Gills free from stem. Stem long; with ring; bulbous.	Lepiota procera (85)

IDENTIFICATION BY **CHARACTER** OF **CAP** (*Continued*)

Character of Cap	Color of Cap	Remarks	Name
Silky	White, covered with silky down	2 to 8 inches broad. Gills flesh-colored. Large cup at base.	Volvaria bombycina (128)
Sticky when moist (viscid, glutinous)	Pure white or variable colors	1½ to 5 inches broad. Gills white; free from stem. Stem with ring; cup at base.	Amanita phalloides (6)
	Grayish-brown or smoky-brown	1 to 4 inches broad. Stem long and with long root.	Collybia radicata (35)
	Reddish-yellow or tawny; sometimes darker at center	1 inch or more broad. In tufts on wood. Stem hairy.	Collybia velutipes (36)
	Yellow to golden or tawny yellow	1½ to 3 inches broad. Web under gills when young. Stem also sticky when moist.	Cortinarius collinitus (42)
	Bright or reddish-yellow or rusty	2 to 4 inches broad. Cap furrowed. Stem long; hollow; bulbous at base.	Cortinarius corrugatus (43)
	Wine-buff, orange-buff, often green-tinged. Scales at margin.	1 to 2 inches broad. In clusters on wood. Stem solid; scaly; tough.	Flammula polychroa (53)
	Pale yellow, sometimes red-tinged at center.	¾ to 1¾ inches broad. Gills and stem fragile; pale yellow.	Hygrophorus chlorophanus (58)
	Red or yellow.	½ to 1½ inches broad. Cap strikingly conic. Waxy. Gills and stem yellow.	Hygrophorus conicus (59)
	Bright red; paler or yellow when old	1 to 3 inches broad. Gills yellow or reddish. Stem pied in color.	Hygrophorus puniceus (62)

KEY TO COMMON GILLED FUNGI

Character of Cap	Color of Cap	Remarks	Name
Sticky when moist (viscid, glutinous)	Orange with brighter zones	2 to 5 inches broad. Milky juice.	Lactarius deliciosus (73)
	Tawny-reddish	2 to 5 inches broad. Milky juice turning yellow after exposure.	Lactarius theiogalus (77)
	Tawny or rusty	1 to 2 inches broad. Cap hemispheric. Gills rusty. Stem long.	Naucoria semiorbicularis (92) (slightly viscid)
	Tan, gray or brownish	½ to 1½ inches broad. Cap conic or bell-shaped, with cracks. Stem long.	Panæolus retirugis (97)
	Grayish-buff, rusty brown or yellowish	3 to 4 inches broad. Margin turned down and in. Stem sometimes off center.	Paxillus involutus (100)
	Yellow	1 to 4 inches broad. On wood. Scales on surface. Flaky ring on stem.	Pholiota adiposa (101)
	Watery cinnamon when moist; pale yellow when dry	1 to 2 inches broad. On wood. Stem with ring. "Fading pholiota."	Pholiota discolor (103)
	Dingy brown; rarely whitish, yellowish ashy or blackish	2 to 2½ inches broad. Gills pink; free from stem. Stem easily detached.	Pluteus cervinus (110) (slightly viscid)
	Red, dark purple, olivaceous or green	2 to 4 inches broad. Gills yellow or tan.	Russula alutacea (113)
	Blood red or rosy	2 to 4 inches broad. Gills chalk white. Taste acrid.	Russula emetica (115)

IDENTIFICATION BY **CHARACTER** OF **CAP** (*Continued*)

Character of Cap	Color of Cap	Remarks	Name
Sticky when moist (viscid, glutinous)	Yellowish or dingy-rusty	3 to 5 inches broad. Radiating lines at edge. Stinking odor.	Russula fœtens (116)
	Light yellowish	½ to 1½ inches broad. Cap hemispheric. Gills yellow. Stem also viscid, with incomplete ring.	Stropharia semiglobata (121)
	Pale pink, rosy or flesh-color	2 to 5 inches broad. Stem short; solid; thick.	Tricholoma russula (125)
	Tawny-red, turning reddish-brown when old	2 to 4 inches broad. Gills whitish, turning dingy or spotted when old.	Tricholoma transmutans (127)
Tomentose (see Downy)			
Water-soaked in appearance when moist, but opaque when dry. Often changing color as moisture evaporates. Hygrophanous	Sooty-brown, brown-ish-yellow or dingy yellow when moist; grayish or brown-ish when dry	1 to 2 inches broad. Gills narrow; far apart; forked. Stem slender; smooth; hollow.	Cantharellus infundibuliformis (17)
	Blackish-brown or grayish-brown when moist; paler when dry	1½ to 3 inches broad. Gills far apart; united at stem.	Clitocybe cyathiformis (23)
	Pale tan or flesh-red when moist; whitish when dry	1 to 2 inches broad. In tufts on wood. Gills whitish. Stem hollow; dark; usually downy at base.	Collybia acervata (31)
	Reddish-brown or grayish red when moist; whitish or gray-ish when dry	¾ to 1½ inches broad. Stem slender; long; downy; color of cap. Dries without putrifying.	Collybia confluens (32)

KEY TO COMMON GILLED FUNGI

IDENTIFICATION BY **CHARACTER** OF **CAP** (*Continued*)

Character of Cap	Color of Cap	Remarks	Name
Water-soaked in appearance when moist, but opaque when dry. Often changing color as moisture evaporates. Hygrophanous (cont.)	Watery-white when moist; opaque white when dry	⅛ to 1 inch in diameters. Attached to wood by edge or by short hairy stem. Gills white, turning cinnamon when old.	Crepidotus applanatus(45)
	Watery-brown when moist; whitish or yellowish when dry	⅔ to 2 inches broad. Cap with small scales. Attached to wood by edge or short marginal stem.	Crepidotus calolepis (46)
	Watery-white when moist; opaque white when dry	1 to 2½ inches broad. On wood, in groups or clusters. Caps irregular in shape. Gills white; rusty when old. Stem marginal, short or absent.	Crepidotus malachius (47)
	Umber (brown); shiny	¾ to 1¾ inches in diameter. Gills whitish when young; flesh-color when mature.	Entoloma strictus (51)
	Watery cinnamon when moist; yellowish or buff when dry	¼ to ½ inch broad. Gills often downy at edge.	Galera hypnorum (54)
	Tan or brownish slightly darker at center. Rusty when dry	½ to 1 inch broad. Conic or bell shaped. Stem long and slender.	Galera tenera (55)
	Bay or tawny-brown when moist; brownish yellow when dry	1 to 2 inches broad. On wood. In clusters. Fragments of veil at edge when young.	Hypholoma appendiculatum (63)

IDENTIFICATION BY **CHARACTER** OF **CAP** (*Continued*)

Character of Cap	Color of Cap	Remarks	Name
Water-soaked in appearance when moist, but opaque when dry. Often changing color as moisture evaporates. Hygrophanous (cont.)	Whitish, yellow-tinged when moist; paler when dry	1 to 3 inches broad. On ground; open places. Splitting at edge. Stem splits easily.	Hypholoma incertum (64)
	Flesh-red, buff-red or pale red when moist; pale-ochre, grayish or buff when dry	½ to 2 inches broad. On ground in woods. Gills flesh-red or violet; powdered white when old.	Laccaria laccata (69)
	Grayish or pale tan when dry; purplish-brown when moist	2 to 4 inches broad. On ground; open places. Waxy Gills and stem color of cap or paler.	Laccaria ochropurpurea (70)
	Brownish-flesh color when moist; paler when dry	½ to 2 inches broad. In tufts on or about old stumps. Tough. Gills saw-like on edge. Stem often at side.	Lentinus cochleatus (80)
	Yellow-rusty to dull yellow	¼ to 1 inch broad. On wood, in clusters. Stem very slender; hairy at base.	Omphalia campanella (93)
	Watery cinnamon when moist; pale yellow when dry	1 to 2 inches broad. On wood in woods. Stem with ring.	Pholiota discolor (103)
	Yellow or brown	½ to 1 inch broad. On wood in woods. Network of furrows. Gills whitish or yellowish when young; flesh-color when old.	Pluteus admirabilis (109)
	Whitish, grayish or grayish-brown	¼ to ½ inch broad. In clusters. Radiating lines on thin, fragile cap. Resembles coprinus micaceus.	Psathyrella disseminata (111)

KEY TO COMMON GILLED FUNGI

IDENTIFICATION BY **CHARACTER** OF CAP *(Continued)*

Character of Cap	Color of Cap	Remarks	Name
Hygro-phanous (cont.)	Smoky-brown or reddish-brown; paler when dry	½ to 1 inch broad. On ground; in grassy places. Gills brown. Stem slender; fragile; hollow.	Psilocybe fœnisecii (112)

IDENTIFICATION BY **COLOR** OF CAP

Color, as a means of identifying gilled mushrooms, is used here only when it is a distinct, bright or noticeable hue. Confusion would result from attempts to distinguish species by reference to such common and indeterminate shades as buff, tawny, brownish, grayish and the like.

Color of Cap	Size of Cap	Remarks	Name
	1½ to 5 inches broad	On ground. Gills white: free from stem. Stem with ring; cup at base.	Amanita phalloides (6)
	1½ to 3 inches broad	On ground; August. Cap tough; fragrant (anise;) fading when dry.	Clitocybe odora (28)
Green or greenish	2 to 4 inches broad	On ground in woods. Gills pale yellow, turning rusty when old.	Russula alutacea (113)
	2 to 4 inches broad	On ground. Patches on surface. Stem short; firm; white.	Russula vire-scens (119)
	1 to 3 inches broad	Cap fleshy; fragile; knob at center; streaked with dark lines.	Tricholoma sejunctum (126)
	3 to 6 inches broad	On ground in woods. Cap smooth, with radiating lines at edge. Gills yellow; free from stem. Stem yellow; with ring; cup at base.	Amanita cæsarea (4)
Orange	3 to 8 inches broad	On ground. Cap with warts or smooth. Gills white; free from stem. Stem with ring; ill-defined cup at base.	Amanita muscaria (5)

IDENTIFICATION BY **COLOR** OF **CAP** (*Continued*)

Color of Cap	Size of Cap	Remarks	Name
Orange	1 to 3 inches broad	On ground in woods. Cap plane or funnel-shaped. Gills narrow; forked; reddish orange; stem color of cap.	Cantharellus aurantiacus (11)
	3 to 6 inches broad	On wood. Odor strong. Stem away from center. Clustered.	Clitocybe Illudens (25)
	½ to 1 inch broad	In clusters on ground. Waxy. Gills whitish or yellowish. Stem fragile.	Hygrophorus cantharellus (57)
	2 to 5 inches broad	Orange-milky juice. Bright zones on cap.	Lactarius deliciosus (73)
	2 to 5 inches broad	Milky juice. Gills (white) turn yellow or dark where bruised.	Lactarius volemus (79) (Dull orange)
Pink, flesh-color or salmon	2 to 5 inches broad	Gills pink when young, blackish-brown when old. Stem with ring; base bulbous but without cup.	Agaricus silvicola (3) (White, pink-tinged.)
	¾ to 1¼ inches broad	Variable in color and shape. Entire plant of one color.	Mycena pura (91)
	2 to 4 inches broad	Taste acrid. Gills chalk-white; of equal length. Stem thick; white or pink.	Russula emetica (115)
	2 to 4 inches broad	Taste mild. Gills white when young; yellowish when old.	Russula Peckii (118)
	2 to 5 inches broad	Gills notched near stem; white, spotted red when old or where bruised. Stem short and thick.	Tricholoma russula (125)

IDENTIFICATION BY **COLOR** OF **GILLS**

Color of Gills	Color of Cap	Remarks	Name
Pink, flesh-color or salmon	Hazel-nut or umber	1 to 2 inches broad. Taste, odor branny. Gills notched.	Entoloma commune (49)

KEY TO COMMON GILLED FUNGI

Color of Gills	Color of Cap	Remarks	Name
Pink, flesh-color or salmon	Whitish or brown-ish-gray	1 to 3 inches broad. Taste branny. Gills whitish when young.	Entoloma grayanum (50)
	Umber-brown	¾ to 1¾ inches broad. Gills grayish - white when young. Cap shiny. Flesh-brown.	Entoloma strictius (51)
	Brownish-flesh	½ to 2 inches broad. In tufts on wood. Cap thin; tough. Gills with saw-like edge.	Lentinus cochleatus (80)
	Some shade of brown or gray	¼ to 1¼ inches broad. Conic. In clusters on wood. Stem hairy at base.	Mycena galericulata (90)
	Yellow or brown	½ to 1 inch broad. Network of furrows. Gills whitish or yellowish when young. Stem downy at base.	Pluteus admirabilis (109)
	Dingy-brown; rarely white, yellow, ashy or grayish	2 to 2½ inches broad. Gills free from stem. Stem easily separable from cap.	Pluteus cervinus (110)

Color of Cap	Size of Cap	Remarks	Name
Purple	1 to 3 inches	Cap with knob or umbo. Webby veil under young cap. Violet tints in gills and stem.	Cortinarius alboviolaceus (40)
	2 to 4 inches	Cap with hairy scales. Gills purple when young, rusty when old. Stem bulbous at base.	Cortinarius violaceus (44)
	1 to 2 inches	Edge curved in when young. Sticky when moist. Colored spots at edge of cap.	Flammula polychroa (53)

IDENTIFICATION BY **COLOR** OF **CAP** (*Continued*)

Color of Cap	Size of Cap	Remarks	Name
Purple	¾ to 1½ inches broad	Cap thin; bell-shaped. Fine radiating lines at edge. Stem long.	Mycena pura (91)
	2 to 4 inches broad	On ground in woods. Gills pale yellow; rusty when old. Stem stout. Taste mild.	Russula alutacea (113)
	1 to 3 inches broad	Gills white when young; yellowish when old. Color of cap rubs off when moist.	Russula mariæ (117)
	2 to 5 inches broad	Margin frosted and rolled in when young. Gills color of cap; free from stem. Stem short; stout.	Tricholoma personatum (124)
Red	3 to 6 inches broad	On ground in woods. Cap smooth, with radiating lines at edge. Gills yellow; free from stem. Stem yellow with ring and white cup.	Amanita cæsarea (4)
	3 to 8 inches broad	On ground. Cap warty or smooth. Gills white; free from stem. Stem with ring; ill-defined cup at base.	Amanita muscaria (5)
	1 to 1½ inches broad	Cap irregular. Gills narrow; forked; color of cap.	Cantharellus cinnabarinus (13)
	½ to 1 inch broad	In clusters on ground. Cap thin; convex. Gills waxy; far apart; forked; whitish, yellowish or red-tinged. Stem long.	Hygrophorus cantharellus (57)
	½ to 1½ inches broad	Cap strikingly conic. Waxy gills. Stem yellow.	Hygrophorus conicus (59)
	½ to 2 inches broad	Cap thin; fragile. Gills yellow or red; waxy; far apart. Stem slender.	Hygrophorus miniatus (60)
	1 to 3 inches broad	Cap thin; fragile; sticky when moist. Gills broad; thick; far apart; yellow or reddish.	Hygrophorus puniceus (62)

IDENTIFICATION BY **COLOR** OF **CAP** (*Continued*)

Color of Cap	Size of Cap	Remarks	Name
	Russula. Many species.		
Red	2 to 5 inches broad	Smooth or dotted with fine scales. Gills slightly notched; white. Stem short; thick; solid.	Tricholoma russula (125)
White	1½ to 3 inches broad	Never in woods. Gills pink when young; turning brown and black when old. Stem with ring.	Agaricus campestris (2)
	2 to 5 inches broad	On ground in woods. Gills pink when young, turning brown or backish brown. Stem with ring—sometimes a double one.	Agaricus silvicola (3)
	1½ to 5 inches broad	On ground. Gills white; free from stem. Stem with ring; cup at base.	Amanita phalloides (6)
	2 to 4 inches broad	Deep striations at edge; fragile. Gills free from stem. Stem long; with cup at base but no ring.	Amanitopsis vaginata (8)
	2 to 3 inches broad	Dry, soft, even surface. Gills white; some forked at base. Stem smooth; solid; white.	Clitocybe albissima (20)
	½ to 1¼ inches broad	Rarely stem is at side. Gills very thin; attached or decurrent. Stem waxy; rooting; hairy at base.	Clitocybe candicans (21)
	1 to 1½ inches broad	Cap glossy; tough. Gills attached to stem; white; stem mealy at top.	Clitocybe dealbata (24)
	½ to 1 inch by ⅛ to ¾ inches	Kidney - shaped. Attached by edge or by short hairy stem to wood. Hygrophanous.	Crepidotus applanatus (45)
	1 to 2½ inches broad	Kidney - shaped. In groups. Hygrophanous.	Crepidotus malachius (47)
	3 to 5 inches broad	On ground in woods. Acrid, milky juice.	Lactarius piperatus (75)

IDENTIFICATION BY **COLOR** OF **CAP** (*Continued*)

Color of Cap	Size of Cap	Remarks	Name
	2 to 5 inches broad	On ground in woods. Soft wooly surface. Milky (slightly acrid) juice.	Lactarius vellereus (78)
	2 to 4 inches broad	On wood. Cap tough; hard when dry. Gills white with saw-like edge.	Lentinus lepideus (81) (white with brown scales)
	2 to 5 inches broad	On ground. Gills white; free from stem; stem with ring; no cup at base.	Lepiota americana (82) (white with reddish scales)
	4 to 12 inches broad	Gills white when young, green when mature; free from stem. Stem with large ring.	Lepiota molybdites (83) (with brown scales)
	2 to 3 inches broad	Gills free from stem; white; pinkish or smoky-brown when old. Stem with ring; no cup at base.	Lepiota naucina (84)
	8 inches or more broad	Cap hairy; stem at edge; on wood.	Panus strigosus (98)
White (cont.)	2 to 5 inches broad	On wood in clusters. Stem at edge of cap. Spores white (Those of P. sapidus lilac.)	Pleurotus ostreatus (106) sapidus (107) ulmarius (108)
	2 to 2½ inches broad	Gills free from stem; white when young; pink when mature. Stem easily separable from cap.	Pluteus cervinus (110) (rarely white)
	2 to 4 inches broad	Cap sometimes stained yellowish. Gills white or faintly greenish when old. Stem short; thick.	Russula delica (114)
	2 to 4 inches broad	On ground in woods. Taste acrid. Gills chalk white. Fragile.	Russula emetica (115) (rarely white)
	2 to 4 inches broad	Cap dry; margin turned in when young. Gills and stem white. Taste bitter.	Tricholoma album (122)
	2 to 8 inches broad	Cap silky-white. Gills pink. Stem with large cup.	Volvaria bombycina (128)

KEY TO COMMON GILLED FUNGI

Color of Cap	Size of Cap	Remarks	Name
	3 to 6 inches broad	On ground in woods. Cap smooth; radiating lines at edge. Gills yellow; free from stem. Stem yellow; with ring; cup at base.	Amanita cæsarea (4)
	3 to 8 inches broad	On ground. Cap warty or smooth. Gills white; free from stem. Stem with ring; ill-defined cup at base.	Amanita muscaria (5)
	1 to 6 inches broad	Cap hairy or smooth; tough; slightly acrid taste. Stem with ring. Gills attached to stem.	Armillaria mella (10) (honey yellow)
	1 to 3 inches broad	Cap funnel shaped. Margin turned and irregular. Gills narrow; forked. Plant all yellow.	Cantharellus cibarius (12) (egg-yolk)
Yellow	½ to 1 inch broad	In groups. All yellow. Gills far apart; decurrent. Stem slender.	Cantharellus minor (18)
	1½ to 3 broad	Cap shiny when dry. Sticky when moist. Veil under cap when young. Whitish gills turn rusty when old.	Cortinarius collinitus (42)
	2 to 4 inches broad	Cap corrugated; sticky when moist; convex. Stem bulbous and sticky at base.	Corinarius corrugatus (43)
	1 to 2 inches broad	On wood in woods. Taste bitter. Pale gills turn rusty when old.	Flammula flavida (52)
	1 to 2 inches broad	On wood in woods. Edge curved in when young. Sticky when moist. Colored spots at edge.	Flammula polychroa (53) (orange buff, etc.)
	½ to 1 inch broad	In clusters on ground. Cap thin; convex. Waxy. Gills yellow; far apart; forked. Stem fragile.	Hygrophorus cantharellus (57)

IDENTIFICATION BY **COLOR** OF **CAP** (*Continued*)

Color of Cap	Size of Cap	Remarks	Name
	¾ to 1¾ inches broad	Waxy. Cap thin; fragile. Entire plant yellow.	Hygrophorus chlorophanus (58)
	½ to 1½ inches broad	Cap strikingly conic. Waxy. Gills and stem yellow.	Hygrophorus conicus (59)
	½ to 2 inches broad	Color uniform. Waxy. Cap thin; fragile.	Hygrophorus miniatus (60)
	¼ to 1 inch broad	On wood in large clusters. Cap thin; with pit at center. Gills narrow; yellow; connected by veins.	Omphalia campanella (93) (dull yellow)
	⅛ to ½ inch broad	Cap thin; pit at center; yellow or pale orange. Gills decurrent. Stem long.	Omphalia fibula (94)
Yellow	1 to 4 inches broad	On wood in woods. All yellow. Sticky; scaly Cap with flaky, disappearing ring.	Pholiota adiposa (101)
	2 to 4 inches broad	Cap often scaly and wrinkled. Whitish gills turn rusty when old. Stem with thick ring.	Pholiota caperata (102)
	1 to 2 inches broad	Watery-cinnamon when moist. Gills pallid when young; rusty when old. Stem with ring.	Pholiota discolor (103)
	½ to 1 inch broad	On wood in woods. Network of furrows. Gills pallid when young; flesh-colored when old. Gills free from stem.	Pluteus admirabilis (109)
	¾ to 1½ inches broad	Cap hemispheric; viscid. Stem long; slender; ring near top.	Stropharia semiglobata (121) (light yellow)

KEY TO COMMON GILLED FUNGI

IDENTIFICATION BY **FORM OF CAP**

Form of Cap	Color of Cap	Remarks	Name
Attached by its top (resupinate)	White (downy)	⅓ to 1 inch broad. Kidney shaped. Attached to wood.	Crepidotus versutus (48)
	White or whitish	On dead branches in woods. Tough; leathery; margin lobed; dries without putrifying.	Schizophyllum commune (120)
Bell-shaped (Campanulate) when mature	Whitish with scattered yellowish scales	1 to 3 inches high. On ground; open places. Cap cylindric. Gills whitish, liquefy and black when old.	Coprinus comatus (38) Frontispiece
	Buff-yellow or tawny yellow	1 to 2 inches broad. In clusters. Radiating lines on surface. Gills liquefy black when old.	Coprinus micaceus (39)
	Tan or brownish; darker at center	½ to 1 inch broad and high. Gills not attached to stem. Stem long; hollow; fragile; slender.	Galera tenera (55)
	Tanned leather	½ to 1 inch broad. Cracks on surface; Gills whitish when young, rusty when old.	Inocybe abundans (67)
	Yellowish-brown	1 to 2 inches broad. Gills pallid or tan. Stem slightly swollen at base.	Inocybe rimosa (68)
	Rusty-red	¼ to ½ inch broad. Cap dry; smooth; radiating furrows. Gills far apart; whitish. Stem tough, shiny; 1 to 2 inches long.	Marasmius siccus (86)
	Some shade of gray or brown	¼ to 1¼ inches broad. In clusters on wood. Stem hairy at base.	Mycena galericulata (90)
	Brownish, with leaden tints	½ to 1 inch broad. Open places. Edge often scalloped or fringed. Stem 4 to 6 inches.	Panæolus campanulatus (95)

IDENTIFICATION BY **FORM** OF **CAP** *(Continued)*

Form of Cap	Color of Cap	Remarks	Name
Bell-shaped (Campanulate) when mature (cont.)	Whitish, grayish or brownish	¼ to ½ inch broad; conic or bell-shaped. In clusters. Thin; fragile; with radiating furrows.	Psytharella disseminata (111)
	Smoky-brown or reddish brown	½ to 1 inch broad. In grass. Gills brown. Stem 2 to 3 in.	Psilocybe fœnisecii (112)
	Silky white	2 to 8 inches broad. Large cup at base.	Volvaria bombycina (128)
Cap conic when mature (apex up)	Watery-cinnamon when moist, buff when dry	¼ to ½ inch broad. Long stem. Often in moss.	Galera hypnorum (54)
	Tan or brownish; darker at center	½ to 1 inch broad and high. Gills crowded; tawny; easily separated from stem. Stem long.	Galera tenera (55)
	Bright red or sulphur yellow	½ to 1½ inches broad. Gills waxy; yellow. Stem yellow; hollow.	Hygrophorus conicus (59)
	Rose or purple	¾ to 1¼ inches broad. Entire plant of one color. Veins between gills.	Mycena pura (91)
	Tan, gray or brownish	½ to 1½ inches broad. Conic or bell-shaped. Network of cracks. Gills gray or black.	Panæolus retirugis (97)
	Smoky-brown or reddish-brown	½ to 1 inch broad. In grass. Gills brown. Stem fragile; 2 to 3 inches long.	Psilocybe fœnisecii
Conic Inverted (Obconic)	Yellowish to rusty	2 to 4 inches broad, 3 to 6 inches high (long). Surface scaly. Gills narrow; blunt; forked.	Cantharellus floccosus (16)
	Grayish brown	1 to 3 inches broad. Gills cream or white. Stem clubbed.	Clitocybe clavipes (22)

IDENTIFICATION BY **FORM** OF **CAP** (*Continued*)

Form of Cap	Color of Cap	Remarks	Name
Cracks on surface	Hazel-nut or umber	1 to 2 inches broad. Taste and odor branny. Gills rosy-pink; notched near stem. Eat not.	Entoloma commune (49) (Radiating cracks)
	Tanned-leather	½ to 1 inch broad. Bell-shaped or plane. Gills whitish when young; rusty when old.	Inocybe abundans (67) (Radiating cracks)
	Yellowish-brown	1 to 2 inches broad. Gills pallid or tan. Stem slightly swollen at base.	Inocybe rimosa (68) (Radiating cracks)
	Orange-brown	2 to 5 inches broad. Milky juice.	Lactarius volemus (79) (Cracks into angular patches)
	White or pale-rusty, with brownish scales	2 to 4 inches broad. On wood. Dry; tough. Edge of gills saw-like.	Lentinus lepideus (81) (Cracks form brownish scales)
	Tan, gray or brownish	½ to 1½ inches broad. Conic or bell-shaped. Stem long. Gills broad; gray or black.	Panæolus retirugis (97) (Network of cracks)
	Green or grayish-green	2 to 4 inches broad. Gills white; a few are forked. Stem short; stout; white.	Russula virescens (119) (Cracks form scaly patches).
Cylindrical	Whitish, with scattered yellowish scales	1 to 3 inches high. On ground; open places. Gills whitish; liquefying black when old.	Coprinus comatus (38) (Frontispiece)
Funnel-shaped	Egg yolk	1 to 3 inches broad. Edge irregular. Gills far apart; narrow; forked; blunt. Plant all yellow.	Cantharellus cibarius (12)
	Yellowish to rusty	Cap 2 to 4 inches broad; 3 to 6 inches long. Surface scaly. Gills narrow; blunt; forked.	Cantharellus floccosus (16)
	Sooty or brownish to yellowish or grayish	1 to 2 inches broad. Edge irregular. Gills narrow; forked. Stem slender; hollow.	Cantharellus infundibuliformis (17)

IDENTIFICATION BY **FORM** OF **CAP** (*Continued*)

Form of Cap	Color of Cap	Remarks	Name
	Blackish-brown when moist; paler when dry	1½ to 3 inches broad. Cap thin; gills far apart; stem short (¾ to 1½ inches).	Clitocybe cyathiformis (23)
	Reddish or pale tan, fading when old	2 to 3 inches broad. Gills white.	Clitocybe infundibuliformis (26)
Funnel-shaped (cont.)	White; often covered with dirt	3 to 5 inches broad. Milky acrid juice.	Lactarius piperatus (75) (when mature)
	Brownish-flesh color when moist; paler when dry	½ to 2 inches broad. Gills sawlike at edge. Stem often off center of cap.	Lentinus cochleatus (80)
	White, sometimes with yellowish stains	2 to 4 inches broad. Often pit at center. Gills white; often greenish when old. Stem short.	Russula delica (114) (when old)

N.B.—Several of the Lactarii (milky mushrooms) are nearly funnel-shaped when mature.

	Watery cinnamon or rusty when moist; often buff when dry	¼ to ½ inch broad. Gills broad; far apart. Stem long; slender; hollow; downy at top.	Galera hypnorum (54)
Hemispherical	Tawny or rusty	1 to 2 inches broad. Surface often cracked. Stem 3 to 4 inches; slightly enlarged at base.	Naucoria semiorbicularis (92)
	Whitish-gray; often yellowish	½ to 1½ inches broad. May and June; open places. Gills very broad; stem 3 to 5 inches; whitish or stained by fallen black spores.	Panæolus papilionaceus (96)

IDENTIFICATION BY **FORM** OF **CAP** (*Continued*)

Form of Cap	Color of Cap	Remarks	Name
Hemispherical (cont.)	Tan, gray or brownish	½ to 1½ inches broad. Open places. Network of cracks about center. Stem 2 to 6 inches; often with band in upper part.	Panæolus retirugis (97)
	Yellow (all)	1 to 4 inches broad. On wood in woods. Sticky; scaly. Stem with flaky, disappearing ring.	Pholiota adiposa (101)
	Yellow or yellowish (all)	½ to 1½ inches broad. Open places. Viscid. Stem with ring at upper part.	Stropharia semiglobata (121)
Incurved at edge. (Curved downward and inward)	Egg-yolk	1 to 3 inches broad. Funnel-shaped when mature. All yellow.	Cantharellus cibarius (12) (Edge turned in when young)
	Grayish-white, grayish-brown, yellowish-brown; blackish-brown or bluish-gray	½ to 1½ inches broad. Gills repeatedly forked; light color. Stem 1 to 3 inches.	Cantharellus umbonatus (15) (Edge turned in when young)
	White; downy	⅛ to 1 inch broad. Attached to wood by edge or top.	Crepidotus versutus (48)
	Umber-brown; shiny	¾ to 1¾ inches broad. Open places; late fall. Gills pink when old.	Entoloma strictius (51)
	White; often covered with dirt	3 to 5 inches broad. Acrid milky juice.	Lactarius piperatus (75) (Edge turned in when young)
	Tawny	¼ to ¾ of an inch broad. Attached to wood by short stem at edge of cap.	Panus stypticus (99)
	Grayish-buff, rusty-brown or yellowish	2 to 4 inches broad. Gills decurrent; forked. Stem short; sometimes eccentric.	Paxillus involutus (100)

IDENTIFICATION BY **FORM** OF **CAP** (*Continued*)

Form of Cap	Color of Cap	Remarks	Name
Incurved at edge. (Involute. Edge turned downward and inward)	White, yellowish, grayish, lilac or brownish	2 to 5 inches broad. In clusters. Attached to wood by stem at edge of cap.	Pleurotus ostreatus,(106) Pleurotus sapidus (107)
	White; sometimes yellowish, especially at center	2 to 4 inches broad. Taste acrid or bitter.	Tricholoma album (122)
	Lilac or violet, pale grayish or whitish	2 to 5 inches broad. Stem 1 to 3 inches.	Tricholoma personatum (124)
Infundibuliform See Funnel-shaped.			
Kidney-shaped (Reniform)	White	½ to 1 inch by ⅛ to ¾ of an inch broad. Attached to wood at margin.	Crepidotus applanatus (45)
	Brown, rusty, or pale-yellowish	⅔ to 2 inches broad. Attached to wood by its edge.	Crepidotus calolepis (46)
	White	1 to 2½ inches broad. Attached to wood by its edge.	Crepidotus malachius (47)
	White; downy	⅓ to 1 inch broad. Attached to wood by its top surface.	Crepidotus versutus (48)
Knob (umbo) at center of cap	Grayish, yellowish or brownish	½ to 1½ inches broad. Gills narrow; forked; whitish; extending down the stem.	Cantharellus dichotomus (15)
	Pale violet or white, with violet tint	1 to 3 inches broad. Gills purplish when young; rusty when old. Stem violaceous; tapering upward.	Cortinarius albo-violaceus (40)
	Cinnamon-brown	1 to 2 inches broad. Webby veil under cap when young.	Cortinarius cinnamomeus (41)

KEY TO COMMON GILLED FUNGI

IDENTIFICATION BY **FORM** OF **CAP** (*Continued*)

Form of Cap	Color of Cap	Remarks	Name
Knob (umbo) at center of cap	Hazel-nut or umber	1 to 2 inches broad. Cracks on surface. Margin lobed when mature. Gills pink.	Entoloma commune (49)
	Umber; shiny	¾ to 1¾ inches broad. Open places; late autumn. Gills pink when mature.	Entoloma strictius (51)
	Wine-buff or orange-buff; often greenish with colored scales at margin	1 to 2 inches broad. Sticky when moist. Stem scaly.	Flammula polychroa (53)
	Cinnamon to buff	¼ to ½ inch broad. Cap conic. Gills cinnamon. Stem 1 to 2 inches long.	Galera hypnorum (54)
	Tawny, rusty	1 to 2 inches broad. Edge turned in. Gills notched. Pallid to tawny. Stem cream-colored.	Hebeloma precox (56)
	Yellowish-brown silky	1 to 2 inches broad. Radiating cracks. Gills attached to stem; pallid or tan. Stem solid; slightly swollen at base.	Inocybe rimosa (68)
	White, with reddish-brown scales	1 to 4 inches broad. Gills white; free from stem. Stem with ring.	Lepiota americana (82)
	Brownish; scaly	3 to 5 inches broad. Gills 5 to 10 inches long; stem with a collar. Gills free from stem.	Lepiota procera (85)
	Buff or tawny	1 to 2 inches broad. In grass. Dries without putrifying. Stem slender; tough.	Marasmius oreades (87)
	Some shade of brown or gray	½ to 1½ inches broad. On wood. In clusters. Cap conic. Stem hairy at base.	Mycena galericulata (90)
	Entire plant rose, purple or lilac	¾ to 1½ inches broad. Cap thin; bell-shaped; fine radiating lines at edge. Stem long.	Mycena pura (91)

IDENTIFICATION BY **FORM** OF **CAP** (*Continued*)

Form of Cap	Color of Cap	Remarks	Name
Knob at center of cap	Whitish, yellow-ish, or greenish yellow	1 to 3 inches broad. On ground in woods. Gills and stem white.	Tricholoma sejunctum (126)
	Yellowish-brown	4 to 8 inches broad. Stem at edge of cap or absent. Gills wavy; forked.	Cantharellus crispus (14)
	Sooty-brown, brownish-yellow or dingy-yellow when moist; gray, grayish-yellow or grayish-brown when dry	1 to 2 inches broad. Pit at center or funnel-shaped. Gills narrow; forked.	Cantharellus infundibluli-formis (17)
Lobed at edge	Grayish-brown, often yellow-tinged	1 to 3 inches broad. Gills liquefying black when old.	Coprinus atrament-arius (37)
	Buff-yellow or tawny yellow	1 to 2 inches broad. In clusters. Gills lique-fying black when old.	Coprinus micaceus (39)
	Hazel-nut or umber brown	1 to 2 inches broad. Gills pink; notched.	Entoloma commune (49)
	Pale yellow, some-times red-tinged at center	¾ to 1¾ inches broad. All yellow. Thin; fragile. Gills waxy; far apart.	Hygrophorus chlorophan us (58)
	Red or sul-phur-yel-low	½ to 1½ inches broad. Strikingly conic cap.	Hygrophorus conicus (59)
	Bright-red; paler or yellow when old	1 to 3 inches broad. Waxy; sticky when moist. Gills broad; far apart.	Hygrophorus puniceus (62)

KEY TO COMMON GILLED FUNGI

IDENTIFICATION BY **FORM** OF **CAP** (*Continued*)

Form of Cap	Color of Cap	Remarks	Name
Lobed at edge	Brownish-flesh-color when moist; paler when dry	½ to 2 inches broad. In clusters on wood. Gills sawlike at edge.	Lentinus cochleatus (80)
	Tawny	¼ to ¾ inch broad. On wood. Taste acrid and puckery. Stem at edge of cap.	Panus stypticus (99)
With PIT or small depression at center (Umbilicate)	Sooty or brownish to yellowish or grayish	1 to 2 inches broad. Sometimes funnel-shaped. Gills narrow; forked. Stem hollow; slender.	Cantharellus infundibuliformis (17)
	Yellow	½ to 1 inch broad. All yellow.	Cantharellus minor (18)
	Whitish; brown-tinged when moist. Whitish when dry	¼ to 1½ inches broad. Taste and odor branny. Gills attached to or extending down the stem.	Clitocybe albidula (19)
	White; shiny when dry	½ to 1¼ inches broad. All white. Gills decurrent. Stem rooting and hairy at base.	Clitocybe candicans (21)
	Red, orange or yellow	½ to 1 inch broad. Gills yellow; waxy. Stem, color of cap.	Hygrophorus cantharellus (57)
	Deep red, vermilion or yellow	½ to 2 inches broad. Gills yellow Stem like cap.	Hygrophorus miniatus (60)
	Tanned leather	½ to 1 inch broad. Cracks on surface. Gills whitish when young, rusty when old.	Inocybe abundans (67)
PIT or depression at center	Pale-red, buff-red or flesh-red when moist; buff or grayish when dry	½ to 2 inches broad. Gills broad; flesh or purplish.	Laccaria laccata (69)

IDENTIFICATION BY **FORM** OF **CAP** (*Continued*)

Form of Cap	Color of Cap	Remarks	Name
PIT or depression at center	White or whitish	2 to 5 inches broad. Soft wooly surface. Acrid milky juice.	Lactarius vellereus (78)
	Whitish	¼ to ½ inch broad. Cap thin, with radiating furrows.	Marasmius rotula (89)
	Dull-yellow or yellowish-rusty	¼ to 1 inch broad. In clusters on wood. Stem hairy at base.	Omphalia campanella (93)
	Yellow or pale orange	¼ to 1 inch broad. Cap thin. Gills decurrent. Stem long; slender.	Omphalia fibula (94)
	White, sometimes with yellowish stains	2 to 4 inches broad. Funnel-shaped when old. Often pit at center. Gills white, often greenish when old. Stem short; thick.	Russula delica (114)
With Radiating marks or furrows at edge. (Striate)	Orange or red; paler at edge	3 to 6 inches broad. Gills yellow; free from stem. Stem yellow; with ring.	Amanita cæsarea (4)
	Bright red or orange when young; yellow on margin when mature	3 to 8 inches broad. Gills white; free from stem. Stem with ring.	Amanita muscaria (5) (slight striations.)
	Brownish-red or red-tinged; warty	3 to 5 inches broad. Chalk white gills. Ringed stem, bulbous at base.	Amanita rubescens (7)
	Reddish-white to reddish brown or leaden-colored	2 to 4 inches broad. Cap thin; fragile. Gills white; free from stem. Stem sheathed at base.	Amanitopsis vaginata (8)
	Dull-white, yellowish or reddish-brown	1 to 3 inches broad. Gills white; free from stem; very large, lobed sheath at base.	Amanitopsis volvata (9)

KEY TO COMMON GILLED FUNGI

IDENTIFICATION BY **FORM** OF CAP (*Continued*)

Form of Cap	Color of Cap	Remarks	Name
With Radiating marks or furrows at edge. (Striate)	Buff-yellow or tawny-yellow	1 to 2 inches broad. Cap bell-shaped. In clusters. Gills liquefying black when old.	Coprinus micaceus (39)
	Umber brown; shiny	¾ to 1¾ inches broad. Gills pink when mature; attached to stem; notched.	Entoloma strictius (51)
	Watery-cinnamon when moist; yellowish or buff when dry	¼ to ½ inch broad. Gills cinnamon. Stem 1 to 2 inches.	Galera hypnorum (54)
	White, with reddish-brown scales	1 to 4 inches broad. Gills white; free from stem. Stem thicker at base; sometimes with ring.	Lepiota americana (82)
	Rusty-red; darker at center	¼ to ½ inch broad. Thin; conic or bell-shaped. Stem dark; shiny. Dries without putrifying.	Marasmius siccus (86)
	Light yellowish or pale brick-red; paler when old	1 to 2 or more inches broad. Shriveled, leathery when dry. Stem curved and hairy at base.	Marasmius peronatus (88)
	Whitish	¼ to ½ inch broad. Cap thin; black spot at center. Dries without putrifying.	Marasmius rotula (89)
	Some shade of brown or gray	¼ to 1¼ inches broad. In clusters on wood. Stem hairy at base.	Mycena galericulata (90)
	Entire plant some shade of rose or purple	¾ to 1¼ inches broad. Veins between gills.	Mycena pura (91)
	Dull yellow or yellowish-rusty	¼ to 1 inch broad. In clusters on wood. Pit at center of cap.	Omphalia campanella (93)

IDENTIFICATION BY **FORM** OF **CAP** (*Continued*)

Form of Cap	Color of Cap	Remarks	Name
	Yellow or pale orange	1/6 to 1/2 inch broad. Cap thin; pit at center Stem very long.	Omphalia fibula (94)]
	Yellow or brown	1/2 to 1 inch broad. Cap thin; elevated at center. Gills flesh-pink when old.	Pluteus admirabilis (109)
With Radial marks or furrows at edge of cap (Striate)	Whitish, grayish, or grayish-brown	1/4 to 1/2 inch broad. On ground in clusters. Cap conic. Stem white; 1 to 1 1/2 inches.	Psathyrella disseminata (111)
	Red, dark purple olivaceous or green	2 to 4 inches broad. Gills yellowish.	Russula alutacea (113)
	Blood-red or rosy	2 to 4 inches broad. Gills chalk white. Taste acrid.	Russula emetica (115)
	Yellowish or dingy rusty	2 to 5 inches broad. Bad odor. Gills whitish or yellowish; some forked.	Russula fœtens (116)
Reniform See Kidney-shaped			
Revolute See Edge Turned up			
Sessile See Stem absent			
Split at the Edge	Grayish-brown; often yellow-tinged	1 to 3 inches broad. Gills liquefying black when old.	Coprinus atramentarius (37)
	Whitish with yellowish scales	Cylindrical cap, 1 1/2 to 3 inches high before expansion. Turning to ink when old.	Coprinus comatus (38) Frontispiece

KEY TO COMMON GILLED FUNGI

Form of Cap	Color of Cap	Remarks	Name
	Buff-yellow or tawny-yellow	1 to 2 inches broad. In clusters. Conic or bell-shaped. Gills liquefy black when old.	Coprinus micaceus (39)
Split at the Edge	Pale yellow; sometimes red-tinged at center	¾ to 1¾ inches broad. All yellow. Cap thin; fragile	Hygrophorus chlorophanus (58)
	Whitish; yellow-tinged when moist	1 to 3 inches broad. On ground; open places. Gills white turning purplish-brown.	Hypholoma incertum (64)
Striatulate, Striate, See Radial marks			
Umbilicate See Pit at Center			
Umbonate See Knob at center			
	White or with dingy hues	1½ to 3 inches broad. Gills pink; turning brown and black when old.	Agaricus campestris (2)
	Bright yellow, reddish-yellow or rusty	2 to 4 inches. Cap furrowed. Stem long; bulbous.	Cortinarius corrugatus (43)
Veil, Fragments of, at edge of Cap	Bay or tawny-brown when moist; brownish-yellow when dry	1 to 2 inches broad. On wood; in clusters.	Hypholoma appendiculatum (63)

IDENTIFICATION BY **FORM** OF **CAP** (*Continued*)

Form of Cap	Color of Cap	Remarks	Name
	Whitish; yellow-tinged when moist; paler when dry	1 to 3 inches broad. On ground; open places. Splitting at edge.	Hypholoma incertum (64)
	Brownish, gray- or leaden tinted; sometimes red tinted	½ to 1 inch broad. Cap bell-shaped. Stem dusted with black spores when old ½ to 1½ inches long.	Panæolus campanulatus (86)
	Tan, gray or brownish	½ to 1½ inches broad. A network or cracks on surface.	Panæolus retirugis (97)
Cap with a WAVY Edge	Egg yellow	1 to 3 inches broad. Funnel-shaped.	Cantharellus cibarius (12)
	Sooty, brownish, yellowish or grayish	1 to 2 inches broad. Funnel-shaped.	Cantharellus infundibuliformis (17)
	Yellow	½ to 1 inch broad. Funnel-shaped.	Cantharellus minor (18)
	Ivory white	1 to 1½ inches broad. In grass. Tough; glossy.	Clitocybe dealbata (24)
	Green or dingy-green	1½ to 3 inches broad. Odor of anise.	Clitocybe odora (28)
	Tan, yellowish or chestnut	½ to 2 inches broad. Gills light, stem dark.	Collybia dryophila (33)
	Grayish-brown or blackish-brown	3 to 5 inches broad. Gills broad; white. Stem white.	Collybia platyphylla (34)
	Buff-yellow or tawny yellow	1 to 2 inches broad. In clusters. Conic. Radiating lines at edge. Liquefying black when old.	Coprinus micaceus (39)
	Umber (brown) with a silvery sheen when dry	¾ to 1¾ inches broad. On ground in grassy-places. Gills flesh-colored when mature; notched.	Entolma strictius (51)

KEY TO COMMON GILLED FUNGI

IDENTIFICATION BY **FORM** OF **CAP** (Continued)

Form of Cap	Color of Cap	Remarks	Name
Cap with a WAVY EDGE	Pale yellow	1 to 2 inches broad. In woods on wood. Stem downy at base. Taste bitter.	Flammula flavida (52)
	Deep red, vermilion or yellow	½ to 2 inches broad. Gills like cap or paler; waxy. Stem 1 to 3 inches.	Hygrophorus miniatus (60)
	Bright red; paler or yellow when old	1 to 3 inches broad. Gills yellow or reddish; waxy. Stem pied in color.	Hygrophorus puniceus (62)
	Whitish; yellow-tinged when moist; paler when dry	1 to 3 inches broad. On ground; open places. Splitting at edge. Stem splits.	Hypholoma incertum (64)
	Brownish-red or tawny	½ to 2½ inches broad. Funnel-shaped when old. Milky juice; mild or slightly bitter.	Lactarius subdulcis (76)
	Lilac or violet, grayish or almost white	2 to 5 inches broad. Gills color of cap or duller. Stem short; stout.	Tricholoma personatum (124)
	White, yellowish, gray, lilac or brownish	2 to 5 inches broad. On wood; stem at edge; in clusters.	Pleurotus ostreatus (106) (sapidus) (107)
WRINKLED surface	Yellow or rusty	2 to 4 inches broad. Sticky when moist. Stem bulbous and sticky at base.	Cortinarius corrugatus (43)
	Whitish, tinged with yellow when moist	1 to 3 inches broad. On ground. Gills whitish when young, purplish-brown when old.	Hypholoma incertum (64)
	Chestnut, paler when old	3 to 5 inches broad. Milky juice.	Lactarius corrugis (72)
	Sooty-brown	1 to 4 inches broad. Milky juice, mild or slightly acrid.	Lactarius lignyotus (74)

IDENTIFICATION BY **FORM** OF **CAP** (*Continued*)

Form of Cap	Color of Cap	Remarks	Name
	Marasmius all species when dry.		
WRIN-KLED surface	Tan, gray or brown-ish.	½ to 1½ inches broad. Cap sticky when moist. Fragments of veil at margin. Long, hollow stem.	Panæolus retirugis (97)
	Yellow with whitish flakes	2 to 4 inches broad. Stem with a ring.	Pholiota caper-ata (102)

IDENTIFICATION BY **SIZE** OF **CAP**

N.B.—The extremes of size only, are used here for identification.

Gilled Mushroom with Broad Caps

Size of Cap	Name
LARGE Cap; Four or more inches broad	Agaricus arvensis (1) Agaricus silvicola (3) Amanita cæsarea (4) Amanita muscaria (5) Amanita phalloides (6) Amanita rubescens (7) Amanitopsis vaginata (8) Armillaria mellea (10) Cantharellus crispus (14) Cantharellus floccosus (16) Clitocybe illudens (25) Clitopilus abortivus (29) Collybia platyphylla (34) Collybia radicata (35) Cortinarius corrugatus (43) Cortinarius violaceus (44) Laccaria ochropurpurea (68) Lactarius corrugis (72) Lactarius deliciosus (73) Lactarius lignyotus (74) Lactarius piperatus (75) Lactarius theiogalus (77) Lactarius vellereus (78) Lactarius volemus (79) Lentinus lepideus (81) Lepiota americana (82) **Lepiota molybdites (83)** Lepiota naucina (84) Lepiota procera (85) Panus strigosus (98) Paxillus involutus (100) Pholiota adiposa (101) Pholiota caperata (102)

KEY TO COMMON GILLED FUNGI

Gilled Mushrooms with Broad Caps (*Continued*)

Size of Cap	Name
LARGE Cap; Four or more inches broad	Pholiota squarrosa (105)
	Pleurotus ostreatus (106)
	Pleurotus sapidus (107)
	Pleurotus ulmarius (108)
	Russula alutacea (113)
	Russula delica (114)
	Russula emetica (115)
	Russula fœtens (116)
	Russula Mariæ (117)
	Russula Peckii (118)
	Russula virescens (119)
	Tricholoma album (122)
	Tricholoma equestre (123)
	Tricholoma personatum (124)
	Tricholoma russula (125)
	Tricholoma transmutans (127)
	Volvaria bombycina (128)

IDENTIFICATION BY **SIZE** OF **CAP**

Mushrooms with Small Caps

N. B.—Some of the Species in this table also occur of larger size than one inch.

Size of Cap	Name
SMALL Cap; One inch or less in diameter	Cantharellus cinnabarinus (13)
	Cantharellus umbonatus **(15)**
	Cantharellus minor **(18)**
	Clitocybe albidula (19)
	Clitocybe candicans (21)
	Clitocybe clavipes **(22)**
	Clitocybe dealbata (24)
	Collybia acervata (31)
	Collybia confluens (32)
	Collybia dryophila (33)
	Coprinus micaceus (39)
	Cortinarius cinnamomeus **(41)**
	Crepidotus applanatus (45)
	Crepidotus calolepis **(46)**
	Crepidotus malachius (47)
	Crepidotus versutus (48)
	Entoloma grayanum (50)
	Entoloma strictius (51)
	Flammula flavida (52)
	Flammula polychroa **(53)**
	Galera hypnorum (54)
	Galera tenera (55)
	Hygrophorus cantharellus **(57)**
	Hygrophorus chlorophanus **(58)**
	Hygrophorus conicus (59)
	Hygrophorus miniatus (60)
	Hygrophorus pratensis (61)
	Hygrophorus puniceus (62)

IDENTIFICATION BY SIZE OF CAP (*Continued*)

Mushrooms with Small Caps (*Continued*)

Size of Cap	Name
ONE INCH or less in diameter	Hypholoma appendiculatum (63) Hypholoma incertum (64) Inocybe abundans (67) Inocybe rimosa (68) Laccaria laccata (69) Lactarius camphoratus (71) Lactarius lignyotus (74) Lactarius subdulcis (76) Lentinus cochleatus (80) Lepiota americana (82) Marasmius siccus (86) Marasmius oreades (87) Marasmius peronatus (88) Marasmius rotula (89) Mycena galericulata (90) Mycena pura (91) Naucoria semiorbicularis (92) Omphalia campanella (93) Omphalia fibula (94) Panæolus campanulatus (95) Panæolus papilionaceus (96) Panæolus retriugis (97) Panus stypticus (99) Pholiota discolor (103) Pholiota praecox (104) Pluteus admirabilis (109) Psathyrella disseminata (111) Psilocybe fœnisecii (112) Russula mariæ (117) Schizophyllum commune (120) Stropharia semiglobata (121)

GILLS

IDENTIFICATION BY CHARACTER OF THE GILLS

Character of Gills	Color of Cap	Remarks	Name
	Grayish-brown or blackish-brown	3 to 5 inches broad. Gills broad; white stem white.	Collybia platyphylla (34) (brittle when old.)
BRITTLE	Red, dark purple, olivaceous or green	2 to 4 inches broad. Gills yellow; of equal length.	Russula alutacea (113)
	Rosy or blood-red	2 to 4 inches broad. Gills chalk white; Acrid taste	Russula emetica (115)

IDENTIFICATION BY **CHARACTER** OF THE **GILLS** (*Continued*)

Character of Gills	Color of Cap	Remarks	Name
BRITTLE	Yellowish- or dingy rusty	2 to 5 inches broad. Sticky when moist. Radial marks at edge. Bad odor.	Russula fœtens (116)
	Rosy pink, yellowish or light yellow	1½ to 2½ inches broad. Gills white; yellowish when old. Stem red.	Russula Peckii (118)
	Green or grayish-green	2 to 4 inches broad. Scaly surface.	Russula virescens (119)

Gills far apart (distant) see under Gills, form of.
Gills free from stem. See under Gills, form of

Milky Juice. See under Mushroom, character of

LIQUE-FYING when old.	Grayish-brown; often yellow-tinged; blackening when old	1 to 3 inches broad. Egg-shaped. Gills whitish when young, pinkish, then black when old.	Coprinus atramentarius (37)
	Whitish with yellow scales	Oblong or cylindric cap; 1½ to 3 inches long before expansion. Split at edge when old.	Coprinus comatus (38) (Frontispiece)
	Buff yellow; often brighter at center	1 to 2 inches broad. Conic. In clusters. Thin; radial marks at edge.	Coprinus micaceus (39)
FAR APART (distant.)	Egg yolk yellow	1 to 3 inches broad. All yellow. Funnel-shaped.	Cantharellus cibarius (12)
	Sooty-brown or yellowish when moist; gray, grayish-yellow or grayish-brown when dry	1 to 2 inches broad. Depressed at center; often wavy at edge. Gills narrow; forked.	Catharellus infundibuli-formis (17)

IDENTIFICATION BY **CHARACTER** OF THE **GILLS** (*Continued*)

Character of Gills	Color of Cap	Remarks	Name
FAR APART (distant.) (cont.)	Yellow, whitish or pale yellow	½ to 1 inch broad. Depressed at center; edge often wavy. Gills narrow; yellow.	Cantharellus minor (18)
	Blackish-brown or grayish-brown when moist; paler when dry	1½ to 3 inches broad. Depressed at center. Hygrophanous. Cap fleshy but thin.	Clitocybe cyathiformis (23)
	Whitish or grayish	2 to 3 inches broad. Bloom on surface. Odor branny. Gills salmon when old.	Clitopilus prunulus (30)
	Grayish-brown or smoky-brown	1 to 4 inches broad. Stem long and deeply rooted.	Collybia radicata (35)
	Dark violet	2 to 4 inches broad. Hairy scales. Gills turn from violet to rusty when old.	Cortinarius violaceus (44)
	Red, orange or yellow	½ to 1 inch broad. Sometimes depressed at center. Gills broad; decurrent. Stem 1 to 3 inches long.	Hygrophorus cantharellus (57)
	Red, vermilion or yellow	½ to 2 inches broad. Thin; fragile; often pit at center.	Hygrophorus miniatus (60)
	Tawny, reddish, buff, ashy or whitish	1 to 3 inches broad. Gills whitish or yellowish with veins between them; waxy.	Hygrophorus pratensis (61)
	Flesh-red or buff-red when moist. Pale ochre, grayish or buff when dry	½ to 2 inches broad. Gills thick, broad, sometimes purplish and dusted.	Laccaria laccata (69)
	Purplish-brown when moist; tan or grayish when dry	2 to 4 inches broad. Waxy; gills color of cap or paler; thick; broad.	Laccaria ochropurpurea (70)

KEY TO COMMON GILLED FUNGI

Character of Gills	Color of Cap	Remarks	Name
		Marasmius, all species.	
Separable easily from cap	Tan-colored or brownish; darker at center	½ to 1 inch broad and high (conic). Stem fragile; hollow; 3 to 4½ inches long.	Galera tenera (55)
		Paxillus, all species.	
Waxy		**Cantharellus, all species.**	

IDENTIFICATION BY **COLOR** OF THE **GILLS**

N.B.—Color of gills is used for identification of species only in cases where it differs from the color of the cap and where it is of a noticeably clear, distinct or unusual hue.

Color of Gills	Color of Cap	Remarks	Name
	White or yellowish	2 to 5 inches broad. Gills whitish when young, turning pink and then brown and black when old. Stem with double ring.	Agaricus arvensis (1)
	White or with dingy hues	1½ to 3 inches broad. Gills pink when young, turning brown and then black when old. Stem ringed when young.	Agaricus campestris (2)
Black	White or tinged with yellow or pink	2 to 5 inches broad. Gills pink, turning brown and then black when old. Ring (sometimes double) on stem.	Agaricus silvicola (3)
	Grayish-brown; often yellow-tinged; blackening when old	1 to 3 inches broad. Gills whitish when young, turning pinkish to black when old. Cap egg-shaped.	Coprinus atramentarius (37)

IDENTIFICATION BY COLOR OF THE GILLS (*Continued*)

Color of Gills	Color of Cap	Remarks	Name
Black	Buff yellow; often brighter at center	1 to 2 inches broad. In clusters. Conic. Thin; radial marks at edge. Whitish gills turn black when old and liquefy.	Coprinus micaceus (38) (Frontispiece)
	Brownish; leaden or reddish-tinted	½ to 1 inch broad. Bell-shaped. Stem 4 to 6 inches.	Panæolus campanulatus (95)
	Whitish-gray, often yellow-tinged	½ to 1½ inches broad. Hemispheric. Stem 3 to 5 inches.	Panæolus papilionaceus (96)
	Tan, gray or brownish	½ to 1½ inches broad. Surface cracked. Conic. Stem 2 to 6 inches.	Panæolus returugis (97)
	Whitish, grayish or grayish-brown	¼ to ½ inch broad. In clusters. Very thin; conic. Stem 1 to 1½ inches long	Psathyrella disseminata (111)
Green	Yellowish-brown	4 to 8 inches broad. On wood. Gills often forked; wavy. Stem lateral or absent.	Cantharellus crispus (14)
	White with brown scales	4 to 12 inches broad. Gills free from stem. Ring on stem but no cup.	Lepiota molybdites (83)

N. B.— Hypholoma perlexum (65) and sublateritium (66) } have sometimes a greenish tinge to the gills when old.

Russula delica (114) Gills often tinged greenish when old.

Color of Gills	Color of Cap	Remarks	Name
Pink, flesh-colored or salmon	White or yellowish	2 to 5 inches broad. Gills change color with age. Stem with double ring.	Agaricus arvensis (1)
	White or with dingy hues	1½ to 3 inches broad. Never in woods. Gills change color with age. Stem ringed when young.	Agaricus campestris (2)

KEY TO COMMON GILLED FUNGI

Color of Gills:	Color of Cap	Remarks	Name
Pink, flesh-color or salmon	White or tinged with yellow or pink	2 to 5 inches broad. Gills change color with age. Ring (sometimes double) on stem.	Agarisus silvicola (3)
	Gray or grayish-brown	2 to 4 inches broad. Taste and odor slightly branny. Gills whitish when young.	Clitopilus abortivus (29)
	Whitish or grayish	2 to 3 inches broad. Bloom on surface. Odor branny. Gills whitish when young. Stem white.	Clitopilus prunulus (30)
	Pale tan or flesh-color when moist; whitish when dry	1 to 2 inches broad. In tufts; in woods. Gills whitish or pinkish. Stem reddish- or purplish-brown; long (2 to 3 inches).	Collybia acervata (31) (gills slightly pinkish)
	Whitish, with yellow scales	Oblong or cylindric cap, 1½ to 3 inches high before expansion. Gills change color with age and liquefy black.	Coprinus comatus (38) Frontispiece
	Hazel-nut or umber	1 to 2 inches broad. Taste, odor branny. Gills notched.	Entoloma commune (49)
	Whitish or brownish-gray	1 to 3 inches broad. Taste branny. Gills whitish when young.	Entoloma grayanun (50)
	Umber-brown	¾ to 1¾ inches broad. Gills grayish-white when young. Cap shiny. Flesh brown.	Entoloma strictius (51)
	Brownish-flesh	½ to 2 inches broad. In tufts on wood. Cap thin; tough. Gills with saw-like edge.	Lentinus cochleatus (80)
	Some shade of brown or gray	¼ to 1¼ inches broad. Conic. In clusters on wood. Stem hairy at base.	Mycena galericulata (90)
	Yellow or brown	½ to 1 inch broad. Network of furrows. Gills whitish or yellowish when young. Stem downy at base.	Pluteus admirabilis (109)

IDENTIFICATION BY **COLOR** OF THE **GILLS** (*Continued*)

Color of Gills	Color of Cap	Remarks	Name
Pink, flesh-color or salmon	Dingy-brown; rarely white, yellow, ashy or grayish	2 to 2½ inches broad. Gills free from stem. Stem easily separable from cap.	Pluteus cervinus (110)
	Silky white	2 to 8 inches broad. Gills free from stem. Stem with large cup at base.	Volvaria bombycina (128)
Purple or Purplish	Flesh-red or buff-red when moist, pale ochre, grayish or buff when dry	½ to 2 inches broad. Gills broad; powdered white when old.	Laccaria laccata (69)
	Dark violet	2 to 4 inches broad. Hairy scales. Gills rusty when old. Bulbous stem.	Cortinarius violaceus (44)
	Pale violet; buff or silvery-white	1 to 3 inches broad. Gills thick; far apart; broad; violet to rusty.	Cortinarius alboviolaceus (40)
	Purplish-brown when moist, grayish or pale tan when dry	2 to 4 inches broad. Gills thick; far apart; broad.	Laccaria ochropurpurea (70)
	Violet, lilac, grayish or white	2 to 5 inches broad. Stem short and stout. Gills nearly free from stem.	Tricholoma personatum (124)
White	Red or orange when young; yellow at edge when mature	3 to 8 inches broad. Cap warty. Gills free from stem. Stem with ring and cup at base.	Amanita muscaria (5)

KEY TO COMMON GILLED FUNGI

IDENTIFICATION BY **COLOR** OF THE **GILLS** (*Continued*)

Color of Gills,	Color of Cap	Remarks	Name
	White, yellow, gray, blackish, brown or smoky-olive.	1½ to 5 inches broad. Gills free from stem or extending to it; broad. Stem with ring and with cup at base.	Amanita phalloides (6)
	Reddish or brownish-red	3 to 5 inches broad. Cap warty. Gills free from stem. Stem with ring; bulbous at base.	Amanita rubescens (7)
	Reddish-white, reddish-brown or leaden brown	2 to 4 inches broad. Radial marks at edge. Gills free from stem. Stem with cup at base.	Amanitopsis vaginata (8)
	Dull-white, yellowish, or reddish-brown	1 to 3 inches broad. Gills free from stem. Stem with large lobed sheath or cup at base.	Amanitopsis volvata (9)
White	Honey yellow to dark reddish-brown	1 to 6 inches broad. Stem with ring.	Armillaria mellea (10)
	Grayish-white, grayish-brown, yellowish-brown, blackish-brown or bluish-gray	½ to 1½ inches broad. Gills repeatedly forked.	Cantharellus umbonatus (15)
	Grayish-brown or sooty-brown	1 to 3 inches broad. Stem club-shaped.	Clitocybe clavipes (22)
	Reddish-tan or pale tan	2 to 3 inches broad. Funnel-shaped.	Clitocybe infundibuliformis (26)
	Green or dingy-green	1½ to 3 inches broad. Odor of anise.	Clitocybe odora (28)

95

IDENTIFICATION BY **COLOR** OF THE GILLS (*Continued*)

Color of Gills	Color of Cap	Remarks	Names
White	Grayish-brown or blackish-brown	3 to 5 inches broad. Gills broad. Stem white.	Collybia platyphylla (34)
	Grayish-brown or smoky-brown	1 to 4 inches broad. Stem deeply rooted and long.	Collybia radicata (35)
	Reddish-yellow or tawny; sometimes darker at center	1 to 2 inches broad. In tufts. Stem brown; hairy when mature.	Collybia velutipes (36)
	Grayish-brown; turning black when old	1 to 3 inches broad. Egg-shaped. Gills liquefying black when old.	Coprinus atramentarius (37) (gills white when young)
	Whitish, with yellow scales	Oblong or cylindric cap, 1 to 3 inches broad before expansion. Split at edge when old.	Coprinus comatus (38) (gills white when young) (Frontispiece)
	Brownish-orange or golden-tawny	2 to 5 inches broad. Milky juice of mild taste.	Lactarius volemus (79)
	Brownish or reddish-brown, with scales	3 to 5 inches broad. Gills free from stem. Stem 5 to 10 inches; with ring.	Lepiota procera (85)
	Rosy or blood-red	2 to 4 inches broad. Taste acrid. Radial marks at edge. Stem white or red-tinged.	Russula emetica (115)
	Rosy-pink, fading to light yellow	2 to 4 inches broad. Taste mild. Edge often split. Stem rosy-pink. Gills yellowish when old.	Russula Peckii (118)
	Green or grayish green	2 to 4 inches broad. Taste mild. Flaky patches on surface.	Russula virescens (119)
	Rosy-red or flesh-color	2 to 5 inches broad. Sometimes small scales. Gills white, often red-spotted. Stem short; thick.	Tricholoma russula (125)

KEY TO COMMON GILLED FUNGI

IDENTIFICATION BY FORM OF THE GILLS

Form of Gills	Name
(Adnate) Attached broadly to the stem	Armillaria mellea (10)
	Clitocybe, all species
	Clitopilus abortivus (29)
	Cortinarius, all species
	Flammula flavida (52)
	Galera hypnorum (54)
	Hebeloma precox (56)
	Hygrophorus miniatus (60)
	Hypholoma appendiculatum (63)
	Hypholoma incertum (64)
	Hypholoma perplexum (65)
	Hypholoma sublateritium (66)
	Inocybe abundans (67)
	Inocybe rimosa (68)
	Laccaria, all species
	Lactarius theiogalus (77)
	Lactarius vellereus (78)
	Lactarius volemus (79)
	Marasmius siccus (86)
	Marasmius rotula (89)
	Mycena galericulata (90)
	Naucoria semiorbicularis (92)
	Panæolus campanulatus (95)
	Panæolus papilionaceus (96)
	Pholiota adiposa (101)
	Pholiota caperata (102)
	Pholiota discolor (103)
	Pholiota squarrosa (105)
	Psathyrella disseminata (111)
	Psilocybe fœnisecii (112)
	Stropharia semiglobata (121)
	Tricholoma, all species except personatum
(Adnexed) extending as far as the stem but not attached to it	Collybia acervata (31)
	Collybia dryophila (32)
	Collybia platyphylla (34)
	Collybia radicata (35)
	Collybia velutipes (36)
	Entoloma commune (49)
	Entoloma grayanum (50)
	Entoloma strictius (51)
	Galera tenera (55)
	Hygrophorus chlorophanus (58)
	Hypholoma perplexum (65)
	Hypholoma sublateritium (66)
	Marasmius peronatus (88)
	Marasmius rotula (89)
	Panæolus retirugis (97)
	Pholiota praecox (104)
	Pleurotus ulmarius (108)
	Russula fœtens (116)
	Russula virescens (119)

IDENTIFICATION BY **FORM** OF THE **GILLS** (*Continued*)

Form of Gills	Color of Cap	Remarks	Name
	White, yellow, greenish, gray, brown or blackish	1½ to 5 inches broad. Gills white; free from stem. Stem with ring and cup.	Amanita phalloides (6)
	Whitish, yellowish or reddish-brown	1 to 3 inches broad. Stem with cup but no ring; Gills free from stem.	Amanitopsis volvata (8)
	Grayish-brown or sooty-brown	1 to 3 inches broad. Cap the shape of an inverted cone. Stem swollen below.	Clitocybe clavipes (22)
	Grayish-brown or blackish-brown	3 to 5 inches broad. Cap fragile. Gills white. Stem white.	Collybia platyphylla (34)
Broad	Grayish-brown or smoky-brown	1 to 4 inches broad. Deeply rooted stem; 2 to 8 inches long above ground.	Collybia radicata (35)
	Reddish yellow or tawny	1 to 2 inches broad. In tufts on wood. Stem velvety.	Collybia velutipes (36)
	Pale violet, buff, or white with violet tint	1 to 3 inches broad. Gills violet when young, cinnamon when old. Stem tapering upward.	Cortinarius albo-violaceus (40)
	Golden-yellow or tawny-yellow	1½ to 3 inches broad. Very slimy. Stem scaly.	Cortinarius collinitus (42)
	Whitish, yellowish, or pale rusty	⅔ to 2 inches broad. On wood. Stem at edge. Cap irregular shape.	Crepidotus calolepis (46)
	White; downy	⅛ to 1 inch broad. Attached to wood by its edge or top surface.	Crepidotus versutus (48)
	Cinnamon, rusty or buff	¼ to ½ inch broad. Gills far apart. Stem long; hollow; slender.	Galera hypnorum (54)

KEY TO COMMON GILLED FUNGI

IDENTIFICATION BY **FORM** OF THE **GILLS** (*Continued*)

Form of Gills	Color of Cap	Remarks	Name
	Bright red	1 to 3 inches broad. Waxy; fragile. Stem sometimes vari-colored, red, yellow and white.	Hygrophorus puniceus (62)
	Pale red, buff, flesh-colored or rusty	½ to 2 inches broad. Gills flesh-red but powdered white when old.	Laccaria laccata (69)
	Purplish-brown, grayish or pale tan	2 to 4 inches broad. Waxy. Stem fibrous; solid.	Laccaria ochro-purpurea (70)
	Brownish-flesh-color when moist; paler when dry	½ to 2 inches broad. Gills with saw-like edge. Stem grooved.	Lentinus coch-leatus (80)
Broad	White, with brown scales	4 to 12 inches broad. Gills green; free from stem. Stem with ring.	Lepiota molybdites (83)
	Rusty-red; darker at center	¼ to ½ inch broad. Shrivels when dry; revives when moist. Stem long; blackish-brown; shining.	Marasmius siccus (86)
	Buff or *café au lait*	1 to 2 inches broad. Large knob at center in some. Stem tough. Open places.	Marasmius oreades (87)
	Brownish; black spot at center	¼ to ½ inch broad. Cap thin; dry. Gills far apart. Stem black; shiny.	Marasmius rotula (89)
	Tawny or rusty	1 to 2 inches broad. Cap often hemispheric. Stem long. Difficult.	Naucoria semi-orbicularis (92)
	Tan or gray	½ to 1½ inches broad. Fragments of veil at edge of cap; network of cracks on surface. Long stem.	Panæolus retirugis (97)

IDENTIFICATION BY **FORM** OF THE **GILLS** (*Continued*)

Form of Gills	Color of Cap	Remarks	Name
	White; hairy	8 inches or more broad. Stem at edge of cap. Gills extending down the stem.	Panus strigosus (98)
	Shelf (gilled) fungi growing on wood.		Pleurotus os-treatus (106) sapidus (107) ulmarius (108)
	Yellow or brown	½ to 1 inch broad. Network of folds on surface. Usually knob at center.	Pluteus ad-mirabilis (109)
	Dingy brown; ashy; rarely white or yellow	2 to 2½ inches broad. Gills pinkish; free from stem. Stem separable easily from cap.	Pluteus cervinus (110)
Broad	Smoky-brown or reddish-brown	½ to 1 inch broad. Gills brown. Stem fragile; slender. In grass.	Psilocybe fœnisecii (112)
	Red, purple or oliva-ceous	2 to 4 inches broad. Gills pale yellow when young; rusty when old. Not forked.	Russula alutacea (113)
	Rosy or blood-red	2 to 4 inches broad. Acrid taste. Gills white; brittle.	Russula emetica (115)
	Whitish, yellowish or green-ish-yel-low; streaked with brown	1 to 3 inches broad. Gills white; notched. Stem stout; solid.	Tricholoma se-junctum (126)
	Silky white	2 to 8 inches broad. Usually on wood. Gills flesh-colored; free from stem. Large cup at base of stem.	Volvaria bomby-cina (128)

KEY TO COMMON GILLED FUNGI

IDENTIFICATION BY **FORM** OF THE GILLS *(Continued)*

Form of Gills	Name
(De-current) Extending down the stem	Armillaria mellea (10) Cantharellus, all species Clitocybe, all species Clitopilus abortivus (29) Clitopilus prunulus (30) Crepidotus applanatus (45) Flammula polychroa (53) Hygrophorus cantharellus (57) Hygrophorus pratensis (61) Laccaria, all species Lactarius camphoratus (71) Lactarius deliciosus (73) Lactarius piperatus (75) Lactarius subdulcis (76) Lactarius theiogalus (77) Lactarius vellereus (78) Lactarius volemus (79) Lentinus cochleatus (80) Lentinus lepideus (81) Mycena galericulata (90) Omphanella campanella (93) Omphalia fibula (94) Paxillus involutus (100) Pholiota squarrosa (105) Pleurotus ostreatus (106) Pleurotus sapidus (107) Tricholoma russula (125)

Form of Gills	Color of Cap	Remarks	Name
Far apart; (Distant)	Egg-yolk yellow	1 to 3 inches broad. All yellow. Cap funnel-shaped. Gills narrow; thick.	Cantharellus cibarius (12)
	Sooty-brown, brown-ish-yellow or dingy yellow when moist; gray, grayish-yellow or grayish-brown when dry	1 to 2 inches broad. Funnel-shaped. Stem slender; 1 to 4 inches long.	Cantharellus infundibuli-formis (17)
	Yellow	½ to 1 inch broad. Gills decurrent, yellow. Stem slender; 1 to 1½ inches long.	Cantharellus minor (18)

IDENTIFICATION BY **FORM** OF THE **GILLS** (*Continued*)

Form of Gills	Color of Cap	Remarks	Name
For apart; (Distant)	Blackish-brown or grayish-brown when moist; paler when dry	1½ to 3 inches broad. Funnel-shaped. Gills attached to stem. Stem ¾ to 1¼ inches long.	Clitocybe cyathiformis (23)
	Whitish or grayish	2 to 3 inches broad. Bloom on surface. Odor branny. Gills whitish when young, salmon when old.	Clitopilus prunulus (30)
	Grayish-brown or smoky-brown	1 to 4 inches broad. Gills white. Stem very long and deep-rooted.	Collybia radicata (35)
	Orange or yellow or red	½ to 1 inch broad. Gills waxy; arched; extending down the stem. Stem slender; 1 to 3 inches long.	Hygrophorus cantharellus (57)
	Deep red, vermilion or yellow	½ to 2 inches broad. Gills waxy; yellow or reddish; attached to stem.	Hygrophorus miniatus (60)
	Tawny, reddish, buff, ashy or whitish	1 to 3 inches broad. Gills waxy, thick; extending down the stem.	Hygrophorus pratensis (51)
	Bright red when moist; paler or yellow when old	1 to 3 inches broad. Gills broad; thick; but slightly attached to stem.	Hygrophorus puniceus (62)
	Pale-red, buff-red or flesh-red when moist; pale ochre, grayish or buff when dry	½ to 2 inches broad. Gills broad, flesh-colored to purplish; dusted white by spores when old.	Laccaria laccata (69)

KEY TO COMMON GILLED FUNGI

IDENTIFICATION BY **FORM** OF THE **GILLS** (*Continued*)

Form of Gills	Color of Cap	Remarks	Name
Far apart; (Distant)	Purplish-brown when moist; grayish or pale tan when dry	2 to 4 inches broad. Firm; fleshy. Gills purplish; thick, broad.	Laccaria ochropurpurea (70)
	Rusty-red; darker at center	½ to 1½ inch broad. Convex; dry. Gills few; whitish. Stem tough, shiny; 1 to 2 inches.	Marasmius siccus (86)
	Buff or tawny	1 to 2 inches broad. Leathery and wrinkled when dry. Broad knob at centre. Stem tough.	Marasmius oreades (87)
	Brownish; darker at center	¼ to ½ inch broad. Cap thin; dry. Gills few; broad; whitish. Stem slender; tough; black.	Marasmius rotula (89)
Forked or branched	— All species of Cantharellus, e. g.		
	Yellowish-orange; sometimes brown-tinged	1 to 3 inches broad. Funnel-shaped; downy surface. Gills narrow.	Cantharellus aurantiacus (11)
	Egg-yolk yellow	1 to 3 inches broad. Funnel-shaped. Gills blunt; narrow. All yellow.	Cantharellus cibarius (12)
	Cinnabar red	½ to 1½ inches in diameter. Wavy edge. Irregular shape. Gills narrow; decurrent. On ground. Entire plant red.	Cantharellus cinnabarinus (13)
	Yellowish brown	4 to 8 inches. On wood. Stem at edge. Gills wavy; greenish.	Cantharellus crispus (14)

IDENTIFICATION BY **FORM** OF THE **GILLS** (*Continued*)

Form of Gills	Color of Cap	Remarks	Name
Forked or branched	Grayish-white, grayish-brown, yellow-ish-brown, blackish-brown or bluish-gray	½ to 1½ inches broad. Gills whitish or yellowish; narrow; near together. Extending down the stem. (Decurrent).	Cantharellus umbonatus (15)
	Sooty-brown, brown-ish-yellow or dingy-yellow when moist; gray, grayish-yellow or grayish-brown when dry	1 to 2 inches broad. Funnel-shaped. Gills narrow; dusted when old. Stem slender; 1 to 4 inches.	Cantharellus floccosus (16)
	Yellowish, inclining to rusty	Trumpet-shaped; 2 to 4 inches broad and 3 to 6 inches deep.	Cantharellus infundibuliformis (17)
	Yellow	½ to 1 inch. Depressed at center; thin. Gills far apart; decurrent. Smaller and more slender than C. cibarius.	Cantharellus minor (18)
	Pure white	2 to 3 inches broad. All white. Stem 1½ to 3 inches.	Clitocybe albissima (20)
	Yellowish with zones of deeper hue	2 to 5 inches broad. Slightly acrid milky juice.	Lactarius deliciosus (73)
	White; often covered with debris or dirt	3 to 5 inches broad. Acrid milky juice. Stem short.	Lactarius piperatus (75)
	Tawny or brown-ish-red	½ to 2½ inches broad. Slightly bitterish milky juice.	Lactarius subdulcis (76)

KEY TO COMMON GILLED FUNGI

Form of Gills	Color of Cap	Remarks	Name
	Tawny-reddish	2 to 5 inches broad. White milky juice, turning sulphur-yellow after exposure to air.	Lactarius theiogalus (77)
	White or whitish	2 to 5 inches broad. Downy surface; acrid milky juice.	Lactarius vellereus (78)
	Grayish-buff, rusty brown or yellowish	2 to 4 inches broad. Edge curled downward and inward. Stem sometimes off center. Stem short.	Paxillus involutus (100)
Forked or branched	White, yellowish ashy, lilac or brownish	2 to 5 inches broad. Stem at edge. In tufts on wood.	Pleurotus ostreatus (106) & sapideus (107)
	White, sometimes with yellowish stains	2 to 4 inches broad. Funnel-shaped when old. Often pit at center. Gills white, often greenish when old. Stem short; thick.	Russula delica (114)
	Yellowish or dingy ochre	3 to 5 inches broad. Bad odor. Radial marks at edge. Gills whitish to yellowish. Cap sticky when moist.	Russula foetens (116)
	Green or grayish-green	2 to 4 inches broad. Flaky patches. Gills and stem white.	Russula virescens (119)

Form of Gills			
Gills free from stem	Agaricus, all species Amanita, all species Amanitopsis, all species Collybia acervata (31) Collybia confluens (32) Inocybe abundans (67)	Lepiota, all species **Marasmius siccus (80)** Pluteus cervinus (110) Russula virescens (119) Tricholoma transmutans (**127**) Volvaria bombycina (128)	

IDENTIFICATION BY **FORM** OF THE **GILLS** (*Continued*)

Form of Gills	Color of Cap	Remarks	Name
	Cantharellus. All species.		
	Whitish, grayish, yellowish or brownish	1 to 3½ inches broad. In tufts on ground; open places.	Clitocybe multiceps (27)
	Tan or flesh-red when moist; whitish when dry	1 to 2 inches broad. In dense tufts on wood. Stem downy at base.	Collybia acervata (31)
	Reddish-brown or grayish-red when moist; pallid or grayish when dry	¾ to 1½ inches broad. Cap thin; shriveled when dry. Stem long; slender; tough.	Collybia confluens (32)
Narrow	White	½ to 1 inch long; ⅓ to ¾ inch broad. Stem at edge or absent. On wood.	Crepidotus applanatus (45)
	Whitish, yellow-tinged at center, darker when moist	1 to 3 inches broad. On ground; open places. Gills whitish; purplish-brown when old.	Hypholoma incertum (64)
	Yellowish-rusty to dull yellow	¼ to 1 inch broad. In clusters on wood. Pit at center of cap.	Omphalia campanella (93)
	Yellow or pale orange	⅛ to ½ inch broad. On mossy ground. Cap thin, with pit at center.	Omphalia fibula (94)
	Tawny	¼ to ¾ inch broad. Tough; kidney-shaped; on wood. Stem at edge or absent.	Panus stypticus (99)
	Watery-cinnamon when moist; pale yellow when dry	1 to 2 inches broad. On wood. Stem with ring.	Pholiota discolor (103)

KEY TO COMMON GILLED FUNGI

IDENTIFICATION BY **FORM** OF THE **GILLS** (*Continued*)

Form of Gills	Color of Cap	Remarks	Name
Notched near the stem (Sinuate)	Pale or dark tan, yellowish or chestnut	½ to 2 inches broad. Gills whitish or yellowish; not attached to stem. Stem brown; sometimes bulbous; 1 to 3 in.	Collybia dryophila (33)
	Grayish-brown or blackish-brown	3 to 5 inches broad. Cap thin; fragile. Gills broad; white. Stem white; 3 to 5 inches.	Collybia platyphylla (34)
	Dark violet; with tufts or scales	2 to 4 inches broad. Gills violet when young; rusty when old.	Cortinarius violaceus (44)
	Umber brown; shiny	¾ to 1¾ inches broad. In clusters on ground. Gills whitish when young; pink when old.	Entoloma strictius (51) (slightly notched)
	Wine-buff, orange buff; purplish scales	1 to 2 inches broad. Gills cream; brownish or purple when old. Stem 2 to 3 inches long.	Flammula polychroa (53)
	Tawny-rusty	1½ to 2 inches broad. On ground. Gills notched; pallid or tawny.	Hebeloma precox (56)
	White or pale-rusty; brownish scales	2 to 4 inches broad. On wood. Tough. Gills with saw-teeth.	Lentinus lepideus (81)
	Some shade of brown or gray	¼ to 1¼ inches broad. Conic. Clusters on wood. Stem slender; hairy at base.	Mycena galericulata (90)
	White, whitish or yellowish	3 to 5 inches broad. On dead elm wood. Stem at edge of cap.	Pleurotus ulmarius (108)
	White, or yellowish at center	2 to 4 inches broad. Taste acrid or bitter. Gills close together; white.	Tricholoma album (122)
	Yellowish; sometimes brownish at center	2 to 4 inches. Sticky. Taste branny. Gills pale yellow.	Tricholoma equestre (123)

IDENTIFICATION BY **FORM** OF THE **GILLS** (*Continued*)

Form of Gills	Color of Cap	Remarks	Name
Notched near stem (Sinuate)	Pale pink, rosy or flesh-color	2 to 5 inches broad. Sticky when moist. Gills white, often red-spotted when old. Stem short; thick.	Tricholoma russula (125)
	Whitish, yellowish or greenish yellow	1 to 3 inches broad. Knob at center. Gills and stem white.	Tricholoma sejunctum (126)
	Tawny-red to reddish-brown	2 to 4 inches broad. Sticky when moist or young. Odor and taste branny.	Tricholoma transmutans (127)
Saw-teeth at edge	Brownish-flesh-color when moist; paler when dry	½ to 2 inches broad. In tufts. Thin; tough. Gills whitish; flesh tinged. Stem central or eccentric.	Lentinus cochleatus (80)
	White or pale-rusty with brownish scales	2 to 4 inches broad. On wood; Stem hard; short.	Lentinus lepideus (81)
	Silky white	2 to 8 inches. Large cup at base of stem. Gills flesh-colored.	Volvaria bombycina (128)
Thick and narrow	Cantharellus, all species.		
Veins between gills under surface of cap	Sooty or brownish, yellowish or grayish	1 to 2 inches broad. Gills narrow; forked; Cap funnel-shaped.	Cantharellus infundibuliformis (17)
	Pure white	2 to 3 inches broad. Soft texture. Gills attached to stem or extending down it.	Clitocybe albissima (20)
	Grayish-brown or Blackish-brown	3 to 5 inches broad. Gills broad. Stem white.	Collybia platyphylla (34)
	Tawny, reddish, buff, ashy or whitish	1 to 3 inches broad. Gills whitish or yellowish; far apart; waxy.	Hygrophorus pratensis (61)

KEY TO COMMON GILLED FUNGI

IDENTIFICATION BY **FORM** OF THE **GILLS** (*Continued*)

Form of Gills	Color of Cap	Remarks	Name
Veins between gills under surface of cap	Rose, rose-purple, violet or lilac	¾ to 1¼ inches broad. All of one color. Stem smooth; straight; hollow; few hairs at base.	Mycena pura (91)
	Tawny	¼ to ¾ inch broad. On wood, in groups. Taste acrid and puckery. Kidney-shaped. Short stem at edge.	Panus stypticus (99)
	Red; dark purple, olivaceus or green	2 to 4 inches broad. Radial marks at edge when old. Gills yellowish; of equal length.	Russula alutacea (113)

IDENTIFICATION BY **CHARACTER** OF THE **STEM**

N.B.—When the stem is absent, the cap is attached to the wood from which it grows, by its edge.

Character of Stem	Color of Cap	Remarks	Name
Absent	Yellowish-brown	4 to 8 inches broad. Gills green. Stem lateral or absent.	Cantharellus crispus (14)
		Crepidotus, all species.	
		Panus, all species.	
		Pleurotus, all species.	
	White or whitish	½ to 1½ inches broad. On dead sticks and branches in woods. Gills split lengthwise along the free edge.	Schizophyllum commune (120)
Downy or hairy at the base	Yellow	½ to 1 inch broad. Like Can. cibarius. but smaller and more slender.	Cantharellus minor (18)
	White; shiny	½ to 1¼ inches broad. Gills very thin; close together; white. Stem polished white.	Clitocybe candicans (21)

IDENTIFICATION BY **CHARACTER** OF THE **STEM** (Continued)

Character of Stem	Color of Cap	Remarks	Name
Downy or hairy at the base	Pale tan or flesh-red when moist; whitish when dry	1 to 2 inches broad. In tufts. Gills whitish; close together. Stem long; brown or brownish.	Collybia acervata (31)
	Reddish yellow or tawny; sometimes darker at center	1 inch or more broad. In tufts; on wood. Sticky when moist. Gills lighter color than stem.	Collybia velutipes (36)
	Umber (brown; shiny)	¾ to 1¾ inches broad. Elevated at center. Gills grayish when young; flesh-color when mature.	Entoloma strictius (51)
	Pale yellow	1 to 2 inches broad. Gills pale when young; rusty when old. Slight bitter taste.	Flammula flavida (52)
	Tawny or brownish-red	½ to 2½ inches broad. Sweetish milky juice.	Lactarius subdulcis (76)
	Yellowish or pale brick-red; tan when old	1 to 2 inches broad. Taste acrid. Wrinkled and leathery when dry. Stem 2 to 3 inches; slender; tough.	Marasmius peronatus (88)
	Some shade of brown or gray	¼ to 1¼ inches broad. On wood. Conic. Radial marks at edge.	Mycena galericulata (90)
	Rose, rose-purple or lilac	¾ to 1¼ inches broad. Entire plant rose, purple or violet.	Mycena pura (91)
	Yellowish-rusty to dull yellow	¼ to 1 inch broad. Tufted; on wood. Pit at center.	Omphalia campanella (93)
	Cinnamon when moist; pale yellow when dry	1 to 2 inches broad. On wood. Gills close together. Stem with ring.	Pholiota discolor (103)

KEY TO COMMON GILLED FUNGI

IDENTIFICATION BY **CHARACTER** OF THE **STEM** (*Continued*)

Character of Stem	Color of Cap	Remarks	Name
Downy or hairy at the base	Yellow or brown	½ to 1 inch broad. On wood. Netword of furrows on surface. Gills flesh-pink when old.	Pluteus admirabilis (109)
Eccentric; attached to cap between its center and its edge	Orange or saffron yellow	3 to 6 inches broad. Entire plant same color.	Clitocybe illudens (25)
	Reddish or pale tan	2 to 3 inches broad. Funnel-shaped. Gills whitish; extending down the stem.	Clitocybe infundibuliformis (26)
	Brownish-flesh-color	½ to 2 inches broad. Depressed at center. Gills saw-like on edge.	Lentinus cochleatus (80)
	White or pale-rusty with brownish scales	2 to 4 inches broad. Tough. Gills saw-like at edge.	Lentinus lepideus (81)
	White; hairy	8 or more inches. Woody when old.	Panus strigosus (98)
	Grayish-buff, rusty-brown or yellowish	2 to 4 inches. Edge turned downward and inward.	Paxillus involutus (100)

Pleurotus, all species sometimes.

Separable easily from cap	Agaricus, all species.
	Amanita, all species.
	Amanitopsis, all species.
	Coprinus, all species.
	Lepiota, all species.
	Pluteus, all species.
	Volvaria, all species.

IDENTIFICATION BY FORM OF THE STEM

Form of Stem	Color of Cap	Remarks	Name
	White or yellowish	2 to 5 inches broad. Gills whitish when young; turning pink, then brown and black when old. Stem with double ring.	Agaricus arvensis (1)
	White or tinged with yellow or pink	2 to 5 inches broad. Gills pink, turning brown and then black when old.	Agaricus silvicola (3)
	Amanita, all species.		
	Grayish-brown or sooty-brown; sometimes darker at center	1 to 3 inches broad. Cap conic with its apex downward.	Clitocybe clavipes (22)
Bulbous at the base	Pale or dark tan, yellowish or chestnut	½ to 2 inches broad. In groups. Gills whitish. Stem 1 to 3 inches.	Collybia dryophila (33) (Sometimes bulbous)
	Yellow, reddish-yellow or rusty	2 to 4 inches broad. Wrinkled surface.	Corrinarius corrugatus (43)
	Dark violet	2 to 4 inches broad. Scaly. Gills violet to rusty; notched.	Cortinarius violaceus (44)
	Yellowish-brown; silky	1 to 2 inches broad. Knob at center. Radiating cracks.	Inocybe rimosa (68) (Slight swelling at base)
	White, with reddish-brown scales	1 to 4 inches broad. Elevated center. Gills free from stem.	Lepiota americana (82)
	White, with brown scales that merge at the center	4 to 12 inches broad. Gills white when young, green when mature.	Lepiota molybdites (83)

KEY TO COMMON GILLED FUNGI

IDENTIFICATION BY **FORM** OF THE **STEM** (*Continued*)

Form of Stem	Color of Cap	Remarks	Name
Bulbous at base	White; rarely with yellowish or smoky center	2 to 4 inches broad. Gills free from stem; white. Stem with ring.	Lepiota naucina (84)
	Brownish, with spot-like scales	3 to 5 inches broad. Gills free from stem. Long stem with ring.	Lepiota procera (85)
	Yellow, often with whitish flakes	2 to 4 inches broad. Stem with ring. Gills whitish when young, rusty when old.	Pholiota caperata (102)
Stem at edge of cap	Yellowish-brown	4 to 8 inches broad. On wood. Gills wavy; greenish.	Cantharellus crispus
	Crepidotus, all species.		
	Brownish-flesh-color	½ to 2 inches broad. In tufts. Cap thin; tough. Gills saw-like at edge.	Lentinus cochleatus
	White with brownish scales	2 to 4 inches broad. On wood. Gills white, with saw-like edge.	Lentinus lepideus
	Panus, all species.		
	Pleurotus, all species.		
	White or whitish	½ to 1½ inches broad. On dead sticks and branches. Gills split along edge.	Schizophyllum commune
Rooted	White	½ to 1½ inches broad. Pit at center; stem off center (rarely). Stem waxy; hairy at base.	Clitocybe candicans (21)
	Grayish-brown or smoky-brown	1 to 4 inches broad. Sticky when moist. Gills white. Stem color of cap.	Collybia radicata (35)
	Some shade of brown or gray	¼ to 1¼ inches broad. Conic. On Stumps. Stem hairy at base.	Mycena galericulata (90) (rarely rooted)

IDENTIFICATION BY **FORM** OF THE **STEM** (*Continued*)

Form of Stem	Remarks	Name
With ring, and cup (volva) at base	All species except that ring is slight or missing in the case of A. rubescens and sometimes rudimentary in A. muscaria.	Amanita
With cup (volva) but without ring	Amanitopsis, all species. Volvaria, all species.	
With ring but without cup (volva) at base	Agaricus, all species. Armillaria, all species. Coprinus comatus, in the young plant only. (Frontispiece) (38) Cortinarius, all species in young plants only. Lepiota, all species. Panæolus, retirugis (97). Not a true ring; a mark only. Pholiota, all species. Stropharia, all species.	

Stem LONG when compared with diameter of the Cap

Agaricus silvicola (3)
Amanita phalloides (6)
Amanitopsis vaginata (8)
Armillaria mellea (10)
Clitocybe illudens (25)
Collybia acervata (31)
Collybia confluens (32)
Collybia radicata (35)
Coprinus micaceus (39)
Cortinarius corrugatus (43)
Entoloma strictius (51)
Galera tenera (55)
Hygrophorus chlorophanus (58)

Hygrophorus miniatus (60)
Laccaria laccata (69)
Lentinus cochleatus (80)
Lepiota procera (85)
Marasmius, all species
Mycena, all species
Naucoria semiorbicularis (92)
Omphalia fibula (94)
Panæolus, all species
Pholiota squarrosa (when mature) (105)
Psilocybe fœnisecii (112)
Stropharia semiglobata (121)

Stem SHORT when compared with diameter of the Cap

Cantharellus cibarius (12)
Cantharellus cinnabarimus (13)
Cantharellus floccosus (14)
Lactarius piperatus (75)
Lactarius theiogalus (77)
Lactarius vellereus (78)
Lentinus lepideus (81)

Russula alutacea (113)
Russula delica (114)
Russula virescens (119)
Tricholoma equestre (123)
Tricholoma personatum (124)
Tricholoma russula (125)

KEY TO COMMON GILLED FUNGI

Identification by Color of Spores

Black spored gilled mushrooms (Melanosporæ).

Coprinus, all species mentioned in this book excepting Coprinus micaceus, whose spores are brown.

Panæolus, all species.

Psathyrella, all species.

Brown or Purplish-Brown spored gilled mushrooms (Porphyrosporæ).

Coprinus micaceus, an exception among the Coprini. All other Coprini have black spores.

Hypholoma, all species.

Psilocybe, all species.

Stropharia, all species.

Green spored gilled mushroom.

Lepiota morgani—Green is an exceptional spore color for a Lepiota. Other species have white spores.

Pink spored gilled mushrooms (Rhodosporae).

Clitopilus, all species.

Entoloma, all species.

Pluteus, all species.

Volvaria bombycina.

Rusty spored gilled mushrooms (Ochrosporæ).

Cortinarius, all species.

Crepidotus, all species.

Flammula, all species. N. B.—The spores of Flammula polychroa are light brown, often with a purple tinge when fresh.

Galera, all species.

Hebeloma, all species. The spores of Hebeloma are pale rusty or clay color.

Inocybe, all species.
Naucoria, all species.
Paxillus, all species.
Pholiota, all species.

White spored gilled mushrooms (Leucosporæ).

Amanita, all species.

Amanitopsis, all species.

Armillaria, all species.

Cantharellus, all species mentioned in this book excepting *Cantharellus cibarius* which has pale yellowish spores.

Clitocybe, all species.

Collybia, all species.

Hygrophorus, all species.

Laccaria, all species.

Lactarius, all species mentioned in this book excepting Lactarius deliciosus with yellowish spores; Lactarius theiogalus with yellowish or pale flesh-colored spores.

Lentinus, all species.

Lepiota, all species mentioned in this book excepting Lepiota molybdites whose spores are green when first shed and slowly turn yellow.

Marasmius, all species

Mycena, all species.

Omphalia, all species.

Panus, all species.

Pleurotus, all species excepting *Pleurotus sapidus*, whose spores are pale lilac in color.

Russula, all species excepting *Russula alutacea*, which has yellowish spores; *Russula mariæ*, which has pale yellow spores.

Schizophyllum commune.

Tricholoma, all species.

Yellowish spored gilled Mushrooms.

Lactarius deliciosus and *Lactarius theiogalus*—These *Lactarii*
are exceptional in the color of their spores. All other
Lactarii mentioned in this book have white spores.

Russula alutacea and *Russula mariæ*.

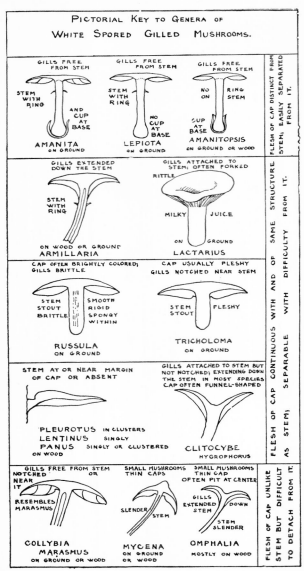

FIG. 5.—Pictorial key to genera of white spored common gilled mushrooms.

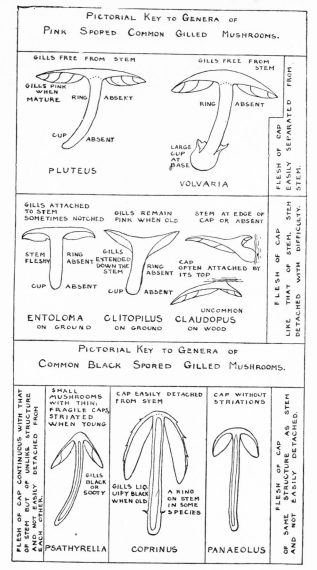

FIG. 6.—Pictorial key to pink spored and black spored common gilled mushrooms.

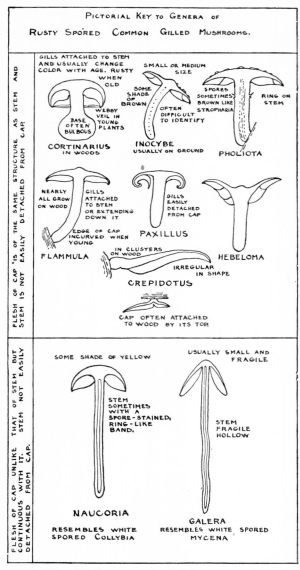

FIG. 7.—Pictorial key to genera of rusty spored common gilled mushrooms.

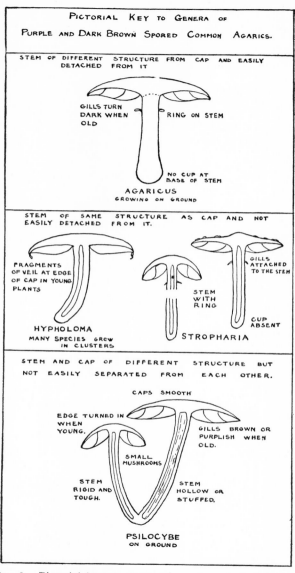

FIG. 8.—Pictorial key to genera of purple and dark brown spored common gilled mushrooms.

TABULAR VIEW OF THE GENERA OF AGARICAE

LEUCOSPORAE (WHITE)	RHODOSPORAE (PINK)	OCHROSPORAE (BROWN)	PORPHYROSPORAE (PURPLE)	MELANOSPORAE (BLACK)
AMANITA AMANITOPSIS	VOLVARIA			
LEPIOTA			AGARICUS (PSALLIOTA)	COPRINUS
	PLUTEUS			
ARMILLARIA		PHOLIOTA CORTINARIUS	STROPHARIA	
TRICHOLOMA LACTARIUS RUSSULA	ENTOLOMA	HEBELOMA INOCYBE	HYPHOLOMA	PANAEOLUS
HYGROPHORUS CLITOCYBE	CLITOPILUS	FLAMMULA PAXILLUS		
PLEUROTUS PANUS SCHIZOPHYLLUM		CREPIDOTUS		
COLLYBIA MARASMIUS	LEPTONIA	NAUCORIA	PSILOCYBE	
MYCENA	NOLANEA	GALERA		PSATHYRELLA
OMPHALIA				

CHAPTER V

DESCRIPTIONS OF GENERA AND SPECIES OF COMMON GILLED MUSHROOMS

GENERA AND SPECIES OF MUSHROOMS

The genus Agaricus

The genus Agaricus includes only such brown spored species as have their gills free from the stem with a ring or collar upon the stem. All of them grow upon the ground only.

SPECIES OF AGARICUS

Agaricus arvensis; horse mushroom. Plate 2, Species 1.

On ground in cultivated fields, grassy pastures and waste places. It is occasionally found under trees and even within the borders of thin woods; scattered or in groups; July to September; edible.

Cap smooth, or slightly flocculent (with a few flakes upon its surface); white or yellowish; 2 to 5 inches broad.

Gills at first whitish or very slightly pinkish; turning dull pink, then blackish brown; near together; free from the stem.

Stem stout; hollow; somewhat thicker or bulbous at the base; white; with a double ring, the upper part membranous, the lower part thicker, split radially, yellowish; 2 to 4 inches long.

Spores brown; elliptic; .0003 to .0004 inches long.

The horse mushroom, also called meadow mushroom, is so much like the common mushroom that some botanists have supposed it to be a mere variety of that species. The most notable differences are its larger size, its hollow, somewhat bulbous stem, its peculiar veil or collar and the paler gills of the young plant. The cap in dried specimens is apt to assume a yellow color which does not pertain to the Common mushroom. No serious harm could come if it should be confused with the common mushroom. Peck.

Agaricus campestris; common mushroom; edible mushroom. Plate 2, Species 2.

On ground in grassy places, in pastures, on lawns and manured ground, in mushroom beds, never in thick woods; singly or in groups; latter part of July to September; edible.

PLATE II.

PLATE II.

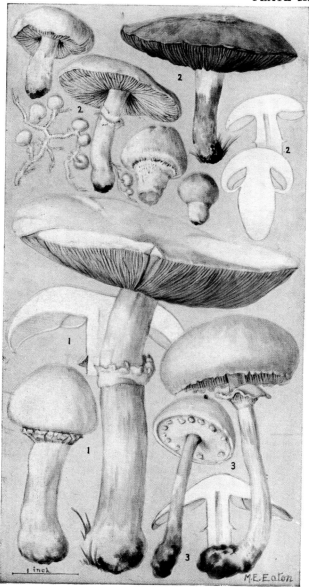

1 inch

M.E.Eaton

GENERA AND SPECIES OF MUSHROOMS

Cap silky or with scales; in very young plants the cap is almost globular or hemispheric and the gills are concealed (buttons); when older the cap expands and the veil separates from the margin revealing the delicate-tinted pinkish gills; when mature the cap is broadly expanded or nearly flat; margin, especially in young plants extends beyond the gills; white or with dingy hues; flesh white or with a tendency to become pinkish when cut; taste mild and pleasant; may be peeled; 1½ to 3 inches wide.

Gills near together; pink when young, turning brown and then black with age; free from stem.

Stem smooth; white or whitish; short; with a ring when young; stuffed; cylindric; 2 to 3 inches long.

Spores brown; elliptic; .00025 to .0003 inches long.

The common mushroom, sometimes called the edible mushroom, as if it were the only edible species known, is perhaps more generally used and better known than any other. It is the one commonly cultivated and the one most often seen on the tables of the rich and of restaurants and public houses. It is so eagerly sought in some of our cities that it is difficult to find the wild ones near these towns, for they are gathered as soon as they appear, and the cultivated ones bring prices above the reach of the poor.

Agaricus silvicola; forest mushroom.   Plate II, Species 3.

On ground in woods and groves; scattered or singly; August to September; edible.

Cap convex or expanded; often with an elevation or umbo in the center; smooth or slightly silky; white or tinged with yellow or pink; flesh whitish or tinged with pink; 2 to 5 inches broad.

Gills thin; close together: free from stem; rounded near the stem; pinkish when young, becoming darker when old; finally brown or blackish-brown.

Stem long; with a ring which is sometimes double; smooth;

bulbous at base; white, often yellowish below; stuffed or hollow; 4 to 6 inches long.

Spores brown; elliptic; .0003 long, .00016 broad.

It is an attractive plant because of its graceful habit and the delicate shades of yellow and white. Atkinson.

The forest mushroom has been regarded by some mycologists as a variety of the common mushroom, from which it is easily distinguished by its longer, hollow bulbous stem and by its place of growth (woods). Peck.

The genus Amanita

The genus of fungi known under this name possess characteristic peculiarities of the stem. At its base is a volva or cup. The very young plants are wholly enveloped in a membrane or universal veil which is ruptured by the growth of the plant, the portion persisting at the bottom forming the above-mentioned cup or sheath. That portion of the universal veil which in the young plant covers the cap, remains in the mature plants of some of the species in the form of patches or warts, often easily separable. It sometimes happens that these warts are washed off by the rain. The gills are free from the stem which is furnished with a membranous collar or ring. The plants are generally large and attractive in appearance. Inasmuch as our most dangerous species belong to this genus the amateur should avoid eating all mushrooms having stems with a cup at the bottom or with a ring upon the stem in connection with any suspicion of a cup at the bottom.

SPECIES OF AMANITA

Amanita cæsarea; Cæsar's mushroom; orange amanita; royal agaric. Plate III, Species 4.

On ground, in woods; scattered; July to September; edible but EAT NOT.

Cap orange or red fading on the margin; smooth except at the margin where it is furrowed or striate; bell-shaped, becoming expanded when old and then the surface may be nearly flat or the center elevated; 3 to 6 inches broad; flesh white or tinged with yellow.

Gills yellow; free from stem.

Stem yellow; with a broad yellowish ring hanging like a broad collar from the upper part; is slightly bulbous at the base where it is covered by the large sac-like white volva or cup; hollow or stuffed; 4 to 6 inches long; ½ inch or more in thickness.

Spores white; elliptical; .0003 to .0004 inch long.

The colors of the plant are generally deeper in large specimens.

The species is not common in America but is described on account of its importance and beauty.

The fly amanita, (Amanita muscaria) resembles this mushroom in size, shape and color of the cap, but in other respects they are quite distinct. Peck.

The chief distinctive characters may be contrasted as follows:

Fly amanita. Cap warty, gills white, stem white or slightly yellowish.

Orange amanita. Cap smooth, gills yellow, stem yellow. Peck.

Amanita muscaria; fly amanita; fly agaric; false orange; fly poison. Plate III, Species 5.

On ground, in woods and open places; June to frost; POISONOUS.

Cap bright red or orange when young, fading to yellow on the margin when mature; occasionally white throughout; smooth, sometimes with minute furrows or striate on margin; adorned with white or yellowish warts or scales, or smooth if these have been washed off by rain; flesh white or yellowish just under the skin or peel; 3 to 8 inches broad; slightly viscid when fresh. Murrill.

PLATE III.

PLATE III.

1 inch

M.E.Eaton.

Gills white; free from stem; rarely tinged with yellow.

Stem furnished with a collar or ring; bulbous at the base; the bulb as well as the base of the stem is scaly at times from the adhering fragments of the wrapper or universal veil, the remains of which do not form such a well-defined cup or sheath as is the case in some other amanitæ, such as Amanita phalloides; white or slightly tinged with yellow; 4 to 6 inches long.

Spores white; broadly elliptic; .0003 to .0004 inch long.

The fly amanita is one of our most common poisonous species. It is also very variable in color and in the size of its cap. It is generally a most showy and attractive plant. I have seen a single cap surrounded by a circle of lifeless flies that had sipped the viscid juice from its moist surface and fallen victims to its virulent properties before leaving the place of their fatal repast. . . . Some of the people of northern Asia make an intoxicating liquor of this fungus by steeping it in water. Peck.

Infusions of it are used as a fly poison. It is a striking and handsome plant because of the usually brilliant coloring of the cap in contrast with the white stems and gills, and the usually white scales on the surface. Atkinson.

The poisonous properties of this fungus are due to a principle known as muscarin which is used as a medicine and the antidote to which is atropin, an alkaloid extracted from the belladonna plant.

Amanita phalloides; poison amanita; destroying angel; deadly amanita. Plate III, Species 6.

On ground, in woods, groves, open places and bushy pastures; July to October; POISONOUS.

Cap bell-shaped or almost globular when young, becoming nearly plane when mature; surface slightly viscid (sticky) when fresh and moist; smooth or decorated with scattered warty patches; margin rarely striated; flesh extremely poisonous but not objectionable to the taste, sometimes with a disagreeable odor; smooth; varying in color from pure white to yellow, yellowish-green, smoky-olive, gray, brown or blackish; 1½ to 5 inches broad. (Pure white cap is A. verna.)

Gills white; free from stem; broad; bellied, sometimes adnexed (adjacent to stem). (Murrill.)

Stem usually white; sharply bulbous at the base; with a wide ring near the upper end; usually white; smooth or slightly scaly; stuffed or hollow; 2½ to 6 inches long; with a volva or cup at bottom.

Spores white; smooth; globular; hyaline (glassy); 7–10 microns in diameter.

The poison amanita is very variable in the color of the cap and yet is so definite in its structural characters that only the most careless observer would be likely to confuse it with any other species. There is, however, a sort of deceptive character about it. It is very neat and attractive in its appearance and "looks as if it might be good enough to eat." This appearance is fortified by the absence of any decidedly unpleasant odor or taste, but let him who would eat it beware, for probably there is not a more poisonous or dangerous species in our mycological flora. To eat it is to invite death.

The differences between Amanita phalloides and the common mushroom are these:

Poison amanita. Gills *persistently white;* stem *equal to* or *longer* than the diameter of the cap; with a *broad distinct bulb* at the base.

Common mushroom. Gills *pink, becoming blackish-brown;* stem *shorter* than the diameter of the cap, with *no bulb* at the base. Peck.

Since the *Amanita Phalloides* occurs usually in woods, or along borders of woods, there is little danger of confusing it with edible mushrooms collected in lawns distant from the woods and in open fields. However, I found several of this species in a lawn distant from the woods. This should cause . . . those not thoroughly familiar with the appearance of the plant to be extremely cautious against eating mushrooms simply because they were not collected in or near the woods. The bulb of the deadly amanita is usually inserted quite deep in the soil or leaf-mold, and specimens are often picked leaving the very important character of the volva in the ground, and then the plant might easily be taken for the common mushroom, or more likely for the smooth lepiota, *Lepiota naucina*, which is entirely white, the gills only in age showing a faint pink tinge. It is very important, therefore, that until one has such familiarity with these plants that they are easily recognized in the absence of some of these characters, the stem should be carefully dug from the soil. Atkinson.

Poisoning by Amanita phalloides when eaten in sufficient quantity was invariably fatal in spite of medical treatment until recently. Dr. Dujarric de la Rivière, head of the Pasteur Institute, Paris, has succeeded in preparing an antitoxic serum which has saved the lives of persons who were apparently fatally poisoned by this so-called "destroying angel." He calls it antiphallinic serum (*serum antiphallinique*). The Government of France has lately passed a law requiring that each *département* of that nation shall keep a supply of it ready for use by physicians.

Yearly deaths in New York City from Amanita poisoning vary in number but have been so high as thirty. It is to be hoped that the new method of treatment may soon be available in this country.

Amanita rubescens; Venenarius rubens; blushing venenarius. Plate III, Species 7.

Cap egg-shaped at first, then convex and later expanded; surface adorned with thin flaky or mealy warts; variable in color but always tinged with reddish or with brownish-red, changing slowly to reddish when bruised; pleasant odor and taste; margin smooth or with slight furrows (striate); flesh white, changing slowly to reddish when bruised; 3 to 5 inches broad.

Gills free from stem or adjacent to it (slightly adnexed); close together; white; characteristically chalky white when dry.

Stem with a ring or collar upon its upper portion; bulbous at the base; with small scales; whitish, but generally with dull reddish stains especially near the base; stuffed; 3 to 6 inches long.

Spores white; ellipsoid; smooth; glassy (hyaline); 10 to 11 × 6 to 7 microns in diameter.

Found commonly in woods and groves from Maine to Alabama and west to Ohio. On ground. Edible but EAT NOT.

The genus Amanitopsis

This genus resembles the amanita family in that each species belonging to it has a cup or sheath enclosing the lower end of the stem. The spores are also white and the gills free from the stem.

The principal feature wherein the genus Amanitopsis differs from Amanita is in the absence of a collar or ring upon the stem.

SPECIES OF AMANITOPSIS

Amanitopsis vaginata; sheathed amanitopsis. Plate IV, Species 8.

On ground or on much decayed wood; singly or scattered in woods and open places; June to October; edible but EAT NOT.

Cap rather thin; smooth or adorned when young with a few adherent fragments of the veil (warty); bell-shaped to expanded; sometimes umbonate; deeply (striated) furrowed at the margin; regular in form but fragile and easily broken; exceedingly variable in color, ranging from reddish white to reddish-brown or leaden-brown; 2 to 4 inches broad.

Gills free from stem; white or whitish; fragile.

Stem without a ring but sheathed at the base by the torn remains of the rather long, thin, flabby volva (veil or wrapper); smooth or adorned with minute scales; variable in color; hollow or stuffed; portions of the conspicuous white volva are sometimes carried up as patches on the cap. Murrill. 3 to 5 inches long, ½ to ¼ inch thick.

Spores white; globular; smooth; glassy (hyaline); 8–10 microns in diameter.

The sheath or wrapper at the base of the stem adheres so slightly to the stem that if the plant is carelessly pulled the sheath is left in the ground. My own experience indicates that it is a fairly good mushroom, but there are many others that I like better. Peck.

This attractive and very variable species is abundant in woods throughout Europe and North America during summer and autumn and possesses excellent edible qualities. It may be distinguished from species of *Amanita*, some of which are deadly poisonous, by the total absence of a ring on the stem, although the conspicuous volva at the base suggests its close relationship to that genus. The variations in color presented by this species are often very bewildering to the beginner. Murrill.

Amanitopsis volvata; Large-sheathed amanitopsis. Plate IV, Species 9.

On ground in and near woods; July to October; POISONOUS.

PLATE IV.

PLATE IV.

1 inch

Mary E. Eaton

Cap 1 to 3 inches broad; hemispheric when young; flat when mature. Dull white, yellowish or rarely reddish-brown. Powdery or flaky surface; fragile.

Gills free from stem; white; rounded near stem; broad; near together.

Stem variable; 2 to 3 inches long; slender; cylindric or tapering upward; enlarged at the base; whitish; downy; stuffed or solid; with a very large volva that is more or less lobed.

Spores white; somewhat elliptical; waxy; 10-12 by 6-7 microns in diameter.

From New England to Alabama and west to Ohio. Its most noticeable feature is the immense cup or volva at base of the stem. Murrill.

The genus Armillaria

This is a white-spored genus which has the gills attached to the stem by their inner extremity. The stem usually has a collar but there is no wrapper or cup at the base as in the genera Amanita or Amanitopsis. The stem is fibrous and not easily separable from the substance of the cap, another feature in which this genus differs from Amanita and also from Lepiota.

Species of Armillaria

Armillaria mellea; honey colored mushroom; honey-colored armillaria; honey agaric. Plate IV, Species 10.

On ground or on decaying wood: in woods or in cleared land; solitary or in groups, tufts or clusters; summer and autumn; edible.

Cap convex to expanded; pale honey yellow to dark reddish-brown; very variable in color and form but once known is easily recognized; adorned with minute tufts of brown or blackish hairs, but sometimes smooth; when old sometimes with minute radial furrows (striate) at the margin; center sometimes prominent (umbonate); flesh white or whitish, somewhat acrid and unpleasant to the taste (raw); 1 to 6 inches broad.

Gills attached to the stem or even extending down it (adnate or decurrent); white or whitish, becoming discolored or spotted with age.

Stem adorned with a collar or ring in its upper portion; this ring is variable, sometimes white and cottony or thin and webby and disappearing when old; (stem) honey-colored, reddish-brown, or dirty brown below, paler above; firm; fibrous; spongy within; usually having flakes or scales upon it below the ring; 1 to 6 inches long; ¼ to ¾ inches thick.

Spores white; elliptic; smooth; glassy (hyaline): 7–10 m. long.

The honey-colored armillaria is very plentiful and extremely variable. The stem may be of uniform thickness or thickened at the base or even narrowed almost to a point here. In one variety it has a distinctly bulbous base, in another a tapering base like a tap root which penetrates the earth deeply. The plants rarely appear plentifully before the last of September. Peck.

Very widely distributed and very abundant on stumps and buried roots of both deciduous trees and evergreens, on which it grows as a parasite, the sporophores (mushrooms) appearing in dense clusters in autumn and the shining brown cords or *rhizomorphs* being often seen in dead logs and stumps. To the forester this is probably the most important species of all the gill-fungi. It is also much used as an article of food in Europe and about New York City, although of inferior quality. Murrill.

Its clustered habit, the usually prominent ring on the stem, and the sharp, blackish, erect scales which usually adorn the center of the cap, mark it as an easy plant to determine in most cases. The colors and markings however, vary greatly, so that some of the forms are very puzzling. Atkinson.

The genus Cantharellus

The genus Cantharellus is distinguished by the character of the gills which have an obtuse or blunt edge and are mostly forked or branched. They are also generally narrow. In general appearance the species are not much unlike species of Clitocybe for the gills extend down the stem (decurrent), but their thick branching habit and blunt edge give the plant a distinct character. In many species the gills look like veins, folds or wrinkles, but in some species, as Cantharellus aurantiacus, they are rather thin and broad. All species grow on the ground except C. crispus.

SPECIES OF CANTHARELLUS

Cantharellus aurantiacus; orange chantarelle; false chantarelle. Plate IV, Species 11.

On ground; in woods and uncultivated places; July to October; edible.

Cap fleshy; soft; plane or depressed at the center (funnel-shaped); covered with a fine wooly surface (minutely tomentose); yellowish-orange, sometimes tinged with smoky-brown, or brownish in the center only; flesh whitish or yellowish; 1 to 3 inches broad.

Gills narrow; extending down the stem (decurrent); close together; reddish orange; repeatedly forked.

Stem cylindric or slightly tapering upward; smooth; solid; color of cap or paler; sometimes becoming hollow with age (Atkinson); 1 to 3 inches long; $1/6$ to $1/2$ inch thick.

Spores white; slightly elliptic; 6–8 x 4–5 microns in diameter.

The orange chantarelle is sharply separated from the other

species by its usually bright orange gills which are regularly and repeatedly forked. . . . The extreme margin is frequently (curved in) decurved or involute.

It was formerly reputed poisonous or dangerous and credited with having a disagreeable flavor. In my own experiments with it the flavor has been found to be agreeable and fair trials of eating it have shown it to be perfectly harmless. I therefore have no hesitation in adding it to our list of edible species. Peck.

This orange cantharellus is very common and occurs on the ground or on very rotten wood, logs, branches, etc., from summer to very late autumn. It is easily known by its dull orange or brownish pileus (cap), yellow gills, which are thin and regularly forked and by the pileus being more or less depressed or funnel-shaped. The taste is somewhat nutty, somewhat bitterish. Atkinson.

Cantharellus cibarius; chantarelle. Plate V, Species 12.

On ground in woods and open places; commonly in groups, but sometimes in curved lines; June to September; edible.

Cap fleshy; firm; convex, becoming expanded or depressed at the center (funnel-shaped); smooth; chrome (egg) yellow; the margin when young turning in but later spreading and often wavy or irregular; flesh white; taste when raw often a little pungent or acrid; 1 to 3 inches broad.

Gills far apart; thick; narrow; forked; extending down the stem (decurrent); yellow.

Stem variable in length; firm; smooth; solid; yellow; often curved; sometimes tapers downward. By some, it is considered as good as the cap for food; 1 to 2 inches long; ¼ to ½ inch thick.

Spores pale yellowish; elliptic; .0003 inch to .0004 inch long.

The chantarelle is beautiful in color if not in shape and is most easily recognized. Its color is a uniform rich egg-

FIG. 9.

FIG. 9.—SPECIES 13.—Cantharellus cinnabarinus.

Photo by author.   See Plate V.

yellow, which is very constant. This extends to all parts of the plant except the inner flesh which is white.

The orange chantarelle or false chantarelle, *Cantharellus aurantiacus*, is the only species liable to be mistaken for the edible chantarelle. It may at once be recognized by the orange color of its gills, which are also thinner and more close and are regularly and repeatedly forked. The color of its cap is a paler and more dingy yellow, varied with smoky-brown tints. Peck.

Cantharellus cinnabarinus; cinnabar chantarelle. Plate V, Species 13, also Figure 9.

In woods and open places; July to September; edible.

Cap firm; convex or slightly depressed in the center; often irregular in shape, with a wavy or lobed margin; smooth; cinnabar red; flesh white; size, ½ to 1½ inches in diameter.

Gills narrow; blunt on edges; far apart (distant); branched or forked; extending down the stem (decurrent)· red like the surface of the cap.

Stem equal or tapering downward; smooth; solid or stuffed; red like the cap.

Spores white; elliptic; .0003 to .0004 of an inch long, .00016 to .0002 broad.

The cinnabar chantarelle is readily recognized by its color. It is externally red in all its parts, the interior only being white. The color is quite constant, but in some instances it is paler and approaches a pinkish hue. It is apt to fade or even disappear in dried specimens.

This mushroom sometimes occurs in great abundance, which adds to its importance as an edible species. The fresh plant has a tardily and slightly acrid flavor, but this disappears in cooking.

It is a small species but often quite irregular in shape. Small specimens are more likely to be regular than large ones.

PLATE V.

PLATE V.

1 inch

Mary E. Eaton

Sometimes the cap is more fully developed on one side than on the other. This makes the stem eccentric or in some cases almost lateral.

Cantharellus crispus; Species 14. No illustration.

On wood, trunks of trees, etc. September to November; in tufts often.

Cap thin; expanded; villous or pubescent (covered with soft hairs, downy); yellowish brown; often lobed; 4 to 8 inches broad.

Gills narrow; close together; dichotomously branched (forked); crisped (wavy or curled); glaucus—(grayish) green.

Stem lateral (at the margin) or absent.

Spores white.

Cantharellus umbonatus; knobbed chantarelle. Plate V, Species 15.

On ground in woods among mosses or in pastures and bushy places among grasses and fallen leaves; in groups; July to September.

Cap rather conical when young, becoming convex, plane or depressed at the center when mature; margin turned in and downy when young; fleshy; soft and flexible; sometimes with a small knob at the center; smooth; dry; color variable, grayish-white, grayish-brown, yellowish-brown, blackish-brown or bluish-gray; flesh white; taste mild; ½ to 1½ inches broad.

Gills narrow; close together; forked 1, 2 or 3 times; extending down the stem; white or whitish; sometimes tinged with yellow.

Stem sometimes tapering upward a little; solid; whitish or pallid or color of the cap, and when growing among mosses is clothed below with a soft white down which binds it closely to the mosses, smooth or with minute fibrils upon it; 1 to 3 inches long.

Spores white; narrow ellipses .0003 to .0004 long by .00016 inch broad.

The dichotomous chantarelle is a small but common species in our hilly and mountainous districts.

It is related so closely to Cantharellus umbonatus that it has been sometimes regarded as a variety of it or has even been confused with it, but the gills of that species have been described as straight, and in our plant they are constantly repeatedly forked as in C. aurantiacus and C. albidus. Peck.

Cantharellus floccosus; floccose chantarelle. Plate V, Species 16.

On ground in woods; in groups; July to September; edible.

Cap funnel-form or trumpet-shaped, deeply excavated; firm; rather thin; surface somewhat scaly; yellowish inclining to rusty; 2 to 4 inches broad at the top, 3 to 6 inches long.

Gills narrow; thick; blunt on the edge; repeatedly forked and branched so that the lower surface of the cap has a coarse network of them; gills and interspaces rusty or yellowish; extending down the stem.

Stem short; smooth or hairy; sometimes elongated and bent.

Spores rusty colored; elliptic; .0005 to .0006 inch long by .0003 inch broad with a small oblique point at one end; usually with one nucleus.

The floccose chantarelle is a large and very distinct species. There is nothing with which it can easily be confused. When young it is narrowly club-shape or almost cylindric, but soon becomes trumpet-shaped. My trial of its edible qualities was very satisfactory, and I consider it a very good mushroom for the table. Peck.

Cantharellus infundibuliformis; funnel-form chantarelle.
Plate V, Species 17.

On ground; in damp woods or mossy, shaded swamps; in groups, sometimes in tufts; June to October; edible.

Cap thin; broadly convex when young becoming pitted at the center or funnel-shaped when older; frequently lobed, wavy or irregular on the margin; water-soaked in appearance (hygrophanous) when moist; sooty brown, brownish-yellow or dingy yellow when moist; sooty brown, brownish-yellow or grayish brown and slightly scaly when dry; 1 to 2 inches broad.

Gills narrow; far apart; extending down the stem (decurrent); irregularly forked or branched; yellowish or slightly ashy, becoming dusted when old or in drying.

Stem slender; smooth; hollow; yellow or yellowish; 1 to 4 inches long.

Spores white; broadly elliptic or globular; .00035 to .00045 inch long.

Its cap is more highly colored when moist and becomes paler with the loss of moisture. In some specimens the margin becomes wavy, folded or lobed and presents a very irregular appearance. The gills appear in maturity as if frosted or covered with a minute whitish dust or mealiness. This is one of the characters distinguishing this species from the yellowish chantarelle. For edible purposes the separation of the funnel-form chantarelle and the yellowish chantarelle is not of much importance. Peck.

Cantharellus minor; small chantarelle. Plate V, Species 18.

On ground in thin woods and open places; June and July; in groups or sparse clusters; edible.

Cap thin; convex or nearly plane; often depressed at center or with pit at center (umbilicate); smooth; yellow; flesh whitish or pale yellow; often wavy or irregular on the margin; size $\frac{1}{2}$ to 1 inch.

Gills far apart; extending down the stem (decurrent); seldom branched or forked; yellow.

Stem slender; smooth; solid when young, hollow when old; yellow; often with whitish down at base; size, 1 to 1 $\frac{1}{2}$ inches long and $^1/_{12}$ to $^1/_6$ inch thick.

Spores white.

The small chantarelle is almost exactly like the chantarelle (Cantharellus cibarius) in color but is easily recognized by its smaller size and more slender appearance, its stem being proportionately longer.

Although of excellent flavor its small size detracts from its importance as an edible mushroom, but sometimes in wet showery weather it appears in sufficient abundance to make it available for the table.   Peck.

The genus Clitocybe

The white-spored genus Clitocybe differs from Tricholoma in the character of the gills.   They are attached to the stem to their extremity as in that genus but they are not notched or excavated on the edge near the stem, and they generally extend down the stem (decurrent).   The flesh is continuous with the stem and hence is not easily separated from it None are known to be fatally poisonous.

SPECIES OF CLITOCYBE

Clitocybe albidula; Clitocybe centralis; whitish clitocybe. Species 19; Figure 10.

On ground; in pine or mixed woods; in groups; September and October; Peck does not say whether edible or not.

Cap thin; convex or nearly plane; with a pit or depression at the center when mature; smooth; whitish tinged with brown; wholly or in the center only when moist, whitish when dry; flesh whitish; taste and odor like bran (farinaceous): ½ to 1½ inches broad.

Gills thin; close together; attached broadly to the stem or extending slightly down it (adnate or decurrent); whitish.

Stem short; cylindric; smooth or slightly frosted; stuffed or hollow; color of the cap; 1 to 2 inches long.

Spores white; slightly elliptic; 5–6 x 2.5–3 microns in diameter.

Common. Peck.

Clitocybe albissima; very white clitocybe. Plate V, Species 20.

On ground; in woods; in groups or sometimes growing in arcs of circles; August and September; Edibility doubtful. whether edible or not.

Cap fleshy, convex or nearly plane; dry; soft; even surface; pure white; inodorous; 2 to 3 inches broad.

Gills attached to the stem or extending down it (adnate or decurrent); some of them forked at the base; white.

Stem smooth; solid; white; 1½ to 3 inches long.

Spores white; ellipsoid; 8 x 5 microns in diameter.

The pure white color and soft texture are retained by the dried specimens. . . . It is an attractive, neat-looking species. Peck.

Clitocybe candicans; whitish clitocybe. Plate V, Species 21.

On ground; among fallen leaves in woods; in groups; September and October. Should not be eaten. It resembles too closely a poisonous species, Clitocybe sudorifica. (See Clitocybe dealbata.)

Cap slightly fleshy; convex, becoming plane or depressed; a pit at the center (umbilicate); regular; rarely, the stem is placed to one side of the center; glossy, with a superficial silky film; white when moist, shining white when dry; diameter $\frac{1}{2}$ to $1\frac{1}{4}$ inches.

Gills very thin; close together; attached to the stem (adnate), later extending down it (becoming decurrent); white.

Stem even; smooth, waxy and polished; cartilaginous hollow or nearly so; often curved; rooting and hairy at the base (villose); $\frac{3}{4}$ inch to 2 inches long.

Spores white; 4–6 x 4 microns in diameter.

Said by Cooke to be farinaceous. Small and somewhat tough. Peck.

Clitocybe clavipes; club stem clitocybe. Plate XIII, Species 22.

On ground; in woods; solitary, in groups or rarely in tufts; July to October; edible.

Cap very fleshy; generally shaped like a cone with its apex downward, sometimes with a small knob at the center of the convex or nearly plane upper surface; soft; grayish-brown, sooty brown, sometimes darker at the center; flesh white; taste mild; 1 to 3 inches broad.

Gills extending down the stem (decurrent); rather broad; cream-colored or white.

Stem tapering upward from a thickened base; solid; elastic; soft and spongy within; smooth or with slight fibrils on the surface; color of cap or paler; $\frac{1}{2}$ to 3 inches long.

Spores ellipsoid; white; 6–8 x 4–5 microns in diameter.

The club stemmed clitocybe may easily be recognized by its peculiar shape and colors. The cap may be compared to a very broad and short inverted cone and the stem to a very narrow elongated cone, the apices of the two being united.

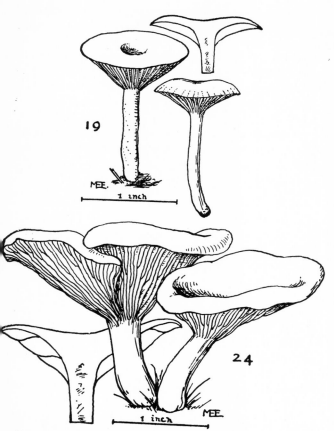

FIG. 10.—Above, SPECIES NO. 19. — Clitocybe albidula. Cap whitish, tinged with brown wholly or in the center when moist; whitish when dry.

Description on page 146.

Below (SPECIES NO. 24).—Clitocybe dealbata. Cap white, almost glossy.

Description on page 150.

Between the brown upper surface of the cap and the similarly colored stem the white gills intervene as if to separate them. Fries says that this species is not edible on account of its spongy texture, but I find it pleasant-flavored and digestible and see no reason why it may not be utilized if taken when dry. After heavy rains it is apt to be water-soaked. Peck.

Clitocybe cyathiformis; cup shaped clitocybe. Species 23. Figure 11.

On decaying wood or on the ground; in woods or open places; August and September; edibility doubtful.

Cap fleshy but thin; depressed at the center or funnel-shaped; water-soaked in appearance when moist (hygrophanous); smooth or nearly so; occasionally with minute radial furrows at the margin (striate) when old; blackish-brown or grayish-brown when moist, paler when dry; 1½ to 3 inches wide.

Gills far apart; broadly attached to the stem or extending down it (adnate or decurrent); united at the stem; dingy or grayish brown.

Stem color of the cap; cylindric or slightly tapering upward; pithy or hollow; an obscure network of fibrils upon the surface; ¾ to 1½ inches long.

Spores white; slightly elliptic; 8–9 x 4–5 microns in diameter.

Clitocybe dealbata; ivory clitocybe. Species 24. Figure 10.

On ground; grassy places, sometimes on (cultivated) mushroom beds; September and October; should NOT be eaten since it closely resembles a poisonous variety Clitocybe dealbata, variety sudorifica.

Cap slightly fleshy; convex, becoming plane when mature or with upturned and sometimes wavy margin; dry; smooth;

FIG. 11.

FIG. 11.—SPECIES 23.—Clitocybe cyathiforme. Cap
brown; 1½ to 3 inches broad.

From Prof. C. H. Kauffman's *Agaricaceæ of Michigan.*

almost glossy; tough; white; taste mild; 1 to 1½ inches broad.

Gills attached to the stem (adnate); close together; thin.

Stem fibrous; cylindric; pithy (stuffed); frosted or mealy at the top; 1 to 1½ inches long.

Spores white; elliptic; 4–5 x 2–2.5 microns in diameter.

This species resembles closely Clitocybe candicans and can be distinguished from it only by minute observation of the various characteristics, particularly of the stem which, in C. candicans, is cartilaginous, somewhat rooting, and is curved and hairy at its base. The spores of C. candicans are broadly elliptical while those of C. dealbata are narrow ellipses.

Clitocybe illudens; deceiving clitocybe; Jack-o'-lantern. Plate VI, Species 25.

On or about old stumps or decaying wood or roots buried in the ground; July to October; woods and open places; in tufts or clusters; POISONOUS.

Cap convex or nearly plane, sometimes depressed in the center, sometimes with a knob at the center even when this is depressed; often irregular or with the stem placed aside from the center; smooth; 3 to 6 inches broad; saffron yellow or orange yellow; flesh white or yellowish; odor strong; taste disagreeable.

Gills color of the cap; close together; extending down the stem (decurrent); narrow at each end.

Stem long, firm; smooth; solid; pithy or rarely hollow; often tapering toward the base; color of the cap or sometimes brownish toward the base; 3 to 6 inches long or even longer.

Spores white; globular; 4–5 microns in diameter.

The deceiving clitocybe is an attractive fungus, forming large

PLATE VI.

PLATE VI.

27

25

27

25

28

28

29

29

30

1 inch

Mary E. Eaton

tufts or even patches on or about old stumps or decaying wood or buried roots. Peck.

A beautiful but unwholesome species. It causes nausea and vomiting if eaten. It is possible to make it comparatively harmless by heating it in salt water for a half hour, then taking it out and frying it in butter. It is phosphorescent. Large fresh specimens when placed in a dark place emit a glowing light. Peck.

From the rich saffron yellow color of all parts of the plant, and especially by its strong phosphorescence, so evident in the dark, it is an easy plant to recognize.

While the plant is not a dangerously poisonous one, it has occasioned serious cases of illness, acting as a violent emetic, and of course should be avoided. Atkinson.

Clitocybe infundibuliformis; funnel form clitocybe. Species 26. Figure 12.

On ground; among fallen leaves in woods; single or scattered, rarely tufted; July and August; edible.

Cap convex and slightly knobbed at center when young; funnel-shaped when mature; margin thin and minutely silky; dry; reddish or pale tan color, fading with age; flesh white; 2 to 3 inches broad.

Gills thin; moderately close together; extending down the stem (decurrent); white or whitish.

Stem generally tapering upward; generally pithy or spongy; soft; elastic; color of cap or paler; 2 to 3 inches long.

Spores white; 5-6 x 3-4 microns in diameter.

Clitocybe laccata. See Laccaria laccata.

Clitocybe multiceps; many cap clitocybe; many-headed clitocybe. Plate VI, Species 27. Figure 13.

On ground; open ground or in grassy places; in tufts or clusters, rarely solitary; June to October; edible.

Cap fleshy; firm; convex; moist in wet weather; watery-white, grayish, yellowish-gray or grayish brown, the center portion more grayish; often irregular in shape from pressure by other caps or stems; flesh milk-white; taste oily and slightly disagreeable; 1 to 3½ inches broad.

Gills attached broadly to stem or extending a little down it (adnate or slightly decurrent); close together; narrow; white or whitish.

Stem thick; cylindric; solid or pithy (stuffed); firm; white or whitish; frosted near the top; 2 to 4 inches long.

Spores white; globular; smooth; glassy; 5-7 microns in diameter.

The tufts may be composed of many or few individuals. The gills are sometimes sinuate (with a bend or tooth upon their edge) on one side of the stem, therein indicating a close relationship with the genus Tricholoma. The flavor of the uncooked mushroom varies. In some it is very disagreeable, in others but slightly so. Some pronounce it among the best of mushrooms when cooked, others say it is unfit to eat. Peck.

This species occurs in wet weather in dense clusters on lawns, especially in rather long grass, and is usually found in great abundance when found at all. Its flesh is firm with a slight oily flavor, and specimens may be kept for several days before cooking. It is known only from New York and a few neighboring states, but should stand transplanting in sod rather easily. Having used it in quantity from my own lawn, I can recommend it as a valuable edible species. Murrill.

Clitocybe odora; sweet clitocybe. Plate VI, Species 28.

On ground in woods and bushy places; scattered or in groups; August.

Cap tough; fleshy; convex, becoming plane or nearly so when mature; smooth; margin regular or sometimes wavy;

FIG. 12.

FIG. 12.—SPECIES 26.—Clitocybe infundibuliformis. Cap 2 to 3 inches broad, reddish or pale tan, fading when old.

From Prof. C. H. Kauffman's *Agaricaceæ of Michigan*. For description, see page 153.

FIG. 13.

FIG. 13.—SPECIES 27.—Clitocybe multiceps. Cap whitish, yellowish, grayish or brownish; 1 to 3½ inches broad.

From Prof. C. H. Kauffman's *Agaricaceæ of Michigan.* See Plate VI.

moist in wet weather; green or dingy green, fading with age or on drying; flesh whitish; odor pleasant, like that of anise; size, 1½ to 3 inches in diameter.

Gills thin; attached to the stem; (adnate) or extending slightly down the stem (decurrent) white, pallid, or grayish-green (glaucous).

Stem cylindrical or slightly thicker at base; stuffed or hollow elastic; smooth; whitish or greenish; thin, ⅙ to ⅓ inches in diameter.

Spores white; 6 to 8 microns by 4 to 5 microns in diameter.

The genus Clitopilus

The species of this pink-spored genus have fleshy stems and gills extending down them (decurrent). Mushrooms with similar gills and stems but white spores, belong to the genus Clitocybe. The pink-gilled species of this genus, Clitopilus, may be distinguished from the pink-gilled common mushroom by the fact that they retain their pink hue when old, not turning dark brown and finally black. Besides in the common mushroom and its family, the gills are free from the stem while in the genus Clitopilus they are attached, as mentioned above. Many species of pink-spored mushrooms, both in this genus and in others have white or whitish gills when they are young, turning to a pinkish hue with advancing age. This is due to the ripening of the pink spores upon their surfaces.

Species of Clitopilus

Clitopilus abortivus; Pleuropus abortivus; abortive clitopilus. Plate VI, Species 29

On ground or on much-decayed wood; in woods or in open places; commonly in groups, sometimes single, sometimes tufted; August to October; edible.

Cap fleshy; firm; convex, plane or slightly depressed at the center; usually regular on the margin but sometimes wavy and irregular; dry; silky when young, smooth when old; gray or grayish-brown; flesh white; taste and odor slightly branny (subfarinaceous); 2 to 4 inches broad.

Gills thin, close together; attached to the stem (adnate) or extending some distance down the stem (strongly decurrent); whitish or pale gray when young, changing to salmon color with advancing age.

Stem solid, slightly downy or fibrous; color of the cap or paler; 1½ to 3 inches long, ¼ to ½ inch thick.

Spores salmon pink; angular; with one nucleus; 8.5 to 10 x 6–7.5 microns in diameter.

The abortive clitopilus takes this name because it is usually found growing with an imperfectly developed subglobose (slightly globular) form in which there is no distinction of cap, stem or gills. It is simply an irregularly rounded mass of cellular tissue of a whitish color, originally described as a subglobose umbilicate (with a pit or depression at its center) downy mass. It is not always umbilicate nor is the surface always downy. It grows singly or in clusters of two or more.

The well developed form is generally a clean neat appearing mushroom but one of a very modest unattractive grayish colored cap and stem and with gills similarly colored when young, but becoming salmon hued when mature. The farinaceous taste and odor are not always distinct unless the flesh is broken.

When taken in good condition and properly cooked it is an excellent mushroom. If stewed gently for a short time it is less agreeable than if thoroughly cooked or fried in butter. The abortive form is also edible and is thought by some to be even better than the ordinary form. Peck.

Common on rich earth or much-decayed wood in woods during late summer and autumn, from Canada to Alabama and west to Wisconsin and Mexico. It is an excellent edible species both in its fully developed and aborted forms, the

FIG. 14.

FIG. 14.—SPECIES No. 29.—Clitopilus abortivus.

Modeled and photographed by Miss Eleanor C. Allen, Amer. Mus.
Nat. History.   Description on page 155.   See Plate VI.

latter being gathered for the market in some parts of Mexico. Murrill.

Clitopilus prunulus; plum clitopilus; prune mushroom. Plate VI, Species 30.

On ground in woods in warm wet weather in July and August; solitary or with but few individuals in a place; edible.

Cap fleshy, broadly convex or nearly plane, sometimes depressed at center; dry; suffused with a bloom; color, whitish or grayish; margin sometimes wavy; flesh white; odor branny (farinaceous); size, 2 or 3 inches broad.

Gills somewhat far apart (distant); extending down the stem (decurrent); whitish when young, becoming salmon colored when older.

Stem white; solid; smooth; 1 to 2 inches long; ¼ to ½ inch thick.

Spores salmon pink (rhodosporæ); oblong elliptical, pointed at each end; .0004 to .00045 inch long.

English writers speak highly of it as an esculent and class it among the most delicious of edible species. Gillet says that it is one of the best mushrooms that can be found.

This species when fresh has a mealy odor and taste. Atkinson.

The genus Collybia

In the white-spored genus Collybia the gills are free from the stem or notched or curved upon their edges near the stem. The stem is either entirely cartilaginous (like gristle) or has a cartilaginous rind while the central portion of the stem is fibrous or fleshy, stuffed (pithy) or hollow. The cap is fleshy and when the plants are young the margin of the cap is incurved or inrolled, i.e., it does not lie straight against the stem as in the genus Mycena.

Many of the species of Collybia are quite firm and will revive somewhat when moistened after drying, but they are not coriaceous (leathery) as in Marasmius, nor do they revive so thoroughly. It is difficult, however, to draw the line between the two genera.

SPECIES OF COLLYBIA

Collybia acervata; tufted collybia. Species 31. Figure 14A.

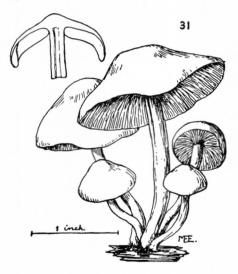

FIG. 14A.—SPECIES No. 31.—Collybia acervata. Cap pale tan or flesh-red when moist; whitish when dry; 1 to 2 inches broad.

Description on page 158.

On wood among decaying leaves or on half buried rotten wood, in woods; in dense tufts; August and September; edible.

Cap slightly fleshy; convex, becoming expanded or nearly plane; smooth; water-soaked in appearance when wet; pale tan or flesh-red when moist, whitish after the escape of the moisture; 1 to 2 inches broad.

Gills narrow; close together; thin; rounded near the stem; adjacent but not attached to the stem (adnexed) or free from it; whitish.

Stem cylindric; hollow; smooth; usually covered with a white down at the base; reddish brown or purplish brown; slender and rigid but brittle; 2 to 3 inches long.

Spores white; elliptic; .00024–.0003 of an inch long.

The tufted collybia is an inhabitant of the woods of our hilly and mountainous districts. It grows in dense tufts on decaying prostrate trunks of trees and among decaying leaves or on bits of rotten wood half buried by fallen leaves.

Though the individual plants are small they grow in such abundance that it is not difficult to obtain a sufficient supply for cooking. They are slightly tough but of good flavor and harmless. Peck.

Collybia confluens. Plate VII, Species 32.

In woods, on ground among fallen leaves; usually in tufts but sometimes in arcs of circles or scattered; July to October; edible.

Cap thin; tough; shriveling when dry, reviving somewhat when moist; flaccid; convex or nearly plane; smooth; water-soaked in appearance when wet (hygrophanous); reddish-brown or grayish red when moist, pallid, whitish or grayish when dry; diameter ¾ to 1½ inches.

Gills close together; narrow; free from the stem; whitish or yellowish-gray.

Stem slender; equal in diameter throughout; hollow; downy; $1/12$ to $1/6$ inch thick, 2 to 5 inches long.

Spores white; ovoid; 5–6 x 4–5 microns in diameter.

PLATE VII.

PLATE VII.

1 inch

Mary E. Eaton.

GENERA AND SPECIES OF MUSHROOMS

The plants if dry and shrunken, revive under the influence of moisture. The cap varies much in color but commonly has a dull russety tinge when moist, sometimes approaching bay red. It fades in drying and becomes grayish white. The stem is long in proportion to the width of the cap. Peck.

Collybia dryophila; Collybidium dryophilum; oak-loving mushroom. Plate VII, Species 33.

On ground or rarely on decayed wood; in woods and pastures; in groups or slightly tufted; May to October; edible (Murrill). Taste nutty.

Cap pale or dark tan, yellowish or chestnut; rather tough; convex to nearly plane, sometimes depressed at the center; edge often wavy, turned in when young; surface smooth and dry; flesh thin, white, ½ to 2 inches broad.

Gills adnexed (adjacent to but not attached to stem) or with a bend or tooth near the stem; whitish or rarely yellowish; rather near together.

Stem cartilaginous (like gristle); smooth; brown; hollow, or stuffed (pithy) in lower portion; sometimes bulbous at base; 1 to 3 inches long.

Spores white; elliptic or egg-shaped; smooth glassy (hyaline); 5-7 x 4-5 microns in diameter.

An edible species of good quality. The early spring form is smaller than the more common summer and autumn form. Murrill.

The oak-loving collybia is one of our most common mushrooms. It occurs in woods, groves, open places and pastures and appears at any time from early spring to late autumn when there is a sufficient degree of warmth and moisture. A favorite place of growth is among fallen pine leaves or under pine trees. It also grows on decaying wood. When it occurs in dense tufts the caps are usually very irregular on account of mutual pressure. The flesh is slightly tough but is agreeable to the taste and perfectly harmless. Peck.

Collybia platyphylla; broad-gilled collybia. Plate VII, Species 34.

About stumps and old prostrate trunks or on much-decayed wood; in thin woods or open places; May to November; sometimes has odor of anise.

Cap thin; fragile; convex to plane and even to margin upturned when old (Atkinson); grayish brown or blackish brown; flesh white; 3 to 5 inches broad.

Gills broad; rather far apart; the edge usually toothed near the stem; white; when old they are more or less broken or cracked (Atkinson).

Stem stout and fleshy but with a fine fibrous and slightly tough or cartilaginous (gristly) rind; pithy (stuffed) or hollow; white, contrasting with the grayish brown of the cap; 3 to 5 inches long.

Spores white; nearly globular or broadly elliptic; .0003–.0004 inches long.

Sometimes this species emits a faint but agreeable odor resembling that of anise, but in decay the odor is very disagreeable and the plants loathsome. Insects are fond of this mushroom, and it is not always easy to find specimens free from their attacks.

In wet weather the caps are apt to have a moist appearance, but they are not truly hygrophanous. Distorted and irregular forms are sometimes found. Peck.

Collybia radicata; rooted collybia. Plate VII, Species 35.

On ground, in woods; scattered; June to October; edible.

Cap thin; convex or nearly plane; sticky (viscid) when moist; grayish-brown or smoky-brown· smooth; 1 to 4 inches broad.

Gills broad; rather far apart; adjacent to but not attached to the stem (adnexed); white.

Stem long and ending below in a long root-like prolongation which penetrates the earth deeply; slender; firm; generally tapering upward; pithy (stuffed); 2 to 8 inches long above the surface of the ground; whitish or color of the cap.

Spores white; elliptic with a slight oblique spur at one end; .0006–.0007 of an inch long, .0004–.0005 inches broad.

The rooted collybia is a common species and one easily recognized if notice is taken of the lower part of the stem. This is a long slender tap-root tapering downward and generally penetrating the earth to a depth about equal to the length of the stem above the surface. The stem is generally thickest at the surface of the ground and tapers slightly from this point in both directions.

After long exposure the spores sometimes assume a yellowish color.

The caps are somewhat tough but agreeable in flavor, and the species is classed as an edible one without any hesitation. Peck.

Collybia velutipes; velvet-stemmed collybia.   Plate VII,
    Species 36.

On dead trunks of trees, either prostrate or standing, on old stumps and decaying wood; in woods or groves; in tufts or clusters or scattered; autumn, winter and spring; edible.

Cap rather thin; convex or plane; smooth; sticky (viscid); reddish yellow or tawny, sometimes yellowish on the margin and darker at the center; sometimes crowded into irregular shape; 1 inch or more broad, larger when not growing in tufts.

Gills broad; rather far apart; rounded near the stem; adjacent but not attached to the stem (adnexed); white or tinged with yellow.

Stem firm; pithy (stuffed) or hollow; brown or tawny brown; velvety hairy when mature; 1 to 3 or 4 inches long.

Spores white; narrow ellipses; .0003 to .00036 inches long, .00016 broad.

The velvet stemmed collybia is one of the few mushrooms that appear late in the season. It has even been called a winter mushroom because it is possible to find it in mild thawing weather in winter. It sometimes develops in spring also. It is easily recognized by its viscid (sticky) tawny cap, its velvety stem and tufted mode of growth. In very young plants the stem is whitish.

Its edible qualities are not inferior to those of the rooted collybia. Its flesh is more tender and quite as agreeable in flavor. It is well to peel the caps before cooking in order to free them from adhering particles of dirt. Peck.

This species is remarkable for its late appearance, being often collected in the winter. It grows on stumps and dead trunks near the ground, and is easily recognized by its viscid, yellowish cap and velvety stem. Murrill.

The genus Coprinus

The genus coprinus is easily distinguished from all others by the character of the gills of the mature plant. These assume a black color and slowly dissolve into an inky fluid which, in the larger plants at least, falls to the ground in drops. The thin caps of some species also partly or wholly waste away in this manner. Because of the production of this black fluid, which has sometimes been used as a poor substitute for ink, these plants have received the name of "inky fungi." A ring is present on the stem in some species. The spores are generally black, rarely brown. Some of the plants literally grow up in a night and perish in a day. Many of the species inhabit dung or manure heaps, as the name of the genus implies. Most of them are so small, thin and perishable that they are not valuable as food. Even the larger ones have thin caps, and those deemed edible should be gathered young and cooked promptly if used as food. The three species described below are common and edible.

SPECIES OF COPRINUS

Coprinus atramentarius; inky coprinus; common ink-cap. Plate VIII, Species 37.

In clusters in rich soil, in gardens, waste places or in woods; late summer and autumn; edible.

Cap egg-shaped when young, becoming expanded; smooth or with a few faint spot-like scales in the center; grayish-brown, often with a yellowish tint, blackening when old; margin sometimes irregularly notched or lobed; flesh white. soon liquefying; 1 to 3 inches broad.

Gills close together (crowded); white when young, soon becoming black and liquefying.

Stem rather slender; smooth; hollow; white or whitish; sometimes with a slight vestige of a ring near the base, but it soon disappears; 2 to 4 inches long.

Spores elliptical; black; .0003 to .0004 inches long.

The inky coprinus is much less attractive than the Shaggy coprinus (Coprinus comatus).

The form growing in woods is generally smaller and more beautiful than that growing in open places.

The cap is sometimes suffused as if with a bloom (powder). It deliquesces rapidly and it is therefore more available for catsup than for food. If intended for the table it must be cooked as soon as brought to the house. Peck.

This excellent edible species is quite common in rich soil on lawns and elsewhere during late summer and autumn. As it appears in close clusters, it may be obtained in greater

PLATE VIII.

PLATE VIII.

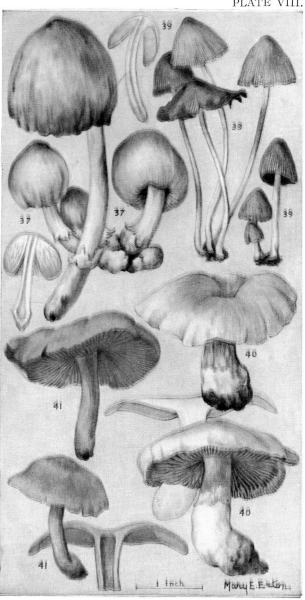

37

39

37

39

39

41

40

41

40

1 inch

Mary E. Eaton

abundance than the shaggy-mane (Coprinus comatus). Owing to its deliquescent character it must be cooked very soon after it is collected. Murrill.

Sometimes the cap is entirely smooth. Other forms present numerous small scales on the top or center of the cap. In others the delicate tufts (scales) cover more or less the entire surface, giving the plant a coarsely granular aspect. This is perhaps the more common appearance, at least so far as my own observation goes. But not infrequently one finds forms which have the entire outer surface of the cap torn into quite a large number of coarse scales, and these are often more prominent over the upper portion. Fine lines mark also the entire surface of all the forms, especially towards the margin, where the scales are not so prominent. The marginal half of the cap is also frequently furrowed. Atkinson.

Coprinus comatus; shaggy-mane mushroom; shaggy coprinus; horse-tail mushroom. Plate I, Species 38. (Frontispiece.)

On ground, in pastures, waste places or dumping grounds; late summer and autumn (in late spring—Atkinson)· in close groups (Murrill); edible.

Cap at first oblong or nearly cylindrical, becoming bell-shaped or expanded and splitting on the margin; whitish, adorned with scattered yellowish scales; turning to a black liquid when old; 1½ to 3 inches long before expansion; the scales make the shaggy appearance which gives it its name.

Gills white and closely crowded together at first, soon pinkish, reddish or purplish tints appear, which quickly turn to black; sometimes all these tints may be seen at one time on one plant; dissolving into a black liquid.

Stem white; smooth; hollow; rather long; smooth or with minute fibres; in the young plant it is furnished with a ring or collar which is movable or but slightly adherent. This collar is easily destroyed and has often disappeared at maturity; 3 to 5 inches long; ¼ to ⅓ inches thick.

Spores black; elliptic; .0005 to .0007 inches long.

The shaggy coprinus or maned agaric as it is sometimes called, is one of the largest and finest species of the genus. It is very tender and digestible and scarcely inferior to the Common mushroom in flavor, though some think it is improved in flavor by cooking a mushroom or two with it. It is fit for the table only before the gills have assumed their black color, but even after that it is sometimes used in making catsup.

When young it is very sapid and delicate, cooked quickly with butter, pepper and salt, it is excellent; in flavor it much resembles the common mushroom, to which it is quite equal if not superior; it is clearly more digestible and less likely to disagree with persons of delicate constitutions. Peck.

The shaggy-mane is a very conspicuous object on lawns in autumn, although it is not so abundant as might be desired. On account of its peculiar shape and decided colors, a single specimen rarely fails to attract attention. It is considered one of the very best of the edible fungi, and is often eaten raw by foreigners. Murrill.

Coprinus micaceus; glistening coprinus; glistening ink-cap. Plate VIII, Species 39.

On ground or on decaying wood; in clusters; May to November; edible.

Cap somewhat bell-shaped or expanded; thin; marked with impressed radiating lines or striations from the margin to or beyond the middle; buff-yellow or tawny yellow; center smooth and often a little more highly colored than the rest; sometimes glistening with minute shining particles when young but these are not often noticeable and when present in young specimens they disappear when the plant is mature; the margin is often notched or lobed and wavy and splitting when the cap expands; when old the color is brownish or dirty, especially if wet; 1 to 2 inches broad.

Gills crowded together; whitish when young, soon becoming pinkish tinted and later, brown and black and liquefying.

Stem white; slender; fragile; smooth; hollow; 1 to 3 inches long.

Spores brown, which is unusual in this genus (others have black spores); elliptical; .00025 to .0003 inch long.

The glistening coprinus is a small but common and beautiful species. Several successive crops often come about a single old stump in one season. It is not uncommon to find it growing from places in the margin of the sidewalks of our cities where shade trees have been cut down. These tufts are sometimes very large and composed of very many plants crowded closely together. Sometimes the caps crack into small areas, the white flesh showing itself in the chinks.

European writers do not record the Glistening coprinus among the edible species, perhaps because of its small size. But it compensates for its lack of size by its frequency and abundance. In tenderness and delicacy it does not appear to be at all inferior to the shaggy coprinus and it certainly is harmless. Peck.

In wet weather this coprinus melts into an inky fluid, but in quite dry weather it remains more or less firm and sometimes it does not deliquesce at all, but dries with all parts well preserved, though much shrunken of course, as is the case with all the very fleshy fungi. Atkinson.

The genus Cortinarius

This genus is distinguished by the rusty yellowish-brown-clay (ochraceous) color of the spores and by the webby character of the veil which, in the young plants, stretches between the stem and the margin of the cap. In many species these fine webby filaments are so numerous that they at first conceal the gills, but they mostly disappear with advancing age, and leave little or no trace of a collar upon the stem.

In the young plants of this family the color of the gills is generally quite unlike that of mature ones. The mature gills become dusted by the spores which collect upon them and assume their color so that the mature plants of all of the species of this genus are colored similarly. It is therefore of the utmost importance in identifying specimens of Cortinarius to know the color of the gills of both the young and old plants.

The gills of all species of Cortinarius are attached to the stem at their inner end and usually their free edges are sharply bent or toothed near the stem (emarginate).

The plants of this genus are usually found growing within or at the borders of woods.

SPECIES OF CORTINARIUS

Cortinarius alboviolaceus; pale violet cortinarius. Plate VIII, Species 40.

On ground among leaves in woods; in groups; late summer and autumn; edible.

Cap convex with a broad elevation at center (umbonate); pale violet to buff, or silvery white with a violet tint; surface smooth, dry, shining; edge turned down; diameter 1 to 3 inches.

Gills attached to stem (adnate) or extending slightly down the stem (decurrent), sometimes notched at stem; rather broad; close together; pale violet to ashy-purplish when young, turning cinnamon-brown when old; irregular on edge.

Stem tapering upward; thick; violaceous above; sometimes stained rusty by fallen spores; 2 to 4½ inches long.

Spores rusty brown; variable size; slightly rough. 6.5–9 x 4–5 microns in diameter.

This pretty, pale-violet species is common through most of temperate North America and Europe. It is abundant enough to use for food. Insects are very fond of it. When dried specimens become so much paler that they are hardly recognizable. Murrill.

Cortinarius cinnamomeus; cinnamon cortinarius. Plate VIII, Species 41.

On ground; in woods, under trees or in mossy swamps; summer and autumn; edible.

Cap thin; convex or expanded, sometimes with a knob at the center (umbonate); dry; smooth, silky; flesh yellowish; cinnamon brown; brownish-rusty or tawny-brown; 1 to 2 inches broad. Young plants show a web between the cap and stem.

Gills thin; close together; some shade of yellow when young turning later to the rusty-ochraceous colors of the spores; attached to the stem (adnate).

Stem slender, rather long; cylindric; pithy (stuffed) or hollow; often bent; silky; yellowish or colored like the cap; 1 to 3 inches long.

Spores ochre; elliptic; .0003 inch long.

The cinnamon cortinarius quite variable in size, shape and color. Like many flowering plants which have a wide range and are not particular as to their habitat, this mushroom is perplexing because of its variability. The fresh plant often has a slight odor of radishes.

Cortinarius collinitus; Cortinarius mucifluus; smeared cortinarius. Species 42. Figure 15.

On ground in thin woods; August to September; edible.

Cap firm; thin; convex to expanded; smooth; glutinous (sticky) when moist, shining when dry; yellow to golden-yellow or tawny yellow; flesh white or whitish; spider-web-like veil extending in young plants from the margin of the cap to the upper part of the stem; 1½ to 3 inches broad.

Gills rather broad; bluish-white or grayish-white when young, turning rusty-colored in mature plants; attached to the stem (adnate).

Stem sticky (viscid) or glutinous when moist, with transverse cracks when dry; straight; solid; 2 to 4 inches long; ¼ to ½ inch thick.

Spores rusty (ochraceous). Slightly elliptic; .0005 to .0006 inch long.

The smeared cortinarius is more common than the Violet cortinarius but is less abundant than the Cinnamon cortinarius. Both the cap and the stem are covered with a viscid substance which makes it unpleasant to handle. The gills are sometimes minutely uneven on the edge.

It is well to peel the caps before cooking since the gluten causes dirt to adhere tenaciously to them. Peck.

It is known by the smooth, even tawny cap, the great abundance of slimy substance covering the entire plant when moist, and, when dry, the cracking of the gluten on the stem into annular (ring-like) patches. Atkinson.

Cortinarius corrugatus; corrugated cortinarius. Species 43. Figure 15.

On ground in woods and bushy places; in groups (gregarious); June to September; edible.

Cap with coarse corrugations or furrows; broadly bell-shaped or very convex; sticky (viscid) when moist; bright yellow, reddish-yellow, tawny or rusty; flesh white; 2 to 4 inches broad.

Gills close together; pallid when young, turning tawny or rusty-colored when mature; uneven on their free edges; attached to the stem (adnate).

Stem long; cylindric; hollow; bulbous at the base; paler

FIG. 15

FIG. 15.—Above, SPECIES 42.—Cortinarius collinitus. Cap 1½ to 3 inches broad; sticky; yellow, tawny or golden.

For description, see page 171.

Below, SPECIES 43.—Cortinarius corrugatus. Cap 2 to 5 inches broad; furrowed; yellow, tawny or rusty.

For description, see page 172.

than the cap except the bulb which is the color of the cap and sticky (viscid) 3 to 5 inches long.

Spores rusty (ochraceous); broadly elliptic; rough; .00045 to .00055 by .0003 to .0004 inch in diameter.

The corrugated cortinarius is a well-marked and easily recognized species. Though the color of the pileus (cap) is variable, its viscid, corrugated surface and the viscid bulb of the stem afford easily recognized characters. Sometimes the wrinkles join with each other in such a way as to give a net-like appearance. The margin in young plants is incurved. The bulb in the young plant is even broader than the cap, which then appears to rest upon it. The plants sometimes grow in considerable numbers and as an edible species it is not to be despised. Peck.

Cortinarius violaceous; violet cortinarius. Plate IX, Species 44.

On ground among fallen leaves in the woods; July and August; edible; scattered or solitary.

Cap convex, later becoming nearly plane; dark violet, adorned with numerous hairy tufts or scales; flesh, tinged with violet; 2 to 4 inches broad.

Gills when young, colored like the cap, but becoming rusty when old; attached to the stem and notched at the stem end.

Stem colored like the cap; bulbous at the base; solid; minute fibres on the surface; 3 to 5 inches long.

Spores rusty; nearly elliptic; .0005 inch long.

The genus Crepidotus

Mushrooms of the genus Crepidotus are very variable in the shape of their caps but are commonly either wedge-shaped or spatulate. The caps quickly curl up on drying unless they ar placed under pressure. They grow in groups and the caps are often stained by the rusty spores. Peck.

PLATE IX.

PLATE IX.

44

44

50

49

50

49

49

56

55

56A

56A

67

55

67

1 inch

Mary E. Eaton

GENERA AND SPECIES OF MUSHROOMS

The species of this reddish-brown genus are usually of small size, thin, soft and fleshy and are especially distinguished by their having the stem attached to the margin of the cap. In some specimens the stem is missing and the cap is attached by its margin to the decayed or dead wood upon which it grows. The cap is resupinate (attached by its top surface) or shelving, lying flat or nearly so, upon the wood. The genus resembles pleurotus among the white-spored mushrooms, or Claudopus among the rosy-spored ones. Atkinson.

SPECIES OF CREPIDOTUS

Crepidotus applanatus; flattened agaric. Plate XI, Species 45.

On old stumps and much-decayed wood; usually growing singly (Atkinson); July to September.

Cap very thin; variable in shape; rounded, kidney-shaped, wedge-shaped or spatulate (shaped like a spatula or spoon); plane or convex; sometimes attached by its margin to the wood from which it grows, or with a short, hairy, stemlike base; smooth; water-soaked in appearance when moist; faint, radial lines on the margin when moist; white; $\frac{1}{2}$ to 1 inch long, $\frac{1}{3}$ to $\frac{3}{4}$ inches broad.

Gills very narrow; crowded together; extending down the stem, if any is present; white, turning cinnamon-colored when old.

Stem at edge of cap; short or absent.

Spores rusty; globular; .0002 to .00025 inch broad.

Creptidotus calolepis; tawny tomentose agaric. Species 46. Figure 16.

On decaying wood of poplar, maple, etc.; June to October; scattered or in groups.

Cap rounded, kidney-shaped or divided into two parts; sometimes attached by its margin or by a short hairy base to the wood upon which it grows; sometimes with a short stem at the margin; water-soaked in appearance when moist; watery-brown and sometimes with faint radial lines or stria-

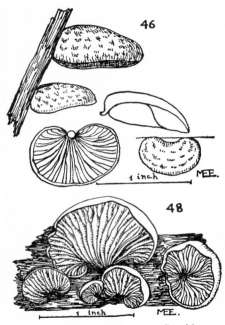

Fig. 16.—Above, Species No. 46.—Crepidotus calolepis. Watery-brown and sometimes with faint radial lines at the margin when moist; whitish, yellowish or pale rusty when dry; scaly.

Description on page 175.

Below, Species No. 48.—Crepidotus versutus. Cap downy pure white.

Description on page 179.

tions on the margin when moist; whitish, yellowish or pale rusty when dry; adorned with small tawny-hairy scales $^2/_3$ to 2 inches broad.

Gills broad; rounded near stem or base; radiating from a lateral (marginal) hairy spot; whitish when young, turning brownish-rusty when old.

Stem very short or absent.

Spores rusty-colored; elliptic; often with a nucleus; .0003 to .0004 inch by .0002 to .00025 inch in diameter.

A pretty species. The cuticle (peel) is separable and is tenacious though it has a jelly-like appearance. Specimens dried in their place of growth are not rare. Peck.

Crepidotus malachius; soft-skinned crepidotus. Species 47. Figure 17.

On damp, decaying wood in woods or shaded places. Much decayed, mossy trunks of trees constitute a favorite habitat; scattered; in groups or with the caps overlapping; June to September.

Cap fleshy, thicker on the margin, and at the base; circular, kidney-shaped or wedge-shaped; convex or nearly plane; smooth or hairy at the base; water-soaked in appearance when moist (hygrophanous); watery-white and with faint radial lines (striations) on the margin when moist, white when dry; flesh white; 1 to 2½ inches broad.

Gills thin; close together; rounded near the stem or base; white or whitish, becoming rusty when old.

Stem absent or very short; placed at the margin of the cap.

Spores rusty; globular; .00025 to .0003 inch in diameter.

In wet weather it has a water-soaked appearance. As the moisture escapes, the cap becomes a clearer white. The moisture disappears from the thickest part of the cap first, the thinnest part last. The species may be distinguished from other white and closely resembling forms by its smoother cap and globular spores. Peck.

Photo by Prof. E. A. White

FIG. 17.

Crepidotus versutus; evasive agaric. Species 48. Figure 16.

On decayed wood.

Cap at first attached by its top surface (resupinate), later bent or turned over; kidney-shaped or divided into two portions; stemless; white; clothed with a soft down; margin curved in; 1/3 to 1 inch broad.

Gills rather broad and far apart; rounded at the base of the cap; radiating from a lateral point on the cap; whitish, turning rusty when old.

Stem absent.

Spores rusty; nearly elliptic; .00035 to .0004 inches long by .00025 to .0003 inch broad.

This little crepidotus has a pure white cap which is covered with a soft white down. The plants grow usually on the under side of rotten wood or bark and then the upper side of the cap lies against the wood, and is said to be resupinate. Sometimes when they grow toward the side of the log the cap has a tendency to be shelving. In the resupinate forms the cap is usually attached to the wood near one edge. Atkinson.

The genus Entoloma

The stems of mushrooms belonging to this genus have neither ring nor cup. The gills are attached to the stem and sometimes extend down it and become pink when old by being dusted with the rosy-colored spores. In this respect the plants might be confused with specimens of the genus Agaricus. As many of the Entolomas are poisonous, the error might have serious consequences. The point of difference is that in the edible mushrooms of the genus Agaricus, the gills are pink when the plant is young and grow brown and then black as the plant ages, while in the Entolomas, on the other hand, the gills remain pink to the last.

Mushrooms of the genus Pluteus have also pinkish gills but they are free from the stem and never attached to it as are those of Entoloma.

SPECIES OF ENTOLOMA

Entoloma commune; common entoloma. Plate IX, Species 49.

On ground in woods; in groups or sparse tufts; taste and odor branny; POISONOUS.

Cap rather thin; convex when young, plane or depressed at center and irregular when old; often with a knob or umbo at the center; surface dry; polished; often with radiating cracks; margin lobed or split when mature. Color that of a hazel nut or umber brown. 1 to 2 inches broad.

Gills rosy-pink; notched near the stem.

Stem white or pale tan; short; often twisted; polished below and frosted near the top; 1½ to 2 inches long.

Spores pink; angular; 6 to 8 microns in diameter.

Common about New York City and found from New England to the mountains of Virginia. Murrill.

Entoloma grayanum; gray entoloma. Plate IX, Species 50.

Among fallen leaves in woods; single, in groups, or, rarely in clusters; July to September; POISONOUS.

Cap fleshy but thin toward the margin; slightly convex or nearly plane; smooth; moist; whitish or brownish-gray; flesh white; taste branny (farinaceous); size variable, 1 to 3 inches.

Gills whitish when young; flesh-pink when mature; extending to the stem; sometimes rounded at the stem end.

Stem cylindrical or nearly so; solid; stuffed or hollow; silky; white or pallid; 1½ to 3 inches long, 1/6 to 1/3 of an inch thick.

Fig. 18.

Fig. 18.—Above, Species 51.—Entoloma strictius. Cap ¾ to 1¾ inches broad, umber (brown).

From Prof. C. H. Kauffman's *Agaricaceæ of Michigan*.

Below, Species 53.—Flammula polychroa. Cap 1 to 2 inches broad; wine-buff or orange-buff, often green-tinged.

Modeled and photographed by Miss Eleanor C. Allen, Amer. Mus. Nat. History.

Spores pink; angular; $7\frac{1}{2}$ microns in diameter.

The gray entoloma is a very variable mushroom, in size, habit and color. The gills remain pink when old and never turn black as do those of the common field mushroom and other species of the genus Agaricus which have pink gills when young. Peck.

Entoloma strictius. Species 51. Figure 18.

In grassy places; in clusters, two or three joined at the bases of their stems; September and October; POISONOUS.

Cap convex, the middle expanded, with a central elevation (umbo); the margin curved in and apt to be wavy at the extreme edge. On drying, the surface of the cap presents a silvery sheen; color of cap umber (brown); smooth; watery in appearance but not sticky, when moist (hygrophanous); flesh brown; $\frac{3}{4}$ to $1\frac{3}{4}$ inches broad.

Gills grayish-white when young, flesh-colored when mature; attached to the stem, with a slight notch in the edge near the stem end (sinuate); rather far apart; rather thick.

Stem colored like the cap but lighter; hollow with white fibers within it; twisted; brittle; cylindric; delicate white fibres at the base.

Spores dull rose color; nearly spherical; 5 to 8 microns in diameter.

The genus Flammula

Almost all of the mushrooms that belong to the genus Flammula grow upon wood. The margin of the cap in young plants is turned downward and inward; when mature, this feature disappears. The gills of these fungi are attached to the stem or extend down it. The stems are fleshy and fibrous. The spores are rust-colored.

SPECIES OF FLAMMULA

Flammula flavida.   Plate XIII, Species 52.

In woods on decaying wood; singly or in clusters; usually in mountainous districts; summer and autumn; edible; taste bitter.

Cap fleshy but thin; broadly convex or nearly plane; smooth; moist; pale yellow; flesh whitish or pale yellow; diameter 1 to 2 inches.

Gills attached to the stem (adnate); pale or yellowish when young, turning rust-color when old.

Stem even; often curved; hollow; whitish or pale yellow; white down at the base; length 1 to 3 inches.

Spores rust-colored; broadly elliptic; 6 to 8 microns in diameter.

The slight bitter taste when raw, disappears on cooking.

Flammula polychroa.   Species 53.   Figure 18.

On wood in woods; in clusters; late summer and autumn.

Cap convex; margin incurved when young; when mature, the cap becomes expanded with a broad elevation at the center; very sticky (viscid) when moist; when mature the cap is covered with delicate hairs on the margin forming scales that vary in color from wine-buff to wine-purple or lavender. The ground-color of the cap is wine-buff or orange-buff, often with shades of green, especially where it has been bruised. Young plants are often purple; 1 to 2 inches in diameter.

Gills notched (sinuate) at the stem end or attached to the stem without a notch (adnate); close together. Before exposure by rupture of the veil they are cream-buff, but later they become drab-brown or take on a purple tinge.

Stem yellowish, often purplish at base; covered with small scales; solid when young, hollowish when old; portions of the veil are attached to the upper part; 2 to 3 inches long, $1/3$ to $1/2$ of an inch thick.

Spores light brown, with a purple tinge when fresh; oval or short oblong; 6–8 by 4–5 microns in diameter.

The genus Galera

The rusty-spored genus Galera resembles Mycena among the white-spored species. The cap is usually bell-shaped and when young the margin fits straight against the stem and is not curved inward. The stem is often very fragile and has neither collar nor cup. The genus does not contain many species.

The species of this ochraceous or rusty-spored genus are small and mostly rather fragile. The cap when young is conical or bell-shaped. When young or moist they have a water-soaked appearance (hygrophanous) and then show radiating lines or minute furrows upon the cap because the gills show through. The colors are whitish or some shade of yellow, tan or brown, and these are paler when the cap is dry.

The stems are slender, fragile and hollow and usually colored like the cap.

SPECIES OF GALERA

Galera Hypnorum. Species 54. Figure 19.

On ground, among mosses in woods or on prostrate, decaying tree trunks; common in hilly or mountainous districts; June to September.

Cap thin; conical or bell-shaped; smooth; watery-cinnamon or slightly rusty when moist; often fading to yellowish or buff when dry; radiating lines when moist; $1/4$ to $1/2$ inch in diameter.

Gills broad; attached to the stem; far apart (distant); tawny or cinnamon colored; often with whitish down on the edge.

Stem slender; hollow; smooth; downy at the top; usually colored like the cap; 1 to 2 inches long; less than $1/12$ inch thick.

Spores rusty; elliptical; .0004–.0005 inch long by .00024–.0003 inch broad.

Galera tenera; Conocybe tenera; slender conocybe; brownie cap. Plate IX, Species 55.

On ground in open places (grassy fields or manured places, Atkinson) spring to autumn; singly (?); edible.

Cap conic or bell-shaped; surface smooth or slightly downy; water-soaked in appearance when moist; tan-colored or brownish, slightly darker at the center; ochre-colored when dry, ½ to 1 inch broad and high.

Gills adjacent to but not adherent to the stem (adnexed); crowded; tawny; (easily separated from the cap, Atkinson).

Stem slender; cylindric; smooth or slightly downy; hollow; fragile; color of the cap; 3 to 4½ inches long.

Spores dark rusty; smooth, nearly elliptical; 12–14 x 6–8 microns in diameter.

This shapely little fungus occurs everywhere on lawns and manured pastures from spring to autumn. When once known it is not easily confused with any other species. Although edible and well-flavored, it would take a long time to gather enough for a meal. Murrill.

This is our most common species of Galera. It sometimes grows in great abundance where cattle have been yarded and in rich lawns and pastures. It is often found growing on dung in company with Panæolus campanulatus. It varies much in size.

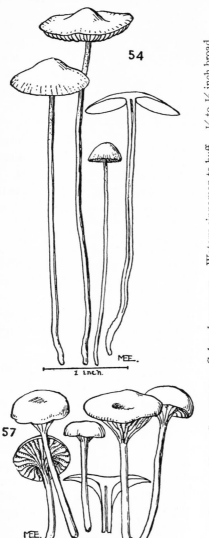

FIG. 19.—Above, SPECIES 54.—Galera hypnorum. Watery cinnamon to buff.   ¼ to ½ inch broad.

Description on page 183.

Below, SPECIES No. 57.—Hygrophorus cantharellus.   Red, orange or yellow.   ½ to 1 inch broad.

Description on page 187.

The genus Hebeloma

Mushrooms belonging to the genus Hebeloma have clay-colored spores but are classed among the rusty spored genera. Their gills extend to the stem but are not attached to it and they are sometimes notched. Their edge is usually whitish and their surface is clay-colored. The veil is seen only in the young stage and then is delicate and composed of fine fibres.

The stem is fleshy and fibrous and is somewhat mealy at its top, and is not easily detached from the cap. The margin of the cap is turned downward and inward in young specimens and the surface is smooth and slightly sticky when moist.

Most of the species of Hebeloma grow on the ground in the autumn and some of them are considered to be poisonous.

SPECIES OF HEBELOMA

Hebeloma precox; early hebeloma. Plate IX, Species 56.

On ground; in groups; June; POISONOUS (?).

Cap convex when young, expanded when mature; slight elevation at center (umbonate); surface smooth; dry; margin incurved; tawny-rusty color; flesh white, taste sweet (Eat not); odor pleasant; 1½ to 2 inches broad.

Gills close together; arched, notched near the stem; pallid when young; tawny (fulvous) when mature.

Stem fleshy; brittle; stuffed or hollow; cream-colored; 1 to 2 inches long.

Spores ovoid; smooth; pale rusty; 5–6 x 3–4 microns in diameter.

Specimens of this uncommon plant were collected and named by Dr. Murrill. Writing of it in *Mycologia*, July, 1911, he says: "This is the first species of Hebeloma to appear in this locality. Although not at all (sticky) viscid when found, it might well become slightly so in wet weather. The remnants of the partial (inner) veil are left clinging to the stipe (stem) as the expansion of the pileus (cap) progresses, leaving none on the margin."

The genus Hygrophorus

In the white-spored genus Hygrophorus the gills of the mature plant have a soft waxy texture which distinguishes them from all others. As in the genus Pleurotus, the gills of some of the species are rounded or notched at the end next to the stem, but the gills of other species are decurrent, that is, they extend down the stem. Those with decurrent gills bear considerable external resemblance to the species of Clitocybe, but the gills are generally thicker and much farther apart than in that genus. No species of Hygrophorus is known to be dangerous, though two or three have been classed as suspicious. Peck.

The waxy character . . . is the chief distinguishing character of the genus. The gills are usually thick and far apart. Species with decurrent gills are similar in appearance to species of Clitocybe but such species may generally be distinguished by the fact that their gills are far apart and their caps and stems are sticky when moist (viscid).

Species of Hygrophorus

Hygrophorus Cantharellus; chantarelle hygrophorus. Species 57. Figure 19.

On damp soil in woods or open places; in clusters; June to August; edible.

Cap thin; convex sometimes with a pit or depression at the center; smooth or with small scales; red, orange or yellow; $\frac{1}{2}$ to 1 inch broad.

Gills rather broad; far apart, waxy; arched; extending down the stem (decurrent); whitish or yellowish; sometimes tinged with red.

Stem slender; fragile; smooth; stuffed or hollow; orange or yellow; 1 to 3 inches long.

Spores white; elliptical; .0003–.0004 by .0002–.00024 inch in diameter.

The margin of the cap may be waved or lobed, the lobes often crowded or overlapping. Peck has given to this variety the name "roseus." Other varieties of this species may have caps and stems of colors differing from each other.

Hygrophorus chlorophanus; sulphury hygrophorus; sulphur-colored chlorophorus. Plate 10, Species 58.

On ground; in damp or mossy places in woods; July to September; edible.

Cap thin; fragile; convex to nearly plane; often irregular, with the margin split or lobed; smooth; sticky when moist (viscid); radiating lines on the margin (striate); pale yellow, sometimes tinged with red in the center; flesh thin; yellowish; ¾ to 1¾ inches in diameter.

Gills extending to but not attached to the stem (adnexed); thin; rather broad; bellied; rather far apart; pale yellow.

Stem smooth; cylindric; color of cap; hollow; sticky when moist (viscid); 1½ to 3 inches long; hollow; pale yellow.

Spores white; egg-shaped, waxy (hyaline); .0002 by .0003 inch in diameter.

Hygrophorus conicus; conic hygrophorus. Plate X, Species 59.

On moist ground in woods and open places; singly or in groups; August to October; probably poisonous. *Do not eat.*

Cap thin; fragile; waxy; sticky (viscid) when moist; conical, usually with an acute tip or apex, rarely with a blunt tip; the margin often lobed; sometimes there are radiating cracks on the surface of the cap. The color is variable, it may be bright red, scarlet, crimson or sulphur yellow; size, ½ to 1½ inches broad.

Gills waxy, rather close together; free from the stem; broad near the outer end but narrow near the stem; yellow.

Stem yellow; hollow; 2 to 4 inches long.

Spores white; elliptical; 9–11 by 6–8 microns in diameter. This species is usually readily distinguished by its conic

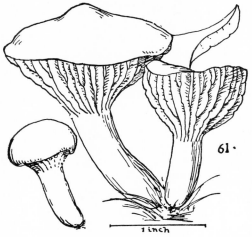

FIG. 20.—SPECIES No. 61.—Hygrophorus pratensis. Cap tawny, reddish, buff, ashy or whitish.

Description on page 191.

cap with acute apex as well as by its change of color to black on drying. It is common in moist woods and grassy places from Greenland to the Bahamas and occurs in Europe. Murrill.

Hygrophorus miniatus; vermilion mushroom. Plate X, Species 60.

On ground in woods and swamps; among mosses and leaves or on bare ground; scattered, in groups or in tufts; June to September; edible.

PLATE X.

PLATE X.

1 inch

Mary E. Eaton

Cap deep red, vermilion or yellow; thin; fragile; smooth or with minute scales; often with a pit at the center; convex, becoming nearly plane when mature; ½ to 2 inches in diameter.

Gills far apart; attached to the stem (adnate); yellow, often tinged with red or, rarely, wholly red; waxy.

Stem slender; smooth; cylindric; stuffed or hollow; polished; color of the cap or a little paler; 1 to 3 inches long.

Spores white; ellipsoid; waxy (hyaline); 8–9 x 4–6 microns in diameter.

This species is very variable in color, size and mode of growth. Specimens always fade to yellow on drying. Murrill.

The vermilion hygrophorus is a very variable but beautiful species. Unfortunately its colors are apt to fade and its beauty to be lost in drying. It is scarcely surpassed by any mushroom in tenderness and agreeableness of flavor. Peck.

Hygrophorus pratensis; meadow hygrophorus. Species 61. Figure 20.

On ground in pastures, grassy places or in woods; scattered, in groups or in tufts; July to September; edible.

Cap firm; convex to expanded or plane; often irregular; smooth; thin at the margin; variable in color; tawny, reddish, buff, ashy or whitish; flesh white or whitish; taste mild; 1 to 3 inches in diameter.

Gills whitish or yellowish; thick; far apart (distant); extending down the stem (decurrent); waxy; the spaces between the gills often veined.

Stem short; cylindric; smooth; solid or stuffed; white or tinged with the color of the cap; 2 to 3 inches long.

Spores white; nearly globular; waxy (hyaline); 6–8 x 5–6 microns in diameter.

Several varieties of this valuable species have been recognized. The names given to them are mostly derived from their color. (Whitish, ashy or rusty white.) Peck.

This variable species is common in late summer in woods and pastures throughout the United States and Europe. Murrill.

Hygrophorus puniceus; red hygrophorus. Plate X, Species 62.

In damp or mossy places in woods and open grounds; July to September; edible.

Cap thin; fragile; conical or bell-shaped (campanulate), becoming expanded and often wavy or lobed at the edge when old; smooth (glabrous); sticky when moist (viscid); bright red; paler or yellow when old; 1 to 3 inches in diameter.

Gills broad; thick; far apart (distant); waxy; yellow or reddish; their attachment to the stem is but slight.

Stem cylindrical or somewhat swollen in its middle (ventriclose); hollow when mature; usually yellow at the top, red in the middle and white at the base; 2 to 3 inches long; 1/3 to 1/2 inch thick.

Spores white; elliptic; .0003 to .0004 inch long, .0002 broad.

The red hygrophorus is a rather large but very tender, fragile species. Its bright red cap makes it a beautiful and conspicuous object. It surpasses our other bright red species in size.

All of the species of Hygrophorus are edible and no harm would come to the eater if one should be mistaken for either of the others. The red hygrophorus is very tender and sapid and may be classed as an excellent though not an abundant mushroom. Peck.

The genus Hypholoma

The fragments of the veil adhering to the margin of the young cap is a distinguishing feature of this genus and is suggestive of its name. Many of the species grow on wood and are tufted (cespitose) in their mode of growth. The spores are brown or purplish-brown. The genus resembles in structure the white-spored genus Tricholoma, the pink-spored Entoloma and the rusty-spored Hebeloma. When there is a well-developed veil hanging from the margin of the cap the specimen must be carefully distinguished from Stropharia on the one hand and from Psilocybe on the other hand if the veil is scanty or missing. Peck.

SPECIES OF HYPHOLOMA

Hypholoma appendiculatum; appendiculate hypholoma. Species 63. Figure 21.

On decaying wood; chiefly in woods of hilly districts; in dense tufts; August to October; edible.

Cap bay-brown or tawny-brown when moist; brownish-yellow and wrinkled when dry; egg-shaped or convex when young, expanded when mature; thin; fleshy; smooth; water-soaked in appearance when moist (hygrophanous); delicate fragments of the veil attached to the margin of the cap in young specimens; 1 to 2 inches broad.

Gills attached to the stem (adnate); close together; white or creamy white when young, turning purplish-brown when old.

Stem slender; cylindric; smooth or frosted at the top; white; hollow; 2 to 3 inches long.

Spores purplish-brown; egg-shaped; smooth; 7 x 4 microns in diameter.

This is everywhere recognized as one of the best and most dainty edible species. It is widely distributed and grows in abundance throughout the season about dead wood or in soil that is rich in decayed wood. Murrill.

The peculiar characters of the species are its tendency to form tufts, to grow chiefly on decaying wood, to be very

FIG. 21.

Above, Species No. 63   *Description on page.*

     Hypholoma appendiculatum. Cap 1 to 2
     inches broad; bay-brown to yellowish. This
     specimen grows from a buried tree root (on
     wood, in woods)   193

Below, Species No. 64

     Hypholoma incertum. Cap 1 to 3 inches
     broad; whitish to yellowish. On ground,
     open places. See Fig. 31.   .   .   .   195

FIG. 21.

hygrophanous, the difference between the moist cap and the dry being well-marked, and in the lateness of its appearance. Peck.

Hypholoma incertum; uncertain hypholoma.   Species 64.
    Figure 21 and 31.

On ground on lawns, pastures, bushy places and by roadsides in showery weather; May to September; in groups or scanty tufts; edible.

Cap whitish, tinged with yellow when moist, especially in the center; thin; fragile; watery in appearance and darker when moist (hygrophanous); surface even or radiately wrinkled; the thin margin sometimes wavy or irregular and adorned when young with fragments of the white veil.   Flesh white; taste mild.   1 to 3 inches in diameter.

Stem cylindric; whitish; hollow; splits easily.   1 to 3 inches long.

Gills whitish, turning rosy and then purplish brown in maturity; attached to the stem (adnate); thin; near together; narrow.

Spores purplish brown; 8–10 x 4–6 microns in diameter.

It differs from the appendiculate hypholoma by its paler cap, its larger spores, its more gregarious habit and in its habitat (on ground).   Peck.

It occasionally has the cap radiately and areolately rimose. (That is, with cracks in the direction from center and at right angles to this.)   Peck.

Hypholoma perplexum; perplexing hypholoma.   Plate X,
    Species 65.

On or about stumps and prostrate tree trunks in woods or open places; generally tufted; August to November; edible.

Cap convex or nearly plane; sometimes with a slight knob at the center; reddish or brownish-red; usually yellowish at the margin. Flesh white or whitish; taste mild; 1 to 3 inches in diameter.

Gills extending to but not attached to the stem (adnexed); thin; close together; slightly rounded near the stem; pale yellow, becoming tinged with green and purplish brown when old (from the ripening spores).

Stem rather slender; cylindric or nearly so; firm; hollow; slightly fibrillose (with fine longitudinal fibres); whitish or yellowish at upper end, reddish-brown at lower end; 2 to 3 inches long.

Spores purplish-brown; slightly oval; smooth; 6–8 x 3–4 microns in diameter.

This mushroom closely resembles hypholoma sublateritium, its distinguishing features being its smaller size, paler margin of the pileus (cap); mild taste, paler and more slender stem, which is always hollow, even when young.   Peck.

This species occurs abundantly on stumps and roots of deciduous trees in autumn, appearing in conspicuous clusters (reddish) of considerable size. It is edible but not very good in quality, being useful because of its very late appearance. Peck separated it in 1872 from Hypholoma sublateritium chiefly because it lacked the bitter taste ascribed to that species, of which it may be only a form.   In collecting this species for food, young and fresh specimens of mild flavor should be selected and they should be cooked for at least 30 minutes.   Murrill.

Hypholoma sublateritium; brick-red hypholoma; brick-
tops.   Species 66.   Figure 22

On or about old stumps, prostrate tree trunks and on decaying wood covered with earth; commonly in tufts; August to November; edible.

Cap dark brick-red, often paler on the margin; convex or

Fig. 22.

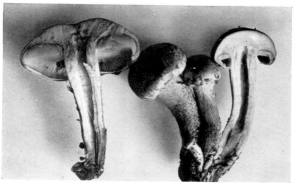

Fig. 22.—Species 66.—Above, Hypholoma sublateritium. Cap 1 to 3 inches broad; brick-red, often paler on margin. Below, section of same.

Photos by author. Description on page 196.

nearly plane; smooth; dry; flesh whitish or yellowish, taste commonly bitter; sometimes mild; 1 to 3 inches in diameter.

Gills extending to the stem or attached to it (adnexed or adnate); close together; whitish or yellowish white, becoming tinged with green when mature, and later, purplish-brown (from the ripened spores).

Stem cylindric or tapering toward the base; occasionally several stems grow from a common base; smooth or slightly fibrous; stuffed; some becoming hollow when old; rust-colored; 2 to 3½ inches long.

Spores purplish-brown; 6–8 × 3–4 microns in diameter.

Murrill considers this species to be identical with Hypholoma perplexum. The gills are quickly attacked by insects which leave their excrement upon portions not eaten and thus, perhaps, may be found an explanation of the occasional bitter taste. Specimens that are collected after frost has checked the ravages of insects, are found to be free from any bitter taste.

The genus Inocybe

Mushrooms belonging to the rusty spored genus Inocybe are generally of small or medium size with some shade of brown as their color and most of them grow on the ground. The gills extend to the stem but are rarely attached to it. Their caps are darker in color when young than when old. The stem is not easily detachable from the cap. The spores are brownish-rust colored, with even, angular or rough contours.

Mushrooms of this genus are difficult to identify. It is often necessary, even for experts, to make use of the microscope in distinguishing the species. The resemblance of some of the Inocybes to others of their genus or to mushrooms of other rusty-spored genera is so close that microscopic examination of the spores cannot be safely omitted.

Many of the species of Inocybe are rare or local, having been found but once, and in a single locality.

None of the species of this genus should be eaten because some of them are poisonous and the distinctions are very difficult to make. Murrill.

SPECIES OF INOCYBE

Inocybe abundans; abundant inocybe. Plate IX, Species 67.

On damp ground in woods; in groups; July and August; probably POISONOUS.

Cap bell-shaped or nearly plane; rarely with a pit at the center (umbilicate); surface dry, with radiating cracks and flaky scales; color of tanned leather with rusty hues at the center and light-brown fibrous lines radiating from it. Taste mild; odor rather strong fungous; ½ to 1 inch broad.

Gills attached to the stem (adnate) or free from it; whitish when young, rusty when old.

Stem whitish at its upper end, inclining to brownish at the base; 2 inches long.

Spores pale rusty; elliptical; 7 x 4 microns in diameter.

Abundant about New York City in late summer. Not easily distinguished from Inocybe infelix (Peck). Murrill.

Inocybe rimosa; cracked inocybe. Species 68. Figure 23.

On ground in woods; singly or in groups; POISONOUS.

Cap thin; convex, bell-shaped or expanded; sometimes with an elevation at the center (umbonate); surface silky, with radiating cracks; yellowish-brown; 1 to 2 inches broad.

Gills pallid or tan; attached to the stem (adnate).

Stem cylindric; firm; slightly swollen at the base; solid; 1 to 2 inches long; thick.

Spores dull-rusty; 7–9 x 3.5–5 microns in diameter.

Very common throughout the northern hemisphere **and** usually recognizable by its very conspicuous radiate splitting. Murrill.

The genus Laccaria

The species of this genus have generally been included **by** botanists in the genus Clitocybe, but they are so peculiar **in**

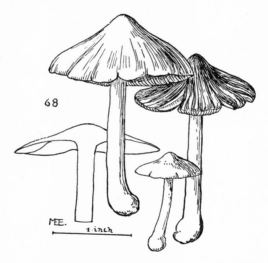

FIG. 23.—SPECIES NO. 68.—Inocybe rimosa. Cap 1 to 2 inches broad; yellowish-brown.

Description on page 198.

their general appearance that it seems best to separate them. The gills are rather thick and far apart and are broadly attached to the stem. When mature they are powdered whitish from the abundant spores. The spores are typically globular (or nearly so) and rough. Peck.

SPECIES OF LACCARIA

Laccaria laccata; laccate laccaria; waxy clitocybe; waxy mushroom.   Plate X, Species 69.

On ground in woods, groves, swamps, mossy places and pastures, in wet, dry or sandy soil and even in sphagnum moss; solitary, in groups or tufts; May to October; edible.

Cap convex or plane, sometimes depressed at the center; surface smooth; hygrophanous; fleshy; rather thin; sometimes with radial lines at the margin (striated); pale red, buff-red, or flesh-red when moist; pale ochre, grayish or buff when dry; margin even; ½ to 2 inches broad.

Gills broad; thick; rather far apart; attached to the stem or extending down it (adnate or decurrent); sometimes slightly toothed near the stem; pale flesh-red and occasionally deep violet; powdered white when old by the spores.

Stem long or short; cylindric or nearly so; fibrous; firm; straight or bent; smooth; stuffed; colored like the cap; 1 to 3 inches long.

Spores white; 8 to 10 microns in diameter; covered with minute warts or elevations.

This is the most common and the most variable species of the genus Laccaria.   It is not particular concerning its habitat or season.   It may be found at any time from spring to late autumn if the weather is not too dry.   As in other species of the genus, the color of the gills is more persistent than that of the cap and is one of the most available characters by which to separate this species from others.   Peck.

This species is very variable in form, size and color; but after all, it is so different from other mushrooms that it is easily recognized.   It is one of the most common species met with, both in woods or fields.   All authors pronounce it harmless, and although poor in quality, it is often eaten. Murrill.

Laccaria ochropurpurea. Plate X, Species 70.

On ground in open, bushy or grassy places; solitary, rarely grouped; July to September; edible.

Cap purplish-brown when moist, grayish or pale tan when dry; unpolished; watery in appearance when moist (hygrophanous); convex or almost hemispheric, with decurved margin; when mature, becoming plane or slightly depressed at the center; firm; fleshy; 2 to 4 inches broad.

Gills attached to or extending down the stem (adnate or decurrent); purplish (color of the cap or paler); thick; broad; far apart.

Stem long or short; variable; cylindric or sometimes thicker in the middle, sometimes thicker at each end; fibrous; solid; color of cap or paler; 1¼ to 3 inches long.

Spores white; globular; warty; 8 to 10 microns in diameter.

This species is often very irregular and very variable in size and shape. The color of the gills is generally darker than those of Laccaria laccata. The cap is much darker when moist than when dry. The stem is very fibrous and firm.

The genus Lactarius

In the white-spored genus Lactarius the gills of the mushrooms exude a milky or colored juice where they are cut or broken. This character alone is sufficient to distinguish this genus from all others but there are also other features which are quite characteristic. The texture of the milky mushrooms is such that while the flesh seems to be firm and rigid it is nevertheless very brittle. The fracture is quite even and not ragged or torn as in more filamentous or fibrous substances. Most of the Lactarius species are stout and fleshy in appearance and resemble in outline those of the clitocybe. In mature plants of this genus the cap is often somewhat funnel-shaped or like a broad inverted cone. The gills are more or less decurrent (extending down the stem) and the stem is generally short and stout. Some of the species have the cap adorned with circular zones or bands that are more highly colored than the adjacent parts. This feature is rarely seen in the mushrooms of any other genus. The taste of the juice and of the flesh in many of these species is very acrid or hot and burning, like that of cayenne pepper. Unless this can be destroyed by cooking or by drying, such species must be considered as wholly unfit for food.

While the taste of the milk is very acrid in some species, in others it is mild or but tardily acrid. This character is of great utility in distinguishing the species and it is necessary to observe it by tasting, but not swallowing the milk or flesh, if we would satisfactorily identify our specimens. Several of the species are edible; others are affirmed by authors to be poisonous. It is most prudent to avoid the use of such acrid species, for, although their acridity is destroyed or dispelled by cooking, they are said to be indigestible, and are acceptable only to the strongest stomachs. Peck.

The spores of all the species of Lactarius are globular, or nearly so and are roughened by minute points or protuberances. Their color may be white or yellowish, according to the species.

SPECIES OF LACTARIUS

Lactarius camphoratus; camphory lactarius. Plate XI, Species 71.

On ground in wet places, swamps and woods; July to September; edible.

Cap bay-red or brownish-red; thin; convex or plane or with a depression at the center, in which is often a small knob; smooth; dry; flesh tinged with the color of the cap; milk white; taste mild; odor sweet; ½ to 1½ inches broad.

Gills dull reddish or with the color of the cap; thin; narrow; close together; attached to the stem or extending down it (adnate or decurrent).

Stem almost cylindric; smooth; stuffed or hollow; with the color of the cap or a little paler.

Spores white; globular; 8 to 9 microns in diameter.

The camphory lactarius closely resembles the sweetish lactarius (Lactarius subdulcis) but differs in its darker red color and by its agreeable odor. Its knob (umbo) when present, is very small and its margin is sometimes wavy. The color is generally bay-red but occasionally it approaches the color of the sweetish Lactarius in which case the odor is the most available character for the separation of these species.

The gills are occasionally paler than usual and thereby tend to the confusion of these two species. The odor is less pronounced in the fresh plant than in the dry. It persists a long time. It is not like that of camphor, as the name would suggest, but resembles more the odor of dried melilot (sweet clover). It is not always dispelled by cooking, but the flavor is not, in our opinion, a serious objection to the edibility of this mushroom. Peck.

Lactarius corrugis; corrugated lactarius. Species 72. Figure 24.

On ground in woods; August and September; edible.

Cap fleshy; compact; firm; convex when young, later becoming expanded or depressed in the center; corrugated, with a spiral network of wrinkles; dark reddish-brown or chestnut-colored, becoming paler as it grows older; suffused as if with a slight frosting or bloom; milk copious, white, with mild taste; 3 to 5 inches broad; flesh whitish or cream-colored.

Gills dark cream-yellow or suggestive of cinnamon, turning paler when old; often showing drops of moisture; becoming dirty or brownish wherever bruised.

PLATE XI.

Species No.		*Description on page.*
45	Crepidotus applanatus	175
71	Lactarius camphoratus	202
73	Lactarius deliciosus	205
74	Lactarius lignyotus	206
75	Lactarius piperatus	207
76	Lactarius subdulcis	207
77	Lactarius theiogalus	208
78	Lactarius vellereus	208
79	Lactarius volemus	209
89	Marasmius rotula	222

PLATE XI.

77

71

78

78

76

74

76

79

79

89

75

73

45

45

45

1 inch

M.E.Eaton

Stem cylindric; solid; firm; paler than the cap; 4 to 6 inches long.

Spores white; large; nearly globular; .00045 to .0005 inch in diameter; with small needle-like points, .0016 to .002 inch long.

This remarkable species resembles Lactarius volemus. It is, however, of a darker color and the surface of the cap is very uneven from the presence of folds which present an appearance much like that of the hymenium (spore-bearing surface) of some species of Merulius (a fungus having a network of pits or pores, instead of gills). The spicules (little spikes) on the gills too, are a peculiar feature of Lactarius corrugis. They are so numerous that under a lens they give a hairy appearance to the edge of the gills. Peck.

Dr. Murrill considers that this species is the most common of the milk-bearing mushrooms (Lactarius).

Lactarius deliciosus; delicious lactarius; orange-milk lactarius. Plate XI, Species 73.

On ground in woods, groves and in mossy swamps; odor not marked; taste often slightly acrid; orange-colored milk exudes when the plant is broken. Wounded places slowly become greenish; July to October; edible.

Cap broadly convex when the plant is young; centrally depressed or funnel-shaped when mature; smooth; moist; yellowish, with circles or mottled zones of deeper hues; flesh whitish, stained with orange in the part nearest to the gills; 2 to 5 inches broad.

Gills orange-colored, but clearer than the cap; attached to the stem or extending down the stem (adnate or decurrent).

Stem smooth; short if growing from the ground, longer if growing among mosses; sometimes tapering toward the base; with the color of the cap or paler, sometimes with a few bright orange spots; 1 to 4 inches long, $^1/_3$ to $^2/_3$ of an inch thick.

Spores yellowish; globular; .0003 to .0004 inch in diameter. The delicious lactarius is well marked by its peculiar colors and is easily distinguished from all other species of Lactarius by its orange-colored juice. The mottled zones upon the cap are less distinct in old plants, and in them the ground-color also fades and becomes tinged with greenish hues. Such plants should not be used as food. There is often a slightly acrid taste to the flesh and milk when the plant is fresh and raw.

The milk or juice pervades the whole plant. Wounds and bruises slowly assume a dull greenish hue.

The stem is usually hollow in mature plants. This species is especially found on pine woods and mossy swamps, though not by any means limited to these. It may sometimes be found in swamps when dry weather prevents its growth elsewhere.

Lactarius lignyotus; sooty lactarius. Plate XI, Species 74.

On ground in shaded, mossy or damp places in woods and swamps; most often in hilly or mountainous places; July to September; edible.

Cap convex, plane or slightly depressed at the center; dry; with or without a small protuberance (umbo) at the center; often with wrinkles radiating from the center; velvety (pruinose); even or lobed at the edge; sooty-brown; flesh white; exuding scanty white milk when bruised or cut; taste mild or slightly acrid; 1 to 4 inches in diameter.

Gills attached to the stem (adnate) or extending slightly down the stem; white or creamy yellow, becoming reddish where they are wounded.

Stem cylindric or tapering upward; stuffed; colored like the cap; 2 to 4 inches long, $1/6$ to $1/3$ inch thick and sometimes thicker; colored like the cap.

Spores globular with small spines (echinulate); white; 8 to 10 microns in diameter.

GENERA AND SPECIES OF MUSHROOMS

The sooty lactarius is a very noticeable species, well marked by its dark-brown color, velvety appearance, its long stem and by the fact that its gills, when wounded, slowly turn a reddish color. It is an excellent edible species. Peck.

Lactarius piperatus; peppery lactarius. Plate XI, Species 75.

On ground in woods; summer and autumn; taste very acrid; edible when properly prepared.

Cap fleshy; thick; firm; convex when young; white, often rough and covered with dirt and debris; when mature, it becomes depressed at the center or funnel-shaped; 3 to 5 inches broad; flesh white; exuding white milk when broken.

Gills white; very narrow; very much crowded together; some of them are forked.

Stem short; solid; cylindric or tapering downward; thick; 1 to 3 inches long.

Spores white; smooth; oval with a small point; 5-7 x 4-5 microns in diameter.

This species is very hot and peppery to the taste and yields abundant white milk. It resembles Russula delica. Atkinson.

In young plants the milk pervades the whole structure.

Lactarius subdulcis; sweetish lactarius. Plate XI, Species 76.

On ground in or near woods; July to October; edible.

Cap thin; fleshy; knob at center (umbonate) when young, becoming funnel-shaped when old; tawny or brownish-red; dry; smooth; margin turned in when young; spreading when old and sometimes wavy; flesh firm; fragile; tinged with tan; milk white, mild or slightly bitterish; ½ to 2½ inches broad.

Gills whitish or tinged with brownish-red; dusted when old; close together; sometimes forked; attached to the stem or extending down it, with a notch near the stem (adnate or decurrent with a tooth).

Stem colored like the cap or paler; cylindric or tapering upward; smooth or sometimes hairy at the base; dry; pithy when young, hollow when old; 1 to 3 inches long.

Spores white; globular or nearly elliptic, with minute spurs; 7 to 8 microns in diameter.

This edible species occurs on the ground in or near woods throughout the Eastern United States and Europe. Murrill.

Lactarius theiogalus; sulphur-milk lactarius. Plate XI, Species 77.

On ground in woods or groves; July to October; "According to Gillet it is pronounced edible by some authors, poisonous by others." Peck.

Cap fleshy; thin; convex when young, becoming depressed at the center when mature; smooth; sticky when moist; tawny-reddish; 2 to 5 inches broad, exuding milk (see below).

Gills attached to the stem or extending down it (adnate or decurrent); close together; pallid or reddish.

Stem pithy (stuffed) or hollow; smooth; colored like the cap; 1 to 3 inches long.

Spores yellowish, inclining to pale flesh-color; nearly globular; .0003 to .00035 inch in diameter.

Milk white, changing to sulphur-yellow after exposure to the air; taste tardily acrid; bitterish.

Lactarius vellereus; fleecy lactarius. Plate XI, Species 78.

On ground in woods and open places; July to September; "Cardier states that it is poisonous according to some authors, edible according to Leveille." Peck.

Cap convex when young and with a pit at the center (umbilicate), later expanded and depressed at the center or slightly funnel-shaped; compact; the whole surface covered with a fine velvety wool (tomentum) that is soft to the touch; white or whitish; exuding milk when cut or broken; this milk is white, with an acrid taste. Cap 2 to 5 inches broad.

Gills rather distant from each other; attached to the stem or extending down it (adnate or decurrent): sometimes forked; whitish when young, cream or yellowish when old.

Stem white; firm; solid; cylindric or tapering downward; downy or woolly; ½ to 2 inches long.

Spores white; nearly smooth; .0003 to .00035 inch in diameter.

The soft, downy tomentum or wool which is characteristic of this species and which covers the cap, gives it a downy or frosted appearance when viewed from a little distance. The stem is short and is sometimes broader than it is long. The gills are about equal in width to the thickness of the cap. They become stained where bruised. The milk that exudes from wounds dries into cream-colored granules. The taste is very acrid. Peck.

Lactarius volemus; orange-brown lactarius. Plate **XI,** Species 79.

On ground in woods and open places; in groups or singly; July to September; edible.

Cap convex or nearly plane when young, becoming depressed at the center or even funnel-shaped when mature; smooth; dry; golden-tawny or brownish-orange, sometimes darker at the center; sometimes with a knob at the center (umbonate); the peel sometimes cracks into small angular patches; flesh white, sometimes tinged with yellow; milk white, abundant, mild to the taste. Cap 2 to 5 inches broad.

Gills attached to the stem or extending a little down it (adnate or decurrent); white or tinged with yellow; close together; a milky fluid exudes when they are bruised or broken; wounds of the gills assume a brownish hue.

Stem colored like the cap or paler; firm; smooth; generally solid; 1 to 4 inches long; not often longer than the diameter of the cap.

Spores white; globular; .00035 to .00045 inch broad.

The orange-brown lactarius is a clean, firm and attractive species. It varies but little in color and is therefore easily recognized. It is most abundant in warm, showery weather. Usually many individuals will be found growing in company so that it is not difficult to obtain a generous supply for the table. It is remarkably free from the attacks of insects, which is a point in its favor as an esculent. Sometimes in drying it emits an unpleasant odor which is, perhaps, an indication that the specimens should not be kept too long before being cooked. Many writers affirm that this fungus

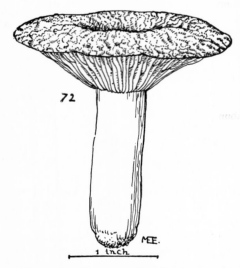

FIG. 24.—SPECIES No. 72.—Lactarius corrugis. **Cap** wrinkled, dark reddish brown, paler when old.

Description on page 203.

FIG. 24A.—SPECIES No. 80.—Lentinus cochleatus. Cap
brownish-flesh color when moist; paler when dry.

Description on page 212.

is quite as good raw as it is cooked, but to me it often has
a slightly acrid or astringent flavor in the raw state. My
own experience with it would scarcely lead me to class it as
more than an ordinarily good mushroom. Perhaps it might
be improved by better cooking than I was able to give it.

There are two or three species somewhat similar to the
orange-brown mushroom in color, but none of them are
hurtful. We are sometimes cautioned against mistaking the
red lactarius for it. This is reported by Fries as very poisonous. I have found this on the high summits of the Catskills
and in the cold mossy swamps and woods of the Adirondack
region, but never in company with the orange-brown lactarius. It is easily distinguished by its more red color,
its smaller size, and especially by its exceedingly acrid.

burning taste. **No one** who had tasted it in the raw state could be **induced to swallow** the least particle of it.   Peck.

This **species was** probably named " volemus " because of the voluminous quantity of milk which exudes when the plant is broken or bruised, though it is not the only species **having** this character.   Atkinson.

The genus Lentinus

Mushrooms belonging to this genus are found growing upon wood. They are variable in form, hard or tough in texture and have white spores. They are easily recognized by the uneven or sawlike edges of their gills.

SPECIES OF LENTINUS

Lentinus cochleatus; shell lentinus. Species 80. Figure 24A.

On or about old stumps or growing from decaying wood buried in the ground; in tufts; July and August; inedible because tough.

Cap thin; tough; flaccid; irregular in shape; often lobed on the margin; plane, depressed at the center or funnel-shaped; smooth; brownish-flesh color when moist, paler when dry; ½ to 2 inches broad.

Gills rather broad; close together; extending down the stem (decurrent); saw-like (serrate) on the edge; whitish, tinged with flesh-color.

Stem placed in the center, to one side or on the edge of the cap; usually united in a tuft; solid; smooth; furrowed or grooved; color of cap or paler; 1½ to 3 inches long.

Spores white; nearly globular; .00016 to .0002 inch in diameter.

The **species is easily** recognized by its tufted mode of

growth and its grooved stem. The plants sometimes emit an agreeable odor. Peck.

Although it is not a common species it is included here on account of its unique grooved stem.

Lentinus lepideus; scaly lentinus. Plate XII, Species 81.

On decaying wood of evergreen trees, often on railroad ties, fence posts and bridge timbers; singly or in tufts; May to October; too tough to be eaten but makes good soup.

Cap fleshy; tough; hard when dry; convex or nearly plane; sometimes slightly depressed in the center; often irregular in shape; the peel (cuticle) cracks and forms brownish, spotlike scales; surface of cap otherwise white or pale rusty; flesh white. 2 to 4 inches broad.

Gills rather far apart; notched near the stem (sinuate); with saw-like teeth along the free edge (serrate-dentate); white; often torn across.

Stem short; hard; solid; often pointed at the base; sometimes scaly; sometimes with a slight ring when young; white or whitish; 1 to 2½ inches long.

Spores white; slightly elliptical; .0004–.0005 inch long, .0002–.00024 broad.

This fungus is often injurious to railroad ties. The cap is occasionally umbonate, that is, there is a knob protruding from its center. The scales may be brown or almost black. The stem is sometimes attached between the center and the side of the cap. When the mushroom emerges from a crack in wood, its stem is pointed at the base.

The genus Lepiota

Mushrooms belonging to the genus Lepiota resemble those of the genera Amanita and Amanitopsis in having their gills free from the stem and in having white spores. They differ in having no removable warts on the cap and no sheath or

PLATE XII.

PLATE XII.

Mary E. Eaton

1 inch

cup at the base of the stem although it may be bulbous. There is a ring or collar on the stem. In some species the epidermis (peel) of the cap breaks into scales which adhere to the cap and this feature suggests the name of the genus which is derived from the Latin word *lepis*, a scale.

SPECIES OF LEPIOTA

Lepiota americana; American lepiota; blushing lepiota. Plate XII, Species 82.

On grassy ground or about old stumps, sawdust heaps or compost heaps; July to October; singly or in tufts; edible.

Cap white with reddish or reddish-brown scales and elevated center; egg-shaped when young, growing convex or expanded when mature; 1 to 4 inches broad; margin striated (with radial marks).

Gills white; close together; free from the stem; sometimes forked or joined near their inner end.

Stem somewhat thickened at or above the base; hollow; usually with a ring or collar, but sometimes this is thin and may disappear when the plant is old; wounds or bruises are apt to assume brownish hues; 3 to 5 inches long.

Spores white; slightly elliptic; with a nucleus; .0003 to .0004 inch long, .0002 to .0003 inch broad.

The American lepiota has one character in which it differs from all other species of this genus. The whole plant when fresh is white except the scales upon the cap and its central portion, but in drying it assumes a dull reddish or smoky color. By this character it is easily recognized   Peck.

Lepiota molybdites; (Lepiota Morgani) green-spored mushroom. Plate XII, Species 83. Figure 25.

On ground in open places (rarely in woods); singly or in groups, sometimes in curved lines or "fairy rings"; June to October; POISONOUS.

Cap soft and fleshy; nearly spherical when young, convex, or even depressed at the center when mature; white, with scattered brown scales which merge together at the center. Flesh white, turning reddish and then yellowish where it is wounded. Cap 4 to 12 inches broad.

Gills broad; close together; free from the stem; white when young, green when mature.

Stem slightly bulbous at the base; firm; stuffed; whitish, tinged with brown; surrounded by a large ring that is often movable; 6 to 8 inches long.

Spores green when first shed, slowly turning yellow; egg-shaped or slightly elliptical; mostly with a single nucleus; 10–13 x 7–8 microns in diameter.

This is one of the largest and handsomest of the lepiotas. It is very abundant in the southern and southwestern states.

Lepiota naucina; lepiota naucinoides; smooth lepiota. Species 84. Figure 26.

On ground in grassy places; rarely in cultivated fields and thin woods; August to November; edible.

Cap white, with the center rarely yellowish or smoky; smooth and even surface; soft; 2 to 4 inches broad.

Gills free from the stem; white; slowly changing with age to a dirty pinkish-brown or smoky-brown color; rounded near the stem.

Stem white or like the cap; furnished with a white collar or ring which is sometimes movable and sometimes disappears in old specimens; bulbous at the base; hollow or nearly so; 2 to 3 inches long.

Spores white; slightly elliptic; with a nucleus; .0003 to .0004 inch long.

Being similar to the common mushroom (Agaricus campestris) in size and color, it is sometimes confused with that species. But a glance at the color of the gills is sufficient

Fig. 25.

Fig. 25, Species 83.—Lepiota molybdites growing in "fairy ring." See Plate XII.

From Prof. C. H. Kauffman's *Agaricaceæ of Michigan.* Description on page 215.

to separate the two. The color of the spores and the character of the stem and collar are also distinguishing differences.

In my estimation this species is scarcely if at all inferior to the common mushroom in its edible qualities. Its flesh is thick and white and usually tender and savory. It is very free from the attacks of insects. Growing as it does often, in places where the grass is short and dense, it has a neat, clean and attractive appearance. Its gills retain their white color for a long time and in this respect it has an advantage over the common mushroom, whose gills soon change from the delicate pink of youth to the repulsive blackish hue of age. Peck.

Since the plant occurs in the same situations as the Agaricus campestris it might be mistaken for it, but of course no harm could come by eating it by mistake for the common mushroom. If one will look at the gills, however, they will not be likely to mistake it for the common mushroom because the gills become pink only when the plant is well expanded and quite old. There is much more danger in mistaking it for the white Amanitas, Amanita phalloides, Amanita verna or Amanita virosa since the gills of these deadly plants are white and they do sometimes grow in lawns and other grassy places where the smooth lepiota and the common mushroom grow. For this reason one should study the descriptions and illustrations of these Amanitas until one is so certainly familiar with their characters that the plants would be known "on sight." Atkinson.

Lepiota procera; parasol mushroom; tall lepiota. Plate XII, Species 85.

On ground in thin woods, in fields and pastures and by roadsides; July to September; unfortunately, not very common; edible.

Cap thin, with a knob or eminence at the center; adorned with brown, spot-like scales; when young, the cap is brownish or reddish-brown and somewhat resembles an egg in shape. Its peel soon breaks up into numerous fragments and as the cap expands, these become separated except on and near the center of the cap; flesh soft, slightly tough and white; mild odor and flavor; 3 to 5 inches broad.

Gills white or yellowish-white; close together; their inner extremity so far from the stem that there is a clear space about it.

Stem very long in proportion to its thickness; with a rather thick, firm collar or ring which, when mature, generally becomes loosened and movable upon it; bulbous at or near the base; with scales or brownish dots below the ring at times; hollow or pithy; 5 to 10 inches long.

Spores white; large; elliptic; .0005 to .0007 inch long.

The parasol mushroom is a very neat, graceful and attractive species. The cap sometimes becomes fully expanded but usually it maintains a convex form like an opened umbrella or parasol.

There is no poisonous species with which it can be confused. The very tall, slender stem with its bulbous base, the peculiarly spotted cap with its prominent darker colored umbo (knob) and the broad space or basin about the insertion of the stem and between it and the gills, easily distinguish this mushroom.

The parasol mushroom has been highly commended and is evidently a first-class edible species. Peck.

This handsome edible species is found in thin soil in meadows, pastures and open woods from New England to Alabama and west to Nebraska. It is widely distributed in Europe and Asia where it is highly esteemed as an article of food, in some places being dried in quantity for winter use. On account of its scaly cap and bulbous stem, it must be carefully distinguished from species of Amanita. Murrill.

FIG. 26.

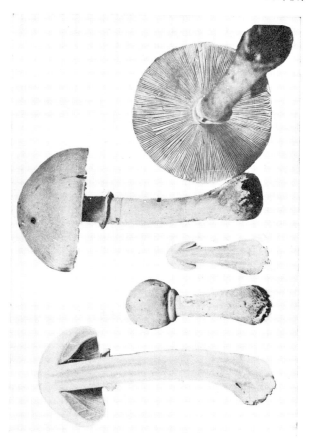

FIG. 26, SPECIES 84.—Lepiota naucina.   Cap white; 2 to 4
inches broad.

From Prof. C. H. Kauffman's *Agaricaceæ of Michigan*.   Description
on page 216.

The genus Marasmius

The tough, leathery texture of the small, thin mushrooms of this white-spored genus is their distinguishing feature. They quickly wither or shrivel in dry weather but revive again in wet weather or when put into water and regain their fresh appearance. The fact that they do not decay is another important feature by which they may be distinguished. Many of the rarer species of marasmius when fresh possess an odor of garlic.

Mushrooms belonging to this genus resemble others of the genera Collybia, Lentinus and Panus. The species of marasmius, though, are usually smaller than those of the two latter species. The central stem of marasmius also differs from the often lateral stems of Panus and Lentinus.

Species of Marasmius

Marasmius siccus; bell-shaped marasmius. Plate XII, Species 86.

On dead leaves in woods; July and August.

Cap thin; dry; convex or bell-shaped; smooth, with radiating furrows; rusty red; a little darker at center; ¼ to ½ inch broad.

Gills few and far apart; broad; narrowed near the stem; free from the stem or slightly attached to it; whitish.

Stem tough; smooth; shining; hollow; blackish brown; 1 to 2 inches long.

Spores white; pointed oblong; variable in size.

Marasmius oreades; fairy-ring mushroom; Scotch bonnet; mousseron; champignon. Plate XII, Species 87.

On ground in open places; common in pastures, lawns and grassy places or by roadsides; appearing in wet weather or after heavy rains; usually in groups. Sometimes in arcs or circles or in complete circles or even in lines; sometimes in clusters; May to October; edible.

Cap fleshy; firm; tough; convex, becoming expanded when mature, often with a large umbo or elevation at the central portion; smooth; buff or tawny (*café au lait*); drying easily and shrinking, reviving when moist; flesh thin, white, of pleasant odor and taste; 1 to 2 inches broad.

Gills rather broad and far apart; scarcely or but slightly attached to the stem; whitish or yellowish.

Spores white; nearly elliptic; .0003 to .00035 inch long.

The fairy-ring mushroom has received this name because of its tendency to grow in rings or circles.

There are two or three mushrooms which are somewhat similar to the fairy-ring mushroom in size and color and which might, by carelessness, be mistaken for it. One of these, the semiorbicular naucoria, Naucoria semiorbicularis, sometimes grows in company with it. It may be distinguished by the color of the gills which, in the mature plant of Naucoria semiorbicularis are rusty-brown. Its spores when caught on white paper have a dark rusty color, and its stem is smooth.

The oak-loving collybia (Collybia dryophila) also resembles it in the color of the cap and gills, but its (C. dryophila's) gills are more narrow and placed very closely, side by side, and the stem is very smooth **and** hollow. This usually grows in woods, but sometimes it occurs in open places and then might be mistaken for the fairy-ring mushroom through carelessness.

It has long been esteemed as edible, but owing to its small size and somewhat tough substance it has not gained the popularity it deserves. Peck.

This very excellent little species is to be looked for in pastures during wet weather in late summer or autumn. Its habit of growing in circles will aid one in recognizing it. I have found it much more abundant in England and other parts of Europe than in this country. If found in sufficient quantity for table use, it should be cooked for some time, owing to its tough texture. Murrill.

Marasmius peronatus. Species 88. Figure 27.

On grounds in woods; single or in groups; August and September; taste acrid; edibility doubtful.

Cap 1 to 2 or more inches broad; light yellowish or pale brick-red, turning paler and wood-color or tan when old.

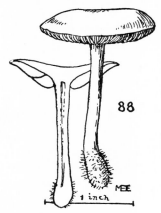

FIG. 27.—SPECIES No. 88.—Marasmius peronatus. Cap yellowish or pale brick-red; wood-color or tan when old.
Description on page 221.

Shrivelled, wrinkled and leathery when dry and radiately lined (striate) at margin. Flesh white.

Gills extending to the stem (adnexed); whitish or pale wood-color when young, turning reddish when old.

Stem 2 to 3 inches long; slender; tough; fibrous; tapering upward; hollow when old; somewhat curved at the base where it is covered with downy hairs.

Spores white; pip-shaped; 7–10 x 4–6 microns in diameter.

Marasmius rotula; little-wheel marasmius. Plate XI, Species 89.

On dead wood or leaves in woods.

Cap thin; dry; convex or nearly flat; brownish with a black spot or depression at the center; smooth, with radiating furrows (striate); ¼ to ½ inch in diameter.

Gills few; far apart; broad; whitish.

Stem slender; black; shiny; tough; paler at the top; hollow.

Spores white; narrow; 6–9 x 3–4 microns in diameter.

The genus Mycena

The species of this white-spored genus are all small and slender with thin caps which are usually conic or bell-shaped and show radiating lines or striations on their upper surfaces. Their stems are smooth and hollow and often covered with down at their bases. There are no rings or cups on the stems.

Species of Mycena

Mycena galericulata. Plate XIII, Species 90.

In woods on dead logs, stumps and branches; late spring to autumn; in clusters; edible.

Cap conic or bell-shaped; sometimes with a knob at the center (umbonate); radial marks on the surface (striate); color variable, but always some shade of gray or brown; ¼ to 1¼ inches broad.

Gills with a notch and tooth at the stem end (emarginate) and extending down the stem (decurrent); connected by veins on the under surface of the cap; white or flesh-color;

Stem slender; firm; whitish; hairy at the base; hollow; 2 to 4 inches long; rarely rooted.

Spores white; waxy (hyaline); 8–10 x 4–6 microns in diameter.

It is a very common and widely distributed species. Atkinson.

Mycena pura. Plate XII, Species 91.

On ground in woods and grassy, open places; single or in clusters; late summer and autumn.

Cap thin; conic or plane, sometimes with a small knob at center (umbonate); smooth; fine radial lines at the edge (striatulate); 2 to 3 centimeters ($^4/_5$ to $^1/_5$) inches broad. Entire plant of uniform color; rose, rose-purple, violet or lilac.

Gills attached to the stem (adnate), sometimes breaking away from the stem; broad at their middle; connected by veins on the under surface of the cap.

Stem sometimes white when young, turning to color of the cap when mature; straight; smooth; hollow; with a few threads at the base.

Spores white; smooth; oblong; 2.5–3.5 x 6–7 microns in diameter.

This beautiful little species is common on the ground in woods throughout North America and Europe. It varies considerably in shape, sometimes being small and bell-shaped with a long stem, and sometimes being quite broad and only slightly rounded on the top or flat, and having a short stem. It has been condemned as being dangerous to eat but its properties have probably not been thoroughly investigated. Even if harmless it is too small and thin to be considered for food. The color varieties were formerly counted as different species. Murrill.

The genus Naucoria

This genus, with dark rusty spores (ferruginous) resembles collybia among the white-spored agarics. The plants grow both on the ground and upon wood. The color of the pileus (cap) is some shade of yellow. The stem is not distinctly ringed, but sometimes a slight, spore-stained band marks the place of the obsolete ring.

PLATE XIII.

PLATE XIII.

102

126

97

97

52

22

90

22

96

90

95

92

100

103

103

99

1 inch

95

99

100

Mary E. Eaton

The members of this genus are, with two or three exceptions, very common. Species of the genus are among the first to appear in the spring and well reward the enterprising mycophagist for his early tramps.

SPECIES OF NAUCORIA

Naucoria semiorbicularis; common naucoria. Plate XIII, Species 92.

On ground in open places; singly or in groups; May to November; edible.

Cap hemispheric, convex, or, rarely, plane; surface often cracked when old; slightly gelatinous (viscid) when moist; tawny or rusty-colored; 1 to 2 inches broad.

Gills adjacent to or attached to the stem (adnexed or adnate); broad; crowded (near together); rusty-colored.

Stem rather tough; slightly enlarged at the base; smooth; pithy (stuffed); yellowish-brown or reddish-brown; 3 to 4 inches long.

Spores rusty; smooth; elliptical; 10–12 x 5–7 microns in diameter.

This excellent edible species is common on lawns and on pastures and along roads and paths from May to November, usually appearing after periods of wet weather. The beginner will have difficulty in distinguishing it because of its homogeneous brownish colors and its lack of definite structural characters. Murrill.

See under *Marasmius oreades*.

The genus Omphalia

Mushrooms of this white-spored genus have thin caps, decurrent gills and cartilaginous, stuffed or hollow stems, somewhat thickened upward.

The species of Omphalia are usually small, the cap rarely exceeding an inch and a half in diameter. They usually have a small pit at the center of the cap, a feature which gives the name to the genus, "omphalia" being derived from the Greek word meaning a navel. When mature a few species assume a funnel shape and then resemble some species of Clitocybe, but from these Omphalia may be distinguished by its cartilaginous stem. From species of Mycena, Omphalia is distinguished by its gills which extend down the stem.

The species of Omphalia grow chiefly on decaying wood or other decaying vegetable matter. Because of their small size, the species of Omphalia are not regarded as important for the table.

Species of Omphalia

Omphalia campanella; Omphalopsis campanella; bell-shaped omphalia. Species 93. Figure 28.

On dead or rotten logs, stumps, etc.; in woods; in clusters; edible

Cap thin; rather tough; convex with a pit or depression at the center (umbilicate); often irregular in shape; with delicate radiating lines on the surface (striate); with a water-soaked appearance when moist (hygrophanous); yellowish-rusty to dull yellow color; $\frac{1}{4}$ to 1 inch broad.

Gills narrow; extending down the stem (decurrent), arched: connected by veins on the under surface of the cap; yellow.

Stem very slender; polished; pale brown; hollow; adorned with brown hairs at the base; $\frac{1}{2}$ to $1\frac{1}{2}$ inches long.

Spores white; nearly elliptic; smooth; glassy (hyaline); 6–7 x 3–4 microns in diameter.

This is one of our prettiest woodland species, found commonly and widely distributed in Europe and North America on dead coniferous wood. Its color is rather sober but it is conspicuous by reason of its clustered habit and is attractive because of its shapely form. It may be found throughout the growing season. Murrill.

GENERA AND SPECIES OF MUSHROOMS

One of the most common and widely distributed species of the genus Omphalia. It is often clustered, large numbers covering a considerable surface of the decaying log. Atkinson.

It is easily recognized by its yellowish-red cap, dark-brown stem and the little tuft of tawny colored hairs at the base of the stem. Peck.

Omphalia fibula. Plate XII, Species 94.

On mossy ground in fields and groves; June to October.

Cap thin; with a pit or depression at the center (umbilicate); smooth; with slight radial lines at the margin (striatulate); yellow or pale orange; $1/8$ to $1/2$ inch broad.

Gills narrow; arched; extending well down the stem (decurrent); whitish.

Stem long and slender; smooth; hollow; colored like the cap; 1 to 2 inches long.

Spores white; somewhat elliptical; smooth; 4–6 x 2–3 microns in diameter.

The cap becomes brighter in color on drying.

The genus Panæolus

In the black-spored genus Panæolus, the cap is somewhat fleshy or thin; the margin without radial lines or striations. The gills do not extend as far as the margin of the cap and are often mottled or spotted with black or brown and with white edges. The veil extending from the margin of the cap to the stem is often well marked, especially in young plants belonging to this genus. It sometimes persists in the form of fragments hanging from the margin of the cap. Peck.

Species of this genus usually occur in manure or rich soil in open places. P. papilionaceus and P. retirugis are said to produce hilarity and a mild form of intoxication in man if eaten in quantity. Ford found the latter species poisonous to guinea pigs. A century ago P. campanulatus was reported poisonous, inducing sleep. McIlvaine has tried it in small quantities without harmful results. Murrill.

SPECIES OF PANÆOLUS

Panæolus campanulatus; bell-shaped Panæolus. Plate
XIII, Species 95.

In open spaces on horse manure or on rich soil; June and July; POISONOUS.

Cap oval or bell-shaped, sometimes with a knob at the center (umbonate); brownish, with a peculiar gray or lead-colored tint, sometimes reddish-tinted; margin often scalloped or fringed remains of the veil; ½ to 1 inch broad.

Gills attached to the stem (adnate); reddish when young, dusted with the black spores when old.

Stem long; slender; hollow; reddish; covered with a bloom; dusted with the black spores when old; 4 to 6 inches long.

Spores black; 16–18 x 10–18 microns in diameter.

Panæolus papilionaceus. Plate XIII, Species 96.

In open places on dung and rich soil; May and June; POISONOUS.

Cap almost hemispheric; sometimes with an elevation at the center (umbonate); sometimes with scales on the surface; whitish gray, often tinged with yellow; ½ to 1½ inches broad.

Gills very broad; gray, becoming black when old; attached to the stem (adnate).

Stem slender; whitish or stained black by the spores; firm; hollow; 3 to 5 inches long.

Spores black; elliptical; 9–10 x 6 microns in diameter.

Panæolus retirugis; wrinkled panaeolus. Plate XIII,
Species 97.

On ground (heavily manured) or dung; open places; in groups; May to August; edible.

FIG. 28.

FIG. 28.—Above, SPECIES 93.—Omphalia campanella.
Cap ¼ to 1 inch broad; yellowish.

Photo by author. Description on page 226.

Below, SPECIES 98.—Panus strigosus. Cap 8 or more
inches broad; white; hairy.

From Prof. C. H. Kauffman's *Agaricaceæ of Michigan.* Description
on page 230.

GENERA AND SPECIES OF MUSHROOMS

Cap conic or bell-shaped, with a slight elevation or knob at the central portion (umbonate); tan, gray or brownish; a network of cracks, especially near the center; sticky (viscid) and dull-colored in wet weather, cracking in dry weather; the margin decorated with fragments of the veil in mature plants; ½ to 1½ inches broad.

Gills adjacent to but not attached to the stem (adnexed); broad; gray or black; often unevenly colored or mottled with black or with dark brown.

Stem slender; hollow; frosted or covered with a fine down; usually gray or reddish-brown; darker toward the lower end; often with a dark band in the upper portion; 2 to 6 inches long.

Veil between the margin of the cap and the stem is white; conspicuous in young plants; does not form a ring on the stem as in other genera, but hangs in fragments from the margin of the cap in old plants.

Spores black; rather elliptic; smooth; 13–16 x 9–11 microns in diameter.

This attractive species is common and widely distributed in temperate regions during spring and summer on heavily manured lawns and about dung in pastures. It is rather easily recognized by its netted and wrinkled cap and the bits of veil that hang from the margin. Although pronounced edible by all authorities, being of nutty flavor and agreeable odor, it does not appeal to mycophagists (mushroom eaters) as most of the other edible species do. Dr. W. W. Ford recently investigated this species and found an extract from it fatal to guinea pigs; but an extract from the famous morel (Morella esculenta) was found to have a similar effect. Murrill.

The color of this plant is not attractive, but it is one of the most beautiful species I have studied, if one regards form and the general features of its development. I have found it on lawns and grassy places, especially made lawns which have been heavily manured. The size of the plant varies greatly according to its environment, being larger in moist soils and in wet weather and smaller in dry soil and dry weather. The plants have several times been eaten raw by me and while they have a nutty flavor and odor, the taste is not entirely agreeable in this condition, because of the accompanying slimy sensation. Atkinson.

The genus Panus

The mushrooms belonging to this white-spored genus are leathery fungi, growing on wood. When mature they are tough and hard. Their caps shrivel when dry but revive when moist. The gills extend down the stem (decurrent) when there is one. The stem is usually attached to the cap aside from the center and in many species are found at its edge or are even lacking altogether.

Some authorities class the mushrooms of this genus among the Lentinuses. The principal feature that distinguishes Panus from that genus is the fact that the edges of its gills are entire, that is, they are not serrate or saw-toothed.

SPECIES OF PANUS

Panus strigosus. Species 98. Figure 28.

On stumps, especially oak; in clusters or singly; September; harmless.

Cap white; covered with hairs; margin thin 8 inches broad or larger.

Gills broad; far apart; extending down the stem (decurrent).

Stem attached to the edge of the cap; hairy like the cap.

Spores white; elongated-oblong; 11–13 x 3.5–4–5 microns in diameter.

A remarkably handsome fungus. Its creamy whiteness and short, hairy stem make it unmistakable among other tree fungi. It is edible when young but it soon becomes woody.

GENERA AND SPECIES OF MUSHROOMS

Panus stypticus; astringent panus. Plate XIII, Species 99.

On stumps of deciduous trees in woods; in groups; autumn and winter; astringent and puckery to the taste; phosphorescent in the dark; POISONOUS.

Cap tough; resembling a shell; kidney-shaped; tawny; attached by a short lateral stem; small scales on the surface; margin even or lobed; curved in when young; flesh watery-white; ¼ to ¾ inch broad.

Gills narrow; thin; close together; tawny; connected by veins on the under surface of the cap.

Stem short; marginal; solid; pale buff or dull-white near the cap, darker near the base.

Spores white; 1–3 by 2–4 microns in diameter.

This small, inconspicuous species is common throughout the temperate regions. It would hardly be collected for food, even if well-flavored, because of its small size and toughness. Murrill.

The genus Paxillus

Fungi belonging to the genus Paxillus are characterized by gills which are easily and smoothly separable from the cap. The spores are rusty-brown (ochraceous).

SPECIES OF PAXILLUS

Paxillus involutus; involute paxillus (that is, paxillus with the margin of its cap turned downward and inward). Plate XIII, Species 100.

On ground or decaying wood in open places or in damp woods; August to October; edible.

Cap compact; flesh tinged with gray; convex when young, expanded and depressed at the center when mature; margin curled downward and inward; nearly smooth; grayish-buff or rusty-brown or yellowish; 2 to 4 inches broad.

Gills close together; extending down the stem (decurrent); branched or forked; connected by veins on the under surface of the cap; whitish when young, yellowish or rusty when old, turning reddish-brown where cut or bruised.

Stem central, or sometimes away from the center of the cap (eccentric); solid; smooth; colored like the cap; 1 to 3 inches long; $^1/_3$ to $\frac{1}{2}$ inch thick; shorter than the diameter of the cap.

Spores rusty; elliptic; .0003 to .0004 inch long.

It is sometimes called the brown chantarelle but it is scarcely a rival of the true chantarelle. Most authorities record it as edible but they do not praise it highly. It is said to be in high estimation in Russia. With us it is scarcely available except to people living near damp woods. Peck.

The genus Pholiota

Pholiota is a rusty or ochraceous-spored genus. Except for the color of the spores, many of the species belonging to this genus resemble closely those fungi of other genera so that the spore color must be observed before identification can be certainly made. Its plants resemble those of Armillaria among the white-spored mushrooms and Stropharia in the brown-spored series. In some of the species of Pholiota growing upon the ground, the spores are brown, enough to cause some difficulty in deciding whether a given species should be regarded as a Pholiota or a Stropharia. Other resemblances make the species of this genus a difficult one for the beginner.

The stem and cap are continuous with each other and cannot be easily separated. The stem has a ring or collar.

Species of Pholiota

Pholiota adiposa; fat pholiota. Plate XIV, Species 101.

On stumps and dead trunks of trees in or near woods; singly or in tufts; September to November; edible.

Cap fleshy; firm; hemispheric or broadly conic; spreading or expanding when mature; sticky (viscid or glutinous); with scales upon the surface; yellow; flesh whitish; 1 to 4 inches broad.

Gills attached to the stem (adnate); close together; yellow or yellowish, becoming darker or rusty when old.

Stem cylindric or slightly thickened at the base; with a slight flaky ring which often disappears; yellow and sometimes reddish or tawny toward the base; 2 to 4 inches long.

Spores rusty (ochraceous); elliptic; .0003 inch long; .0002 inch broad.

The scales are easily separable from the cap and sometimes disappear when the plant grows old. They are usually more highly colored than the cap. The ring is often absent in mature specimens and is by no means conspicuous in young ones.

This species is not classed as edible by European authors but I find its flavor agreeable and its substance digestible and harmless. It is well to peel the caps before cooking them. Peck.

Pholiota caperata; wrinkled pholiota; the gypsy. Plate XIII, Species 102.

On ground in woods, mossy swamps and open places; July to October; edible; scattered or somewhat grouped.

Cap egg or bell-shaped, becoming expanded when mature; smooth; often whitened in the center by whitish flakes or scales; generally more or less wrinkled; thin towards the edge; yellow; flesh white; 2 to 4 inches broad.

Gills attached to the stem (adnate); often uneven on the edge; whitish, turning rusty-colored when old.

Stem stout solid; sometimes bulbous at the base; smooth or slightly flaky; white or whitish; with a thick ring; 2 to 5 inches long.

FIG. 29.

Modeled and photographed by Miss Eleanor C. Allen of the Amer.
Museum Nat. History.

FIG. 29.

Spores rusty; slightly elliptic; .0005 to .0006 inch long .00025 to .0003 inch broad.

This is a fine, large pholiota easily recognized by its peculiar wrinkled cap and the white frosting or flaky covering of the center of the cap. Sometimes, however, specimens may occur in which neither the wrinkles nor the flakes are present. Occasionally there is the semblance of a sheath or cup (volva) enclosing the base of the stem. The ring (annulus) is usually well-developed, white and persistent. Peck.

It is much esteemed in Germany and is eagerly sought as food by the common people who call it familiarly "Zigeuner," the gypsy. Bost. Mycological Club Bull. 1896.

Pholiota discolor; fading pholiota. Plate XIII, Species 103.

On decaying wood and prostrate trunks of trees in woods; singly or in tufts; July to October; edible.

Cap thin; convex when young, becoming nearly plane when mature; viscid or sticky and water-soaked in appearance when moist (hygrophanous); watery-cinnamon colored and with faint radiating lines on the margin (striatulate) when moist; fading to pale yellow when dry; flesh white; taste mild; 1 to 2 inches broad.

Gills narrow; close together; attached to the stem (adnate); pallid when young, becoming pale-rusty when old.

Stem cylindric or slightly tapering upward; with a distinct, persistent ring; slightly fibrous; pallid or brownish; often with a white down at the base; 1 to 2½ inches long.

Spores rusty or brown; nearly elliptic; 6–8 by 5–6 microns broad.

The fading pholiota is a small but common species growing in woods on decaying wood or ra ches. It is easily distinguished by its viscid (sticky) cap. The change of color in the cap by the escape of its moisture is very noticeable and is suggestive of the specific name. It grows singly or somewhat gregariously and very rarely in small tufts. In this case, the caps are apt to be smaller than usual. Peck.

Pholiota praecox; early pholiota; pholiota candicans. Plate XIV, Species 104.

On ground; lawns and other grassy places; solitary or in groups; May to July; edible.

Cap convex or nearly plane; peels readily; soft; smooth; whitish, becoming tinged with tan or with rusty-brown; flesh white; sometimes with a knob or elevation at the center (umbonate); sometimes with cracks in the peel; sometimes with fragments of the veil attached to the margin of the cap; 1 to 2 inches broad.

Gills adjacent to but not attached to the stem (adnexed); close together; whitish, turning brownish or rusty-brown when old.

Stem whitish or nearly of the color of the cap; slender; pithy or hollow when mature; smooth; with a ring near the top; stem easily separable from the cap; 1½ to 3 inches long.

Spores rusty-brown; elliptic; .0004 to .0005 inch long, .00024 to .0003 inch broad.

The early pholiota is a small but variable species. From other similarly colored species that appear in grassy places early in the season, the collar on the stem will easily distinguish it. Sometimes the collar is slight and disappears with age, and sometimes the fragments of the veil remain attached to the cap, leaving nothing for a collar. Peck.

This is one of our best edible species and it occurs quite abundantly during spring and early summer in grassy and open places throughout temperate regions. Murrill.

Pholiota squarrosa. Plate XIV, Species 105.

On or near wood; in clusters; August to December; edible.

FIG. 30.

FIG. 30.—Above, SPECIES 106.—Pleurotus ostreatus.   Cap
2 to 5 inches broad; white, ashy or yellowish.

Photo by author.   Description on page 237.

Below, SPECIES 108.—Pleurotus ulmarius.   Cap 3 to 5
inches broad; white, whitish or yellowish.

From Prof. C. H. Kauffman's *Agaricaceæ of Michigan*.   Description
on page 240.

Cap saffron-rust color; covered with darker, turned up scales; fleshy; convex; dry. Flesh light yellow. 3 to 5 inches broad.

Gills attached to the stem with a tooth; close together (crowded); narrow; pale olive when young, turning rusty when old.

Stem short when young, but long when mature; tapering downward; scaly below the ring that surrounds the upper part.

Spores rusty; elliptical; .0003 inch by .00016 inch broad.

A variable and showy species, growing chiefly in dense tufts. The scales give the cap a very rough appearance, especially in the young plant. Peck.

The genus Pleurotus

The genus Pleurotus scarcely differs from Tricholoma and Clitocybe except for the fact that the stems of plants are attached to the cap at some point to one side of the center. In some species the stem is scarcely developed at all; in others, it is attached to the very margin of the cap. Some of the species of Pleurotus have the gills rounded or notched at their inner extremity, near the stem, as in the genus Tricholoma, while some others have them decurrent, that is, extending down the stem, as in the genus Clitocybe. A distinctive character that is worthy of notice in this genus Pleurotus, is that the plants are found growing on wood only. Generally their flesh is more tough than it is in those mushrooms growing upon the ground. Sometimes they grow from dead spots or dead branches of living trees and are often out of reach, being high above the ground.

SPECIES OF PLEUROTUS

Pleurotus ostreatus; oyster mushroom. Species 106. Figure 30.

The oyster mushroom, or oyster fungus, so named because of its flavor, is very similar to the sapid mushroom.

PLATE XIV.

PLATE XIV.

104

104

105

110

107

112

111

101

Mary E. Eaton   1 inch

According to the descriptions of the European plant, it is there quite variable in color, but in the United States, the prevailing colors are white or ashy-gray, changing to yellowish in the old or dried state. The stem, when present, is usually shorter than in the sapid pleurotus and is often more lateral. It is sometimes hairy at the base and is sometimes absent. But the caps are clustered and overlapped very much as in that species and the gills are the same in both. For table purposes there is little need of keeping the two species distinct. Both are much more liable to be infested with insects than is the elm pleurotus. Both grow on decaying wood and at the same season and under similar conditions. The oyster mushroom is apparently much less frequently found in New York State than is the sapid mushroom. It has long been classed amongst the esculent species but in consequence of the toughness of its flesh it does not rank as a mushroom of the first quality. Peck.

Its **spores** are white; oblong; 7 to 10 microns in length.

Pleurotus sapidus; sapid pleurotus. Plate XIV, Species 107.

On dead trunks or limbs of trees, in tufts or crowded clusters whose stems are more or less united at the base and whose caps crowd and overlap each other; in woods and open places; June to November; edible.

Cap convex or concave (depressed on the top); smooth; often irregular in shape; moist in wet weather; variable in color—white, yellowish, ashy gray, dull lilac or even brownish; flesh white; 2 to 5 inches broad.

Gills broad and rather far apart; extending down on the stem (decurrent); branching and connected with each other on the stem; whitish or yellowish; sometimes ragged or torn.

Stem usually tufted, several growing from a common base;

usually white and smooth; solid; firm; attached to the cap to one side of the center or at its margin; 1 to 2 inches long.

Spores pale lilac; oblong; .00035 to .00045 inch long.

The peculiar character which distinguishes this species and about the only one that is available for separating it in all cases from Pleurotus ostreatus (the oyster mushroom) is the lilac tint of the spores. When these are collected on black or brown paper they have a sordid, whitish appearance, but if caught on white paper, the color of the mass is a very pale dull lilac. It has seemed to me that they are whitish, even when collected on white paper, when first thrown down, but after a short exposure to the air, or after a greater accumulation of them, the lilac tint appears. Notwithstanding this peculiarity in the color of its spores, the species is classed among the white-spored mushrooms and it is, perhaps, a question whether it is, after all, anything more than a variety of Pleurotus ostreatus.

It is quite common and is more abundant in wet weather. Sometimes it appears to grow from the ground, but a careful investigation would show that it starts from some decaying root or buried piece of wood. I have eaten it both fried and stewed and consider it to be about the same in edible qualities as the oyster mushroom. Peck.

Pleurotus ulmarius; elm pleurotus. Species 108.
   Figure 30.

On stumps or cut branches of elm trees; September tc November; in groups or clusters; edible.

Cap convex or nearly flat; firm; smooth; white, whitish or tinged near the center with a yellowish hue; the peel is sometimes cracked in small areas, making the cap look scaly; flesh white; 3 to 5 inches broad.

Gills broad and rather far apart; notched at the end near the stem; white or tinged with yellow when old; adjacent to, but not attached to the stem (adnexed.)

Stem firm and solid; attached to the cap a little to one side of the center; usually curved; smooth or sometimes downy or hairy at the base; 2 to 4 inches long.

Spores white; globular; .0002 to .00025 inch broad.

The elm pleurotus or elm tree mushroom is a conspicuous object, growing as it generally does, from dead places in or on the stumps of cut branches of standing elms. By its large size and white color it easily attracts attention.

It is not uncommon to see this mushroom late in autumn growing on the elms that have been planted as shade trees along the streets of our cities and in our public parks. It grows especially on those trees that have been severely trimmed or have had their tops cut away. Its time of appearance is so late in the season that it is not often infested by insects. It therefore persists a long time and will keep two or three days without harm. Its flesh is not as tender as that of many of the mushrooms that grow on the ground but it has an agreeable flavor and is quite harmless. Most tree-inhabiting mushrooms grow more slowly and are therefore more tough and more slow to decay than are those growing on the ground. They are also less easily collected since they often grow high up on standing trees. In consequence of their persistent character they are easily dried and preserved for winter use.

The elm pleurotus sometimes grows on other than elm trees, as, for instance, the maple and poplar. Occasionally when growing from the cut surface of an upright stump or from the upper side of a branch, its stem is straight and attached to the center of the cap. When dried specimens are soaked several hours in water they resume their original size and are nearly as good as if fresh. Peck.

The genus Pluteus

Mushrooms of the genus Pluteus have pink spores. They resemble the white-spored Lepiotas but have no ring upon the stem. Neither have the Plutei a sheath or cup (volva) enveloping the base of the stem. They are the only pink-spored mushrooms whose gills are free from the stem. The stem can be detached rather easily from the cap. The gills turn pink or flesh colored as the plant grows older.

SPECIES OF PLUTEUS

Pluteus admirabilis. Species 109. No illustration.

In woods on decaying wood; common in hilly districts July to September; edible.

Cap thin; convex or expanded; usually with a broad elevation at the center (umbonate); with a network of folds or furrows; radiate markings at the margin (striate); yellow or brown; ½ to 1 inch broad.

Gills near together; broad; rounded at the stem end; whitish or yellowish when young, flesh-colored when old.

Stem slender; hollow; cylindrical or slightly thickened at the base; yellow or yellowish-white with white down at the base.

Spores pink; 6.5–8 microns in diameter.

Small young specimens sometimes have the stem solid. This character, with its small size, distinguishes it from Pluteus leoninus. Peck.

Pluteus cervinus; fawn-colored pluteus. Plate XIV. Species 110.

On wood and about stumps in woods; solitary or in sparse groups; edible; May to October.

Cap bell-shaped when young, later becoming expanded; smooth or slightly fibrous on the surface; dingy brown, adorned with blackish fibrils, but specimens sometimes occur with the cap white, yellow, ashy, grayish-brown or blackish-brown; slightly sticky (viscid) in wet weather; 2 to 2½ inches in diameter; flesh white; almost tasteless.

Gills free from the stem; broad; white when young, turning pink or flesh-colored when mature.

Stem cylindric or enlarged at the base; upper portion white, the lower portion colored like the cap; usually smooth; nearly solid; brittle; easily separated from the cap; 2 to 6 inches long.

Spores flesh-colored; broadly elliptic; smooth; 6–8 by 5–6 microns in diameter.

This species is very common in New York and very variable, yet it is not abundant. Usually but one or two specimens are found at a time. It grows especially on or about old stumps and prostrate trunks and may be found in wet weather from May to October. The tendency of the gills to liquefy is often shown by their wetting the paper on which the cap has been placed for the purpose of catching the spores. Peck.

Peck wrote that, in spite of its name, he had never seen it brown-colored.

The genus Psathyrella

Plants of this genus of black-spored mushrooms have fragile, thin caps with striations or radial lines upon them and when young, the edge lies straight against the stem. The gills are black to sooty and are of a uniform color and not spotted as in mushrooms of the genus Panæolus. The species are small and can seldom be gathered in quantity. Those tested have the mushroom flavor and are valued for the savor they impart to less gifted species when cooked with them.

Species of Psathyrella

Psathyrella disseminata. Plate XIV, Species 111.

On decaying wood and on the ground, especially about much-decayed stumps, but also on lawns, etc., where buried roots are decaying; crowded together in large tufts; spring until late autumn, sometimes occurring in greenhouses throughout the year, edible.

Cap very thin and fragile; oval, becoming bell-shaped when mature; marked with radiating lines or furrows at the edge; whitish, grayish or grayish-brown; small; ¼ to ½ inch broad.

Gills few; far apart; attached to the stem (Atkinson); whitish, turning when old to pinkish purple (gray, Atkinson) and finally black.

Stem slender; fragile; hollow; white; 1 to 1½ inches long.

Spores black; oblong; 8 by 6 microns in diameter.

This is a very common and widely distributed species, appearing from late spring until late autumn. They resemble small species of Coprinus (and like it, become soft when old). Atkinson.

It resembles the small sulcate-striate (with radial furrows or lines) Coprini but the gills do not dissolve. Peck.

The genus Psilocybe

Almost all of the species of this brown-spored genus are of small size and grow upon the ground. Their caps are smooth, with the edge turned in when young. When old the gills become brown or purplish. The stem is rigid and tough, hollow or stuffed. The veil is not to be seen.

Species of Psilocybe

Psilocybe fœnisecii; mowers' mushroom; harvest mushroom. Plate XIV, Species 112. Fig. 31.

Cap conic, convex or bell-shaped; surface smooth; water soaked in appearance when moist (hygrophanous); smoky brown or reddish-brown; paler when dry than when moist; often of several shades; ½ to 1 inch broad.

Gills attached to the stem (adnate); broad; not crowded together; brown.

Stem pallid or brownish; slender; cylindric; hollow; fragile; smooth or slightly powdered (pruinose); 2 to 3 inches long.

Spores brown; smooth; slightly elliptic; 12–15 by 6–7 microns in diameter.

The harvest mushroom is small but very abundant and therefore may be considered as of use for food, although it can not be classed among the best species. It occurs everywhere on lawns and in fields after rains throughout the season and should be carefully distinguished from certain poisonous species of Panæolus and other genera which grow in similar localities. Murrill.

The haymakers' psilocybe is a small but regular, neat and attractive species which gets its name from its usual place of growth, where it is often destroyed by the mower while he is cutting grass.

When fresh and moist it is dark brown or reddish-brown and is usually marked on the margin by darker parallel radiating lines. By the escape of moisture these lines disappear and the cap becomes paler, assuming a grayish color. The moisture generally escapes first from the center of the cap though the flesh is thicker there than on the margin. This gives a somewhat variegated appearance to the cap while the moisture is escaping, but after the evaporation is completed the color is nearly uniform. Sometimes the center of the cap has a reddish or tan-colored hue, in which case this color is generally retained for a time after escape of the moisture.

Sometimes the mowers' mushrooms appear in great numbers and in successive crops, otherwise it would be unimportant as an edible mushroom on account of its small size.

FIG. 31.

Two species illustrated.

From Prof. C. H. Kauffman's *Agaricaceæ of Michigan.*

FIG. 31.

It has not a very high flavor but it is harmless and relishable when fried in butter and may therefore be classed as an edible species, though some authors say that there are no edible species of Psilocybe. When uncooked its taste is strong and disagreeable. Peck.

The genus Russula

This white-spored genus closely resembles the milky mushroom genus (Lactarii) but is easily distinguished by the absence of a milky juice. The gills of some species when young are adorned with small drops of water, but no milky or colored juice issues from wounds as is the case in the milky mushrooms. The red colors which are so conspicuous in this species are rarely if ever seen in Lactarius. In the flavor of the flesh there is great similarity. In both genera many species have a mild or agreeable flavor and many others have an acrid, hot or peppery taste. This disagreeable flavor is generally destroyed in cooking so that nearly all the species that have been tried have been found to be edible. There is no veil or collar on the stem and no cup at its base. Many species resemble each other closely. Peck.

SPECIES OF RUSSULA

Russula alutacea; tan-colored russula. Plate XV, Species 113.

On ground in woods and groves; singly or in groups; July and August; edible.

Cap fleshy; fragile; convex when young, growing plane or even depressed at the center when mature; covered with a sticky peel; marked with marginal striations or lines when old; variable in color—red, dark purple, olivaceous or green; flesh white; taste mild; 2 to 4 inches broad.

Gills pale yellow, turning rusty or tan-colored when old;

PLATE XV.

PLATE XV.

1 inch

Mary E Eaton

thick; broad; all of equal length; rather far apart; rounded near the stem.

Stem stout; solid or spongy within; white or red; 1 to 2½ inches long.

Spores yellow (ochraceous or rusty-yellow) although the plant is placed in the white-spored genus; nearly globular; .0003 to .0004 inch broad.

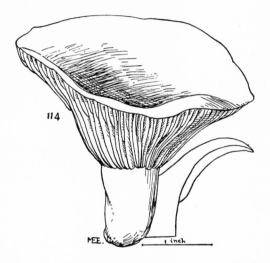

FIG. 32.—(SPECIES NO. 114).—Russula delica. Cap white, sometimes with yellowish stains.

Description on page 250.

A fine species considered edible but I have not tried it. The color of the cap is so variable that the species is not always readily recognized. Peck.

The taste is mild and the plant is regarded as one of the very good ones for food. Atkinson.

Russula delica; weaned russula; short-stemmed russula. Species 114. (Line drawing.)

On ground in woods; singly or in groups; Maine to Alabama and west to Colorado; summer and autumn; edible.

Cap firm, fleshy; broadly convex when young; flat-topped, with a pit at the center (umbilicate), cup or funnel-shaped when old. Surface even; white, sometimes with yellowish stains when soil has been brought up from the ground upon it. The cap has a tendency to become yellowish when old or dried. The edge of the cap is often turned downward and inward. Flesh firm; white; taste slightly peppery (acrid). Cap 2 to 4 inches broad.

Gills thin; far apart; white, or faintly greenish when old; extending down the stem; some of them branched; rather narrow.

Stem short; thick; white; smooth; 1 to 2 inches long.

Spores white; nearly spherical; .0003 to .0004 inch long by .00024 to .0003 inch broad.

This mushroom resembles closely the peppery-milk mushroom, Lactarius piperatus, but is devoid of milky juice and its gill-surfaces are often tinged with glaucus-green. It is more compact and lasts longer than do most other species of russula. Murrill.

Russula emetica; emetic russula. Plate XV, Species 115.

On ground in woods and swamps; singly or in groups; July to September; generally considered to be POISONOUS.

Cap fleshy; firm when young, becoming fragile when old; convex when young, growing plane or depressed at the center when mature; marked with radiating striations or furrows on the margin; sticky (viscid) when moist; rosy or blood-red, sometimes white, or fading to white when old; easily peeled; flesh white except next to the peel when it is reddish; taste very acrid (hot, peppery); 2 to 4 inches broad.

Gills broad; rather far apart; rounded near the stem; free from the stem, or nearly so; white.

Stem solid or spongy within; white or tinged with red; 1½ to 3 inches long.

Spores white; globular; .0003 to .0004 inch broad.

This russula has a very hot peppery taste and is generally considered poisonous by European mycologists but is deemed edible and harmless by some American mycophagists. Thorough cooking probably destroys its harmful properties. I have not tried it (1906). Peck.

This Russula has a very wide distribution, is a beautiful species and is very fragile. The plant is said to act as an emetic. Atkinson.

It is common in woods throughout Europe and the eastern United States, often growing where logs have decayed. It is distinguished by its red color, viscid surface, readily separating cuticle (peel) and very acrid taste. In addition to its acrid quality it is definitely poisonous, containing small quantities of choline, pilzatropine and probably muscarine. When taken in any quantity, it promptly acts as an emetic. It is mainly because of the existence of this species, that most specimens of Russula should be tasted before selecting them as food. Murrill.

Russula fœtens; fetid russula. Plate XV, Species 116.

On ground in woods and bushy places; usually in groups; July to September; POISONOUS.

Cap fleshy; fragile; nearly globular or convex when young, becoming plane or depressed at the center when mature; sticky (viscid) when moist; the very thin margin has noticeable radiating furrows or striations; yellowish, or dingy-ochraceous; flesh pallid; taste acrid; odor of bitter almonds; 3 to 5 inches broad.

Gills rather close together; adjacent to but not attached to the stem (adnexed); unequal in length, some of them are forked; whitish and often studded with drops of moisture when young, becoming yellowish when old; dingy where bruised; connected by veins on the under surface of the cap.

Stem short; stout; pithy, or hollow in places; white or whitish; 1½ to 2½ inches long.

Spores white; nearly globular; .0003 to .0004 inch long and nearly or quite as broad.

Readily recognized by its peculiar odor, acrid taste and widely striate margin. It is gregarious in habit (grows in groups) and is somewhat variable in color. Peck.

This conspicuous species is common throughout most of Europe and the United States, sometimes occurring in great quantity in one spot. Its odor is similar to that of peach-kernels and in some specimens it is strong and unpleasant, although at times it may be scarcely noticeable. This unpleasant odor and the very slimy character of the surface render the plant unattractive and one would hardly collect it for food. It is known to be definitely poisonous to a certain extent and should always be avoided by mycophagists (mushroom-eaters). Murrill.

Russula Mariæ; Mary russula. Plate XV, Species 117.

On ground; in woods and open places; July and August; edible.

Cap nearly hemispheric when young, becoming broadly convex, flat, or even depressed at the center when mature; dry; surface powdery in appearance; dark crimson or purplish, sometimes darker at the center. Flesh white except close to the peel where it is pinkish; taste mild or slightly peppery. 1 to 3 inches broad.

Gills white when young, becoming yellowish when old; close together; attached to the stem.

Stem short; stout; solid or slightly spongy at the center;

colored like the cap or a little paler; usually white at each
end; rarely entirely white.   1 to 2 inches long.

Spores pale yellow; globular; .0003 inch broad.

Mary's russula is easily identified by the pruinose (powdery)
appearance of the surface of its cap. When moistened and
rubbed on white paper it leaves a reddish stain. A few of
the gills are forked near the stem. Those caps that are
purplish sometimes fade as they grow old, especially at the
margin.   Murrill.

This russula is a beautiful and easily recognizable species,
though somewhat variable in its colors, varying from deep
crimson to purple. The center is sometimes more highly
colored than the margin and in old purple specimens the
edge is apt to fade to a whitish color and to acquire radial
marks or furrows. The spaces between the gills are veiny.

The taste of the flesh is mild but occasionally specimens
are found in which it is slightly peppery. Occasionally the
stem tapers downward or is pointed at the base. Forms are
seen in which the stem is entirely white, but it is usually
colored like the cap or a little paler than the cap, with white
ends. Peck.

Russula Peckii; R. Purpurina of American authors;
purpurine russula. Plate XV, Species 118.

On ground in woods and open places; solitary or in groups;
June to September; edible; taste mild.

Cap fleshy; convex when young, flat (plane) when mature
or depressed at center; slightly sticky when moist; edge often
split; skin peels; rosy-pink, paling even to light yellow. 2 to
4 inches broad.

Gills crowded when young; white, turning yellowish when
old; extending to but not attached to the stem; almost all of
equal length; not forked.

Stem spongy; stuffed; rosy pink, paler toward the base; 1 to 2 inches long.

Spores white; spherical; 4 to 8 microns in diameter.

This is a distinct and beautiful species, easily known by its red stem, mild taste and white spores. The gills have a few short ones intermingled and the edge often appears woolly (floccose) under a lens, and red near the margin of the cap. Peck.

Russula virescens; greenish russula. Plate XV, Species 119.

On ground in thin woods and open places; July and August edible.

Cap fleshy; at first nearly spherical, becoming convex as it grows older and later nearly plane or depressed at the center; dry; adorned with small flaky patches or warts on the surface; margin smooth and without striations; green or grayish-green; flesh white; taste mild; 2 to 4 inches broad.

Gills free from the stem or nearly so; narrow near the stem a few of them forked and a few shorter ones sometimes intermingled with the full-length ones; white.

Stem short; stout; firm; white; 1 to 2 inches long.

Spores white; nearly globular; .00024 to .0003 inch long.

The margin of the cap is usually even but occasionally in old specimens it may be partly striate. Peck.

The plant is well known by the green color of the cap and by its surface being separated into numerous quite regular somewhat angular patches where the green color is more pronounced.

It has long been recommended for food both in Europe and in this country. There are several of the russulas in which the cap is green, but this species is readily distinguished from them by the greenish flaky patches on the surface of the cap. Russula furcata is a common species in similar situtions and has forked gills and a cap very variable in color, sometimes reddish, purple, purple-brown, or in one form, green. I know of the Russula furcata having been eaten in rather small quantities, and while in this case no harm resulted, the taste was not agreeable. Atkinson.

Schizophyllum

Schizophyllum commune; Schizophyllum alneum. Species 120. Figure 33.

On dead sticks and branches in woods; all the year; inedible.

Cap tough; leathery; dry; white or whitish; margin lobed; surface downy; ½ to 1½ inches broad. Shrivels when dry, revives when moist.

Gills colored like the cap; their free edges split lengthwise (this splitting can best be seen with the aid of a magnifying lens); woolly.

Stem absent; the cap is attached at its margin or top surface.

Spores white.

Very common in New York State.

The genus Stropharia

The mushrooms belonging to the genus Stropharia possess purple-brown spores; the gills are attached to the stem and the veil forms a ring on the stem, but there is no sheath or cup (volva) at the base of the stem.

SPECIES OF STROPHARIA

Stropharia semiglobata; hemispheric stropharia. Plate XV, Species 121.

On ground or on dung in grassy open places; scattered or in groups; May to Autumn; poisonous.

Cap hemispheric, or nearly so; light yellowish; smooth; very sticky (viscid) when moist; fleshy; ½ to 1½ inches broad.

Gills yellow; attached to the stem (adnate); broad; purple-brown to blackish, darker in color when old than when young, clouded with the ripening spores.

Stem light yellow; sticky (viscid); slender; smooth; cylindric or with a bulb at the base; hollow; ring or collar near the top, but this is sometimes incomplete; 2 to 5 inches long.

Spores brownish purple; ellipsoid; smooth; 15–18 by 9–10 microns in diameter.

Common and widely distributed but rarely abundant. Stevenson says it is considered poisonous, but later authors claim that it is edible, although its favorite habitat and its slimy character are objectionable to most persons. The name is exceedingly well chosen as the shape of the cap is as near an exact hemisphere as one is able to find among living things. Murrill.

The genus Tricholoma

The species of Tricholoma have no collar on the stem. In this white-spored genus the gills are attached to the stem and are excavated or notched on the edge at or near the stem. It often happens that this notch is so near the extremity of the gill that the part attached to the stem is more narrow than the gill just beyond the excavation and causes the gills to appear as if rounded at the inner extremity. This is an important character though not a very conspicuous one. The stem is fleshy and usually short and stout.

The species of Tricholoma are numerous and are mostly rather large, having a fleshy cap and a stout fleshy stem and white spores. The veil is usually very slight and it is not often noticeable except in the young plant.

The genus is distinguished from Armillaria on one hand by the absence of a ring on the stem and from Clitocybe on the other by the notched gills and the fleshy or fibrous-fleshy stem. It is distinguished from the genus Collybia

FIG. 33.

FIG. 33.—SPECIES 120.—Schizophyllum commune.
Photo by the author. Description on page 255.

(in which the gills are similar) by its more fleshy cap and stem and by the fact that it nearly always grows upon the ground. Some of the species of Tricholoma are known to be edible and probably many others are also. None are known to be absolutely poisonous.

SPECIES OF TRICHOLOMA

Tricholoma album; white tricholoma. Species 122. Figure 34.

On ground in woods; singly, in groups or in tufts; taste bitter and unpleasant; August to October; inedible and probably POISONOUS.

Cap fleshy; convex; becoming plane or depressed at the center when old; very dry; smooth; white; sometimes yellowish about the center and rarely wholly yellowish; the margin turned downward and inward in young plants; flesh white; taste acrid or bitter; no decided odor; 2 to 4 inches broad.

Gills notched near the stem (emarginate); close together; white.

Stem solid; elastic; cylindric or tapering upward; surface fibrous; white; 2 to 4 inches long, ⅛ to ½ inch thick.

Spores white; elliptic; .0002 to .00025 inch long.

This species is variable in color and size, being sometimes robust, sometimes slender. It departs from the character of others of its tribe in having a dry cap. Peck.

Tricholoma equestre; equestrian tricholoma; canary mushroom. Plate XVI, Species 123.

On ground in woods or in or near pine woods or groves; autumn and, in southern States, through December; edible. Odor not marked; taste branny.

Cap smooth; sticky (viscid); yellowish, sometimes tinged at the center with reddish-brown—the yellow is more distinct at the margin; flesh white; size, 2 to 4 inches broad; sometimes irregular in shape.

Gills beautiful pale yellow; close together; deeply notched at the stem end.

Stem short; stout; solid; white or yellowish.

Spores white; .00025 inch to .0003 inch long; .00016 to .0002 inch broad.

It is easily recognized by its sticky yellowish cap and its bright sulphur-colored gills. Peck.

Tricholoma personatum; masked tricholoma; blewits. Plate XVI, Species 124.

On ground in thin woods and open places; singly or in groups, occasionally in tufts; September to frost; edible

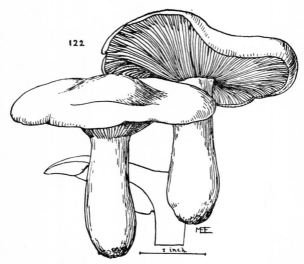

FIG. 34.—SPECIES No. 122.—Tricholoma album. Cap white, rarely yellowish.

Description on page 257.

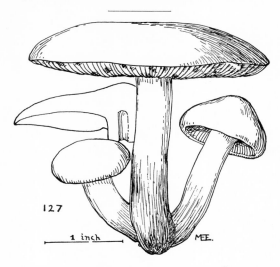

SPECIES No. 127.—Tricholoma transmutans. Cap tawny-red when young, reddish-brown when old.

Description on page 262.

Cap lilac or violet, occasionally pale grayish or almost white, becoming (when old) slightly brownish on the disc; thick; firm; convex or expanded; surface smooth; moist; margin frosted and rolled in when young, sometimes wavy or irregular when old; apt to be water-soaked in appearance in wet weather; flesh firm, white and pleasant to the taste; 2 to 5 inches broad.

Gills close together; rounded near the stem; free from the stem or nearly so; resembling the cap in color; becoming dull in color when old.

Stem short and stout; color of the cap or nearly so; sometimes bulbous at the base; downy when young, smooth when old; 1 to 3 inches long.

Spores dingy white; ellipsoid; smooth; 7 by 10 microns in diameter.

PLATE XVI.

PLATE XVI. *M*

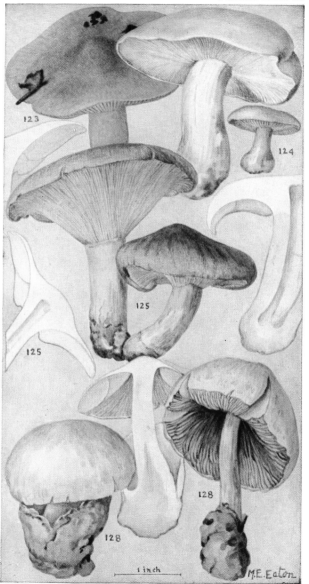

123

124

125

125

128

128

1 inch

M.E.Eaton

This species is of good flavor and is not easily confused with dangerous species. In large, mature specimens the flesh becomes soft and readily absorbs water in wet weather which lessens its value for edible purposes. Murrill.

In Europe it is said to have been sometimes confused with tricholoma nudum, a very closely allied species, and also with Cortinarius violaceus, but such mistakes could result in no harm for both of these are edible. Peck.

Tricholoma Russula; reddish tricholoma. Plate XVI, Species 125.

On ground in woods; solitary or in groups or in clusters; edible.

Cap 2 to 5 inches broad; fleshy; firm; pale pink, rosy red or flesh color; sticky (viscid) when moist; smooth or dotted with small scales; edge covered with fine down in young plants. Flesh white; taste mild.

Gills rounded and slightly notched near the stem; extending slightly down the stem; white, often becoming red spotted when old or where wounded.

Stem solid; thick; firm; whitish or reddish; often scaly at the top; 1 to 2 inches long.

Spores white; .00025–.0003 inch long, .00016 inch broad.

The reddish tricholoma is a pretty mushroom. Its cap as seen in this country is usually pale pink or rosy red though the European plant is sometimes pictured with a much brighter color and the typical form is described as pale purple. The reddish color is similar to that of some russulas as is suggested by the name. It may be distinguished from russulas of a similar color by the downy appearance of the edge of young caps, by the different texture of the flesh and by the different shape of the spores under the microscope. The cap, being sticky is often soiled by adhering particles of dirt or twigs or fallen leaves.

It is an excellent fungus, meaty, easily cooked and of fine flavor. Peck.

Tricholoma sejunctum; separating tricholoma. Plate
XIII, Species, 126.

On ground in mixed woods; September; edible.

Cap fleshy; convex when young, becoming expanded when mature; with a boss or knob at the center (umbonate); slightly sticky (viscid) when moist; whitish or yellowish, sometimes greenish yellow; streaked with brown or blackish fibrils; flesh white, fragile; 1 to 3 inches broad.

Gills broad; rather far apart; rounded or notched near the stem; white.

Stem solid; stout; often irregular· white; 1 to 3 inches long.

Spores white; nearly spherical; .00025 inch broad.

The plants of this species are not uncommon on Long Island, growing in sandy soil in woods of oak and pine. They are usually irregular in shape and the cap becomes fragile. They are quite variable in color, sometimes approaching a smoky-brown hue and again being nearly white. The typical taste is said to be bitter, but those I have tasted can scarcely be said to be bitter. Peck.

Tricholoma transmutans; changing tricholoma. Species
127. Figure 34.

On ground in thin woods and open places in wet weather; in groups or clusters; August to October; edible.

Cap sticky (viscid) when moist and when young and fresh; tawny red when young, becoming reddish-brown when old; sometimes darker at the center; flesh white, with a mealy or farinaceous odor especially when cut; taste also farinaceous; 2 to 4 inches broad.

Gills close together; whitish or pale yellowish becoming dingy or reddish-spotted when old; notched at the inner extremity where they are attached to the stem.

Stem whitish, usually becoming reddish-brown toward the base; about as long as the diameter of the cap; often pithy when young and hollow when old; 2 to 4 inches long.

Spores white; nearly globular; .0002 inch broad.

This plant seems to prefer a light sandy or gravelly soil. It sometimes grows in company with Tricholoma imbricatum in groves of young spruce, balsam-fir and tamarack trees. Its edible qualities are similar to those of Tricholoma imbricatum, from which it is easily known when moist, by reason of the viscidity (stickiness) of its cap. Peck.

The genus Volvaria

Volvaria, a rather rare genus, takes its name from the volva or sheath or cup surrounding the base of the stem, but which entirely envelops the plant when it is young. The genus is characterized by its rosy or reddish spores, the presence of the volva or cup and the absence of any ring on the stem.

SPECIES OF VOLVARIA

Volvaria bombycina; silky volvaria. Plate XVI, Species 128.

On rotting wood, leaf mould and richly manured ground; world-wide in distribution; not common; singly or rarely in tufts; June to October; edible.

Cap more or less globular when young, bell-shaped and later convex when mature; beautiful white, covered with a silky down. Old specimens may appear scaly. Flesh white and not very thick; 2 to 8 inches broad.

Gills free from the stem; close together; very broad at the middle; flesh-colored; edge sometimes ragged.

Stem tapering upward; smooth; solid; white; with a large thick cup (volva) at the base; separates easily from the cap; 3 to 6 inches long.

Spores rosy pink or flesh-colored; somewhat elliptical; 8–10 by 5–6 microns in diameter.

There is no ring on the stem but there is a volva or cup at the base. In this respect the genus Volvaria corresponds with the genus Amanitopsis, but it differs from that genus in the color of its spores. The volva is very large and thick and is usually somewhat sticky. The generic name Volvaria, which signifies that it has a wrapper, was given to this plant because of the large baglike cup. McDougall.

CHAPTER VI
COMMON MUSHROOMS OTHER THAN THOSE WITH GILLS

CHAPTER VI

COMMON MUSHROOMS OTHER THAN THOSE WITH GILLS

Distinguished from the gilled mushrooms previously dealt
with in this book, there remain other common fleshy fungi
to be described. These include the tube fungi (shelf or
bracket fungi and boletes), puffballs, mushrooms with spiny
protuberances on their lower surface (hydnums), the coral
fungi (clavarias), the morels and cup fungi, the stinkhorns
and others.

The form of the spore-bearing surface gives to the many
orders of fleshy fungi their particular appearances. Nature has provided each of the many kind of mushrooms
with some especial means of increasing the area from which
spores may be emitted. In the case of the mushrooms with
gills, these bladelike structures furnish a fruiting surface
enormously greater in area than the plant would possess
without them. The same needed increase of surface is furnished in the polypores or tube fungi by a multitude of vertical cylinders, on whose inner surfaces the spores are formed
and out of lower open ends (pores) they are dropped for
dispersal. The spiny, hedgehog fungi cast their spores from
the surfaces of the multitudes of little awl-like, vertically
hanging teeth. In the case of the coral fungi, augmented
spore bearing surface is provided by the many erect stems
that constitute each plant.

For every spore that falls on fruitful soil, millions come to
naught, but the propagation of the species goes on, so careful
is Nature of the species, so careless is she of the individual.

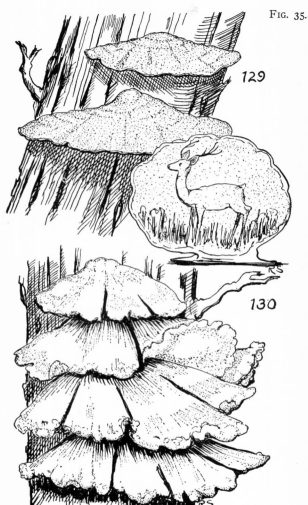

FIG. 35.

129

130

268

Polypores and Boletes

Polypores and Boletes are those mushrooms whose caps bear little hollow tubes on the lower surface of the cap in place of gills. Boletes grow on the ground, are fleshy, soon decay and their tubes may be easily separated *en masse* from the cap. As a rule they have a central stem. Polypores, on the other hand, are usually shelf or bracket fungi attached to wood by the edge of the cap or by a marginal stem and their spore tubes are inseparable from the cap.

As is the case with the gilled mushrooms, spores of the tube fungi (polypori) are produced on an exposed surface but within the vertically placed tubes. When mature, they fall and emerge from the open ends of the tubes. While the fleshy, short-lived fungi produce their propagating spores during a few hours or days only, some of the corky or leathery polypores continue to produce spores intermittently for months and in some cases during many seasons.

SPECIES OF POLYPORES

Ganoderma applanatum; plane brown ganoderma. Fig. 35, Species 129.

A very common perennial woody shelf fungus attached broadly by its margin to the trunk of a deciduous tree. It is usually from 2 to 8 inches broad but may attain a breadth of two feet. Its thickness may be one quarter or less of its breadth. The upper surface is crusted, smooth or irregular and marked by concentric zones, each representing a year's growth. Color, brown to grayish, sometimes covered with rusty brown spores. The pores of the smooth lower surface are whitish and when scratched or marked, become brownish. This property makes this fungus a favorite medium for making pictures on its lower surface.

Polyporus sulphureus; sulphur polypore. Fig. 35, Species 130.

This large and brilliantly colored edible shelf fungus appears on dead trunks of deciduous trees from August to October. Clusters of the bracketlike caps overlap each other, often in profusion. Each fruiting body, attached at its margin to the host is from 2 to 6 inches broad, flattened, often fan shaped and wavy. The upper surface is wooly or smooth, lemon to orange in color, often somewhat zoned. The flesh is yellowish and firm, ½ to 1½ inches thick. The pored under surface is of a light sulphur yellow and with a silky sheen. Spores ovoid, waxy, 6 to 8 microns long by 3 to 5 microns broad.

Best for the table when young and when cooked by broiling.

Polyporus betulinus; birch polypore. Fig. 36, Species 131.

The smooth white or gray, corky shelf fungus found growing abundantly on dead birch trees. It is tough and tasteless though not poisonous.

Polyporus versicolor. Fig. 36, Species 132.

This is one of the common, thin and leathery species of polyporus usually called Polystictus. They grow in clusters on dead wood to which they are attached by their margin. The upper surface of the cap is marked by concentric bands of various colors; grey, purple, reddish or brownish. The tubes are very minute, giving the lower surface a smoother appearance than is usual among other polypores. The polysticti are too tough to suggest edibility.

FIG. 36.

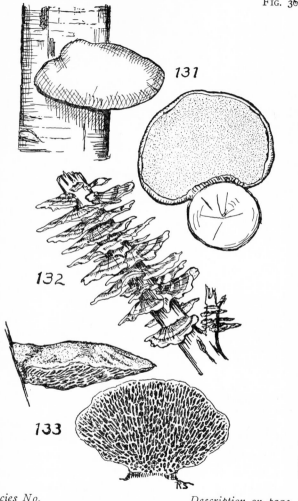

131

132

133

Daedalia quercina; oak-loving bracket fungus. Fig. 36, Species, 133.

A woody, coarse shelf-fungus to be seen on oak stumps and dead trees through the year. Its under surface shows large and small irregular pores, sometimes suggestive of modified gills.

The whitish, corky caps are broadly attached to the stump, thickest at the attachment, and often zoned on the upper surface. The caps are from two to four inches deep, three to six inches from side to side and one to two inches thick. Specimens become blackish when old.

Boletes, Boletuses, Boleti

Boleti resemble, at first sight, the gilled mushrooms. Upon examining the lower surface of the cap, however, one sees a multitude of tiny holes or pores, instead of gills. The pores are the open ends of little tubes which are common to both polypores and boleti.

The chief character by which one may distinguish boleti from polypores is the fact that in boleti the porous substance or mass of tubes on the under surface of the cap may be easily removed by pressing this layer outwardly from the stem toward the margin.

"There are about 80 kinds of boletes in North America and nearly all of them are edible. A few are bitter and two are slightly poisonous; these are the sensitive bolete which turns blue when (the broken flesh is) touched, and the lurid bolete which has red or orange-colored tube-mouths. Many of the boletes occur in great abundance and their flavor can hardly be excelled." W. A. Murrill.

Any boletus, therefore, which does not turn blue when cut

or broken, has not orange-colored or red tube-mouths and is mild in taste, may safely be eaten.

In preparing boletes for the table, specimens infested by larvæ should, of course, be rejected. The stems are too tough to be edible and the mass of tubes must be discarded. The peel, if slimy, must also be removed before cooking.

Boletus felleus; bitter boletus. Fig. 37, Species 134.

A large, handsome mushroom whose appearance suggests that of a baked bun. The convex cap, 3 to 8 inches broad, is smooth and variable in color from pale yellowish to dark brown. The white flesh sometimes darkens a little where wounded and is very bitter in taste. It is firm when the mushroom is young but becomes soft when mature. The long tubes are whitish or flesh colored. The stem sometimes tapers upward, is colored lighter than the cap and usually shows a network of dark lines in its upper portion. The spindle-shaped, flesh colored spores are 12½ to 17 microns long and 4 to 5 microns broad. This conspicuous mushroom is found in woods and grassy places from July into September.

Boletus scaber; rough-stemmed boletus. Fig. 37, Species 135.

This edible species is abundant from July to November on the ground in woods.

The cap is 1½ to 3 inches broad, variable in color (whitish, reddish or brown) and usually smooth. The flesh is white but darkens when bruised or cut. The tubes are long but shorter near the stem; whitish when young but brownish when old and sometimes blackish when bruised. The stem is firm and tapers upward, 2 to 6 inches long and ½ to 1 inch

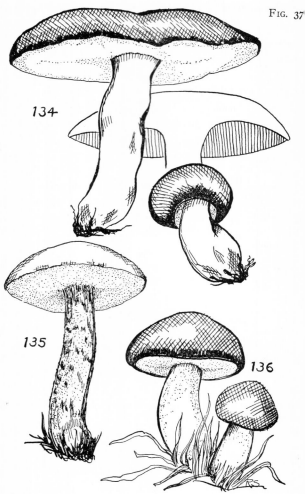

FIG. 37

134

135

136

thick, whitish but roughened by many reddish or brownish scales.

Boletus granulatus; granulated boletus. Fig. 37, Species 136.

An abundant and widely distributed boletus whose season is from August until frost. It is found on sandy, open ground, often near evergreen trees.

The grey or brownish cap is from two to four inches broad and half to one inch thick. It is often spotted near the center. The skin is sticky and peels off easily and the margin is often turned downward and inward. The flesh is firm, thick and white but yellowish next to the tubes. The tube layer is attached to the stem. The solid stem is whitish or pale yellow with brownish specks. The spores are about 8 x 3 microns in size.

It is among the best edible species.

Gyrodon merulioides. Fig. 38, Species 137.

This is perhaps the commonest species. The dull reddish-brown caps are from two to five inches broad, irregular in shape; sometimes lobed at the margin. The yellowish under surface is conspicuously marked by an irregular network making pits in place of circular pores. The stem is inserted off center or even at the margin. Several caps are often found attached to each other.

The species has the soft feel of a boletus and the toughness of a polypore. It is found on ground in woods in the autumn.

Fig. 38.

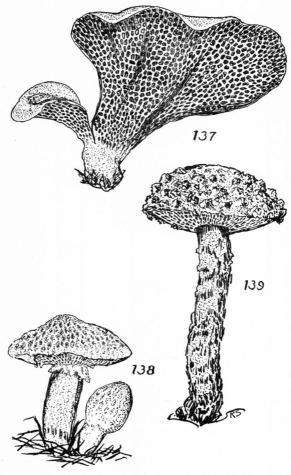

137

139

138

The genus Boletinus

Boletinus is a genus of mushrooms whose species resemble boletus usually. Their spore bearing surface under the cap, however, consists of a network of irregularly shaped, small pits instead of regular round pores or openings of cylindrical tubes. Many of the genus have their stems placed at one side of the center.

> **Boletinus pictus;** painted boletinus. Fig. 38, Species 138.

The cap of this handsome, noticeable species, 2 or 3 inches broad, is covered, when mature, with reddish scales, separated from each other by yellowish cracks. A veil covers the under surface of immature caps and sometimes fragments of it remain attached to the margin of the fully developed cap. It is found in August and September and is edible.

Strobilomyces

This genus, closely resembling Boletus, is represented by but one common species:

> **Strobilomyces floccopus** (S. strobilaceus) ; pine cone mushroom. Fig. 38, Species 139.

The conspicuous, tufted or warty surface of the blackish cap makes this species easily recognizable. The breadth is 2 to 4 inches. The solid, rough, dark stem is 3 to 5 inches long. The tubes change with age from whitish to nearly black. This mushroom grows in woods during July and August. It is rather common but not abundant.

Fistulina

This genus of tube fungi possesses some of the characteristics of Boletus and some of Polyporus. The only common species is Fistulina hepatica.

Fistulina hepatica; beefsteak mushroom, chestnut tongue. Fig. 39, Species 140.

This dark-red, fleshy mushroom grows like a shelf upon chestnut stumps in woods. It has been especially abundant since the occurrence of the blight that killed the chestnut trees in the early years of the present century, thus increasing the number of hosts upon which this fungus might thrive.

The botanical name Fistulina (little pipe or whistle) refers to the spore-bearing tubes on the lower surface of the cap. The term hepatica derives from the liver-like appearance of the flesh.

The cap is thick, fleshy and dark red above and the under surface is yellowish or whitish. The typical cap is somewhat semicircular in shape with the lateral, thick reddish stem attached to the arc at an angle as seen in the illustration. The reddish flesh is juicy and its cut section resembles that of smoked, cooked beef tongue. The upper surface when young and in moist weather, is jelly-like but covered with a sticky pellicle or skin. This jelly disappears when the mushroom dries or becomes old.

The tubes are short, free from one another and cannot be pulled away from the flesh. The upper skin is easily peeled off. The cap when mature, is from 3 to 7 inches broad and from one-half to one inch thick. The stem may grow to a length as great as the breadth of the cap but is usually much shorter.

This mushroom requires a longer time to mature than do many of the other fleshy fungi. Under certain weather conditions I have seen them take ten days to reach their full development. In the neighborhood of New York City their season is from about September 1 until frost.

The elliptical, yellowish spores are from 5 to 6 microns in length.

FIG. 39.

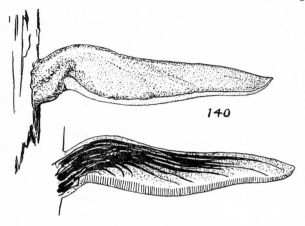

140

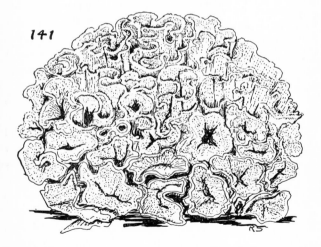

141

The slightly acid taste of this mushroom is not pleasant to all persons but is in high favor with many. When sliced thin and fried or well broiled the acidity is not very noticeable.

The genus Clavaria (Coral Mushrooms)

These fungi are so named because of their resemblance to branched coral. They are found on ground in the woods from August to October and are edible although some of the plants taste bitter. They may be cooked in the same manner as are gilled and other mushrooms. Each plant should be carefully examined before being prepared for the table. If the base is tunneled by larvæ the whole plant must be discarded as it will probably be found to have a bitter taste. The spores are borne on the surface of the branches or plates.

Sparassis crispa. Fig. 39, Species 141.

This large tufted mushroom, though classed with coral fungi, has curled plates or leaves instead of stems and branches, as do other clavaria. It is a conspicuous plant; whitish, grayish or pale yellow in color. It appears as a large, round mass from four inches to two feet in diameter. It grows on ground in woods during the summer and autumn.

The pale ochraceous spores are 5 to 6 microns long by 3 or 4 microns broad. They are formed on the surfaces of the plates or leaves.

This is an excellent edible mushroom.

Clavaria fusiformis; spindled yellow coral mushroom. Fig. 40, Species 142.

This coral fungus appears as a rather sparse cluster of erect yellow cylindrical branches growing from a base which

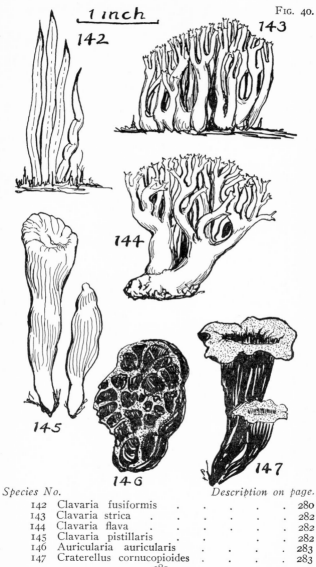

FIG. 40.

1 inch

142

143

144

145

146

147

is also yellow. When the branches are old they become hollow. The branches are about four inches in height, toothed and darker in color at their ends.

The plant is found on ground in woods. The spores are pale yellow, round and 4 to 5 microns in diameter.

Clavaria stricta; straight coral fungus. Fig. 40, Species 143.

There are many branches clustered parallel and straight upright to a height of two or three inches and proceeding from a common base in the ground in woods. The dull yellowish branches end in forks with pointed tips.

It grows in August and September and is edible if uninfested with larvæ. The spores are dark cinnamon in color and 4 microns by 6 microns in diameter.

Clavaria pistillaris; pestle-shaped clavaria. Fig. 40, Species 145.

Although classed with the many-branched corals this mushroom, as its name suggests, is shaped like a club and grows singly or in groups. The rounded, club-like upper end of each stem is puckered, fleshy, white within and spongy. The clubs are from two to ten inches in height. They vary in color; some are yellow, other rusty to chocolate in shade.

The plants grow in woods, mossy or grassy places from August until October.

The elongated, white spores are ten microns in length and five microns broad. This is an edible mushroom.

Clavaria flava; pale yellow, coral mushroom. Fig. 40, Species 144.

A bushy, yellowish plant, from three to six inches high. It is made up of many erect branches whose tips are of a darker shade. The base or main stem is thick, fleshy and white.

"This excellent . . . beautiful species occurs rather abundantly—. The base should be examined for insects which might give a disagreeable flavor to the whole plant. The golden Clavaria, *C. aurea,* is similar, but more deeply colored. The color of the rarer red-tipped clavaria, *C. botrytes* . . . fades out with age. There is also an unbranched, club-shaped clavaria, *C. pistillaris* (pestle-shaped) which is often eaten." Murrill. (See above.)

Auricularia auricularis; little ear. Fig. 40, Species 146.

This gelatinous, almost black mushroom is lobed and folded in a manner suggestive of the form of a human ear. Why the ear of Judas, is not apparent except perhaps as explained by Nina L. Marshall in the Mushroom Book. (N. Y. 1903.) "Its habit of growing on elder has given rise to the belief that Judas Iscariot hanged himself on this tree." The plants are hairy beneath and in spite of their dark color the spores are white. Each fruiting body or cap is from one to four inches in breadth.

Craterellus cornucopioides; Horn of Plenty. Fig. 40, Species 147.

This almost black, velvety trumpet-shaped mushroom appears on the ground in woods in August and September. It is from two to four inches in height and half as much in breadth. The edge of the cap is wavy, split or in folds. The substance is thin but may be either brittle or tough. The outer or under spore-bearing surface has neither gills, pores nor spines.

Hydnums

These mushrooms are characterized by having **teeth** or spines pointing vertically downward in order to make a greater surface on which spores may be formed just as in the clavarias the upright branches serve the same purpose. The hydnums grow both on ground and on wood. Some have their soft spines or teeth on the under surface of a toadstool-like cap while the teeth of others depend from ascending branches, while still others are spread upon the under surface of dead wood.

Hydnum caput-ursi; Bear's head hydnum. Fig. 41, Species 148.

This is a handsome white fungus growing on wood. It shows tufts of long, soft teeth hanging like icicles from branches arising from a single stout stem. The whole tufted mass may grow to a diameter of 8 inches, the teeth being half an inch or more long.

Somewhat similar to the above is the Satyr's beard or Hydnum erinaceum but this plant is usually smaller and grows on a single tuft.

Hydnum repandum. Fig. 41, Species 149.

This resembles a gilled mushroom, having the ordinary cap and stem. The stem is small, not in the center. The under surface of the white or buff cap (1½ to 8 inches broad) however, has straight, white brittle teeth beneath, instead of gills.

The species is edible.

Another species, *Hydnum imbricatum,* is somewhat like H.

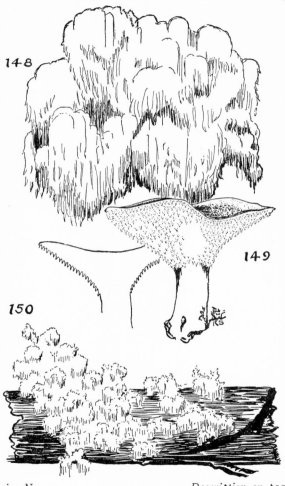

Fig. 41.

148

149

150

repandum except that its brown upper surface is cracked and appears to be covered with scales.

Hydnum coralloides. Fig. 41, Species 150.

This is one of the most beautiful of plants and grows in pure white tufts on decayed wood. Its graceful branches appear lacy with the myriads of fine white spines hanging from them. The divided and subdivided branches all grow from a common stem.

BIRD'S NEST FUNGI

Nidulariaceae

The aptly named *bird's nest fungi* seldom fail to arouse wonder when first seen, with their little eggs resting in a miniature cup-like receptacle. Their spores are contained within the egg-like bodies or sporangia, like minute puffballs. There are four families or genera in this order of nidulariaceae, namely cyathus, nidularia, sphaerobolus and crucibulum. They are somewhat alike in gross appearance and size. All are gastromycetes, that is "stomach fungi" whose spores are formed on the surface of cells but all enclosed in a pouch or skin.

Crucibulum vulgare; common bird's nest fungus. Fig. 42, Species 151.

The commonest species of the bird's nest fungi, is a tan-colored little bowl, ¼ to ½ inch in diameter, containing several tiny white "eggs." When still immature, these are hidden under a thin, yellowish membrane. Each egg is attached to the nest by a thread. Crucibulum vulgare grows in clusters on decayed wood.

FIG. 42.

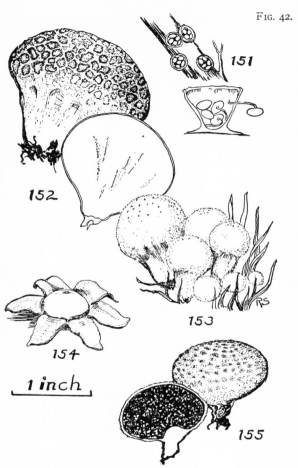

Puffballs

Puffballs are the safest of all fungi for the beginner to eat, since none of them are poisonous. If they are white and firm inside, they are fit to be eaten. If the interior is smooth and homogenous, the fungus is a puffball. The "egg" or young stage of the deadly amanita exhibits the embryo stem and cap when cut open and the ball stage of the beginning stinkhorn shows the stem and a green mass inside, surrounded by a jelly-like substance.

In preparing puffballs for the table, they are peeled, sliced and fried a golden brown, or may be cooked in any of the ways recommended for the ordinary field mushroom. From Murrill.

Calvatia cyathiformis; pasture puffball. Fig. 42, Species 152.

The more or less globular, whitish gray or brown fungus is from 2 to 6 inches in diameter, springing from a short, thick base on the ground in open fields. Its surface is smooth and when old shows a network of cracks. When the fungus is past its prime and the sac and contents have dried and been scattered by the wind, there remains a cupshaped base.

Spores round, with toothed surface, brownish purple, 5 to 7 microns in diameter.

This common puffball is the largest one in the Eastern States with the exception of the rare giant puffball which is the size of a man's head or greater.

Lycoperdon gemmatum. Fig. 42, Species 153.

This small puffball occurs in clusters thickly pressed together, usually growing on the ground but sometimes on dead wood. The plants are white when young but become gray or grayish brown as they mature. The surface is covered with soft erect scales or warts, and the white flesh turns to black powder as the spores become ready to be expelled through the central opening in the apex when mature. The shape of the gemmed puffball is often somewhat like that of a boy's spinning top. It varies in size from one to two and a half inches in height and a little less in breadth.

The brownish spores are about 3 microns by 4 microns in size.

Like other puffballs, this one is edible when the flesh is yet white and firm but the tough skin should be removed and this is not readily done.

Geasters or **Earth-stars** are curiously formed little globes with an outer tough husk which, when mature, separates into pointed fragments, their bases remaining attached to the lower part of the ball or spore-containing sac-like petals of a flower, or a pointed star.

When dry, these segments, seven to twenty in number, fold the ball in their grasp. When wet, they expand or straighten out so as to uncover it again. In some species they bend outwardly and down so far as to rest their tips on the ground and elevate the spore-sac. The spores are discharged through a hole in the top of the sac.

Geaster hygrometricus; water-measuring earth-star. Fig. 42, Species 154.

Is the commonest species and grows upon bare soil. The outer coat is dark gray and rough, the inner sphere smoother and of a lighter shade. When the pointed segments (see above) are unfolded they have a spread of one and a half or two inches. The spores are globular, brown and with fine warts on their surface.

Scleroderma vulgare. Fig. 42, Species 155.

The flesh of this black sheep in the puffball family is a slaty or leaden black. Its tough brownish skin is covered with coarse dark scales separated by lighter colored cracks. The plants grow on the ground in woods, are round or oval and vary in size from one to three inches in diameter. Unlike some others of the puffballs this one opens irregularly for spore dispersal and not by a central apical aperture in its skin. The dingy spores are warty and are 9 to 11 microns in breadth.

Scleroderma vulgare is not edible.

Spore Sac Fungi, Ascomycetes

The mushrooms described hereinafter in this book differ from all of those mentioned in the preceding pages in the way that their spores are produced. The spores of gilled mushrooms, tube fungi, hedgehog mushrooms (Hydna) coral mushrooms, (Clavaria) puffballs (Calvatia, Lycoperdon), bird's nest fungi (Nidularia), are produced on the surface of microscopic cells (basidia). These mushrooms are known to botanists as basidiomycetes.

Those hereinafter described namely, the morels, cup fungi and stinkhorns, produce their minute propagating cells or spores within elongated microscopic sacs (asci), usually in groups of 8 and are known as ascomycetes.

Cup Fungi, Discomycetes

The Pezizas or Cup fungi are ascomycetes bearing their spores in groups of four or eight in microscopic sacs in their upper or concave surface. They are ordinarily shaped like a cup or saucer and vary in size from that of a pin head to several inches in breadth. The cup fungi are as a rule leathery in appearance and to the touch and are never brittle.

Peziza badia; brown peziza. Fig. 43, Species 156.

Edible, but not first class. Grows on ground in woods. One to three inches in diameter; solitary or in groups. Chocolate-brown outside; lighter within. This is one of many kinds of cup mushrooms which vary greatly in size and color. Small red cups (Sarcopsypha) growing on decaying wood are occasionally seen in early spring. Some of these ₊ave hairy margins.

The spores are born in microscopic sacs (asci) in the upper, concave surface of all cup fungi.

Peziza repanda. Fig. 43, Species 157.

This pale brown cup fungus 3 to 4 inches in breadth grows on rotten wood or soil and is one of the most conspicuous of the pezizæ. It is usually sessile but sometimes has a short stem when young. As the plant develops the cup spreads out into a saucer shape, its margin sometimes splitting and the color becoming darker.

The spores are 8-10 microns broad by 14-16 microns long.

Phallus impudicus; common stinkhorn. Fig. 43, Species 158.

The common name describes the conspicuous features of form and odor of this remarkable fungus which grows on the ground in fields and woods and late summer and autumn.

The whole plant, an erect horn three to five inches high, grows out of a white sheath (volva) and is surmounted by a slightly conical pitted cap two inches high and an inch and a

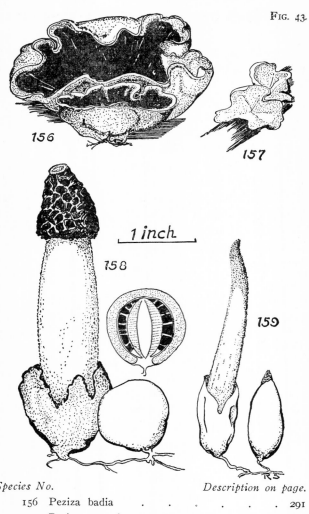

FIG. 43.

156

157

1 inch

158

159

R S

half broad. This olivaceous cap when fresh is covered by a slimy substance with a horrible odor. The stem is white, hollow and an inch or more thick and loosely surrounded by a lacy white veil.

The mucilaginous, stinking matter on the cap contains the spores (ellipsoid, 4 x 2 microns) which are dispersed by being eaten with the mucus by flies.

This species is similar except for absence of the veil to *Phallus ravenelli*.

All species are considered poisonous but the disgusting odor would prevent their being tasted.

Mutinus caninus. Fig. 43, Species 159.

An erect horn-like mushroom three or four inches high, usually a little curved in its upper one-fourth, the spore-bearing portion, red in color, the stem white. It proceeds out of a ragged edged sheath or cup and is found in woods or bushy places.

Some of the specimens are odorless but others have a distinctly disagreeable odor which entitles the plant to be classed as a stinkhorn.

The elliptic spores are 3 to 6 microns long and 2 to 4 microns broad.

McIlvaine is apparently alone in admitting that he has eaten it. He goes so far as to praise its edible quality.

Morels, Morchella

Our common morels belong to the botanical family of ascomycetes known as helvellæ and consist of a stem and a cap or head, both hollow. The cap is pitted in a characteristic manner that suggests the appearance of tripe or honey-comb.

FIG. 44.

1 inch

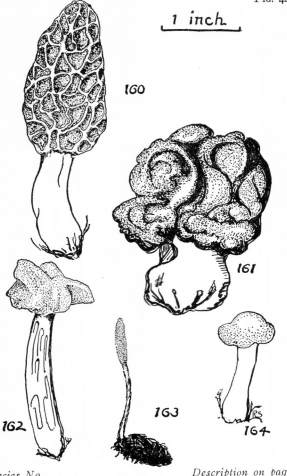

160

161

162

163

164

Spores are borne in the surface of the cap in sacs (asci) and are ellipsoid, yellowish, about 13 x 22 microns.

No morel is known to be poisonous. The only other mushrooms at all resembling morels are stinkhorns but these have such an intolerable odor that no one would eat them.

Morchella esculenta; common morel. Fig. 44, Species 160.

This curious coarse mushroom, its head looking as if covered with tripe, appears in April or May on ground in sparse woods.

It is from two to six inches in height; the somewhat conical cap is from one to two inches thick and its surface is marked by ridges that surround irregular pits. The color is tan or brownish, the stem lighter than the head. Cap and stem are hollow.

The common morel is prized for its edibility when fresh.

The genus Gyromitra

Akin to the morels, the gyromitras bear their spores in sacs or asci and have stems. Their upper, or spore-bearing surfaces are curiously folded so as to resemble somewhat the convolutions of the brain. They are among the largest of the ascomycetes. The name, signifying twisted bonnet, is suggestive of the appearance of these plants.

Gyromitra brunnea; brown gyromitra. Fig. 44, Species 161.

This mushroom is easily confused with *Gyromitra esculenta,* which, while sometimes edible as implied by its name, is reported as the cause of a large number of cases of poisoning. It should be eaten only with great caution, or avoided entirely.

This is a stout fleshy stemmed mushroom, brown as its name suggests. The cap is contorted into folds and is two to four inches across. The stem, an inch or more thick and two inches or more in height, is solid or spongy and white surfaced. It is irregular in cross section and seldom cylindrical.

The plant grows on the ground in woods.

The oval or spherical spores are hyaline and nucleated and are 11 microns in diameter or 11 microns by 14 microns when oval.

McIlvaine states that the plant is tender and well-flavored.

Helvella lacunosa.   Fig. 44, Species 162.

Elvela Mitra (Linnæus) according to Seaver.*

The blackish-brown cap is supported by a yellowish or smoky stem, is bonnet-like or saddle shaped and its margin is bent and folded. The cap is sometimes attached to the stem for some distance.

The stem is often ribbed on its surface and hollow. Its longitudinal grooves are characteristic.

The ellipsoid spores are 12 microns in breadth by 20 microns long and usually contain a large oil drop.

The plant grows on damp soil and is solitary or found in groups.

Its odor is offensive but according to some British writers on mycology it is said to be edible.

* Seaver, F. J. *The North American Cup-fungi*, New York, 1928.

MUSHROOMS OTHER THAN THOSE WITH GILLS

Cordyceps militaris. Fig. 44, Species 163.

This mushroom consists of an erect or somewhat curved stem, three or four inches in height and surmounted by an elongated or spindle-shaped cap but little broader than the stem. The color is brownish or grayish.

On investigation the stem is found to proceed from a dead larva or chrysalis. Two of these mushrooms may arise from the same insect on or under the ground.

The spores are borne in sacs or asci.

There are a few other species of the Genus Cordyceps, one of which, Cordyceps capitata, is parasitic upon a subterranean, truffle-like fungus called Elaphomyces.

McIlvaine reports that they are delicious stewed but they are not common enough to be of importance as an edible species.

Leotia lubrica. Fig. 44, Species 164.

The Leotias are small slimy mushrooms without gills, pores or spines but produce their spores in microscopic sacs (asci), but with their caps and stems they resemble at a distance the gilled mushrooms. Leotia lubrica is one and a half to two inches high and one-half to three-quarters of an inch broad. The cap and rather thick stem are hollow when mature. The whole plant is a dull olive-yellow color. It grows on damp ground in woods, usually in groups. The hyaline spores are long and narrow, 22-25 microns long and 5-6 microns broad.

It is edibile but not of superior quality.

CHAPTER VII

MUSHROOMS AS FOOD

CHAPTER VII

MUSHROOMS AS FOOD

From the Forty-eighth Annual Report of the New York State Botanist, C. H. Peck.

According to the authority of those who have especially investigated this subject, the dangerously poisonous species found in this country all belong to a single genus, Amanita. About a dozen species of this genus have been found in our State, and of these, two are known to be harmless and edible, three or four only are commonly classed as poisonous, and probably a single one of these is responsible for a vast majority of the fatal accidents resulting from "mushroom poisoning." There are, however, some species in other genera that are capable of causing nausea, vomiting and derangement of the digestive organs. They are unwholesome because of their persistently bitter, acrid or otherwise disagreeable flavor, or because of toughness of texture or the possession of some quality repugnant to the stomach. They may indeed cause sickness and vomiting, but the irritation they induce is soon apparent and quickly causes the rejection from the system of the offending substance and then the normal condition of the system is soon restored. Sometimes recovery in such cases may be hastened by the administration of some simple emetic which will assist the stomach in its efforts to expel the unwholesome material.

For two thousand years or more people have made use of mushrooms for food and from time to time death has resulted from their use, either through ignorance or carelessness. Still men persist in their use, and those who would use them if they dared frequently ask how they may distinguish mushrooms from toadstools, the word "toadstools" indicating to them poisonous or harmful species. Many attempts have been made to answer this question and many rules have been formulated by the observance of which, it has been claimed, all difficulty and danger would be avoided. Some of these rules are entirely unreliable and to others there are so many exceptions that they are misleading and practically worthless. The rules vary according to the standpoint of the one proposing them. One who considers the common mushroom the only edible species seeks to separate it from all others, and says "avoid all which have white gills and a hollow stem." This rule precludes the use of many mushrooms which are just as good as the one it sustains, and at the same time, it is not definite enough to limit the selection to the one intended. Another, thinking of the delicious lactarius which has an orange-colored juice, says "reject all such as have a white milky juice." This rule forbids the use of several species of lactarius that are no more harmful and scarcely less sapid than the delicious lactarius. Again we are told by some one who has in mind the poisonous amanitas, to "discard all mushrooms that have a warty cap or a membranous sheath at the bottom of the stem." This would be a very good rule if we might add to it the sentence, unless you know the species to be edible and safe. The orange mushroom, which is deemed an edible species of first quality has a membranous sheath at the base of the stem, and the reddish amanita has a warty cap and yet is not only harmless but very good, so that the rule which would forbid the use of these species excludes more than is necessary. The same may be said of those directions which require the rejection of all mushrooms having a viscid cap or an acrid taste or whose flesh on being broken quickly changes to a blue color. And as to the old-fashioned silver spoon test by which it was thought that a silver spoon thrust among cooking mushrooms would be quickly tarnished if they were

MUSHROOMS AS FOOD

poisonous and remain bright if they were edible, that was long ago proved to be most unreliable by a fatal experiment in which several persons lost their lives because the cook put confidence in it. We are, therefore, forced to conclude that no abstract rule is at present known by which the good can in every case be separated from the bad. The only safe and reasonable way to do is to learn to recognize each species by its own peculiar specific characters. It is in this way that we recognize the useful and esculent species among flowering plants, and it must be in this way that we select our edible mushrooms. A little more care may be necessary in one case than in the other, because of a closer resemblance in some cases between good and bad mushrooms than between good and bad flowering plants. The principle that is to govern in this matter is the same in both cases. The greater the number of edible species clearly recognizable by any one the greater the field from which he may draw his supplies. If he is acquainted with but one species he should limit his use of mushrooms to that one species, unless he can avail himself of the more extensive knowledge of some one else or unless he is willing to take the risk of eating some poisonous or unwholesome species. In a few instances it is possible to affirm of certain groups of species or of certain genera, that no deleterious species are known in them. He who can discriminate between puff balls and all other fungi does not incur very much risk in eating any puff ball of good flavor, though he may not be able to distinguish the species from each other. The probability is that he will suffer no harm by so doing, but there is not absolute safety. It is possible that some rare species exists having deleterious qualities which have not yet been ascertained by experiment, hence the lack of absolute certainty; for we know by experience among the amanitas that excellent edible species may exist in the same genus with and be closely related botanically to dangerously poisonous species.

Many mushrooms have a farinaceous or branny taste or odor, or both taste and odor are of this character. Some have thought that all species having this meal-like flavor are edible, and indeed many of them are, and no dangerously poisonous species is known to have it. But occasionally a species has this flavor combined with or followed by a bitter or otherwise disagreeable flavor which would at least render the mushroom undesirable if nor unwholesome. So that rules designed to aid in the selection of edible species have their exceptions and their weak points as well as the rules designed to protect us against the poisonous species. There is, therefore, no escape from the necessity of acquiring a knowledge of each species we would utilize, sufficiently clear and exact to enable us to distinguish it from all others. Whatever value investigators and experimenters, who are willing to take some risks for the good of others, may find in such rules or general principles, it is evident that they are not sufficiently definite, exact and reliable for general use. To any one willing to avail himself of the experience of others and to apply himself sufficiently to learn to recognize the species they have found to be edible, nature opens a field productive of much palatable and nutritious food, which is too often left to decay where it grew.

But some care is necessary in the selection of specimens of species known to be edible. The plants selected should be in good condition. Well grown, sound, fresh specimens only should be chosen. Old, partly decayed, water-soaked, worm-eaten or withered plants should be discarded. Even young and sound ones should not be kept too long before they are cooked. They are in some cases very perishable and deteriorate rapidly. If more have been collected at one time than are needed for a single meal it will generally be better to cook them all at once and keep them in a refrigerator in the cooked rather than in the raw state. As a rule it is better to cook them the same day they are collected. In the case of the

MUSHROOMS AS FOOD

inky fungi this will be absolutely necessary, for they will not keep in good condition from one day till the next. Some of the species literally grow up in a night and perish in a day. These also should be cooked with great promptness, for they are only desirable while young and before the gills have begun to change to a black inky liquid. Puff balls should only be used while the inner flesh is pure and white. When the yellowish stains of maturity begin to appear they are no longer fit for food. No one would think of eating them after the flesh has changed to the cottony dusty mass of maturity.

Many insects are fond of mushrooms. Both they and their larvæ feed on them and the latter often live in them. A mushroom may appear fair externally, but if it is cut or broken its flesh may be seen to be full of holes or galleries excavated by larvæ, and perhaps a colony of the larvæ themselves may be found within. It is needless to say that such specimens are unfit for food. Strange as it may seem, a colony of larvæ in the lower part of the stem of a mushroom will sometimes affect disastrously the flavor of the cap or upper part which they have not yet invaded. This fact may explain in part the varying opinions of different writers concerning the flavor and edible qualities of certain mushrooms. Slight differences in flavor may also be attributed to differences in the character of the soil in which they grow, the amount of moisture in the atmosphere, degree of temperature, age and rapidity of growth and exposure to the sun and wind. Old and slowly-developed individuals are likely to be less tender than young and rapidly growing ones. Differences in individual tastes will also account in part for differences of opinion on this point. There are also peculiarities of constitution which have given origin to the saying, "What is one man's meat is another man's poison." One person can eat no egg, nor anything into which egg enters as an ingredient, without suffering or sickness. Another is made sick by eating strawberries, nevertheless egg and strawberries are not classed as poisonous. Still it is possible that some fungi as harmless as egg and strawberries may have been charged with poisonous qualities from some such accidental circumstance or individual peculiarity.

In collecting mushrooms for the table it is well, in all cases in which the stems are too tough for food, to cut the caps from the stems. In this way much dirt and useless material will be left where it belongs, and it will be possible in many cases to ascertain if the caps have been attacked by insects. Most often the larvæ mine their way up from the ground through the central part of the stem to the cap, and by cutting the cap from the stem their holes or galleries are exposed to view. In but few species are the stems sufficiently tender to be used. Some have recommended that the caps be placed in the collecting basket in an inverted position, for if placed in their natural position with gills downward they will drop their spores and their flavor will be impaired. It is very doubtful if this partial loss of spores affects the flavor in any appreciable degree. If more than one species should be taken during the same excursion it would be well to keep them separate from each other by wrapping each species in a piece of paper by itself. This precaution is not necessary if the species are so distinct in color, shape or size that they can readily be separated from each other at home, or if they are so similar in flavor and texture that they may be treated alike in cooking without any detriment to their esculent qualities.

Should a doubt arise at any time, concerning the identity of a supposed edible species, do not use such a mushroom until all doubt on this point has been banished. If it is thought desirable to compare the plant with the published figure and descriptions for the purpose of identifying the species, select for this purpose sound specimens which represent both the young and the mature forms, that all the specific character may be shown. Take the specimens up carefully from their place of growth, removing all the loose dirt from the base of the stem. Wrap the specimens carefully in soft paper or large green leaves that they may be kept as fresh as possible till the time of examination. On reaching home, lose no time in making the examination for in some species there are evanescent characters which will not be available after a few hours' delay. In one family of fungi the color of the spores is an important character and a great aid in the identification of species. The color of the spores in many species is the same as or similar to the color of the mature gills, but there are so many exceptions that explicit directions for ascertaining their color will be given in another place.

In the preparation of mushrooms for cooking, the utmost cleanliness should be observed. Some have the upper surface of the cap covered with a sticky, viscid or glutinous substance when fresh. This often causes bits of dirt, leaves or sticks to adhere to the cap tenaciously. In such cases it is generally best to remove this rubbish by peeling the caps. In other cases the dirt may be wiped away with a damp cloth or towel, or washed off and then the surface dried with a towel. It is also well to peel those having a thick tough skin.

The proper method of cooking will depend somewhat on the kind of mushroom, the tastes of those that are to eat them and the conveniences at hand. Many of them can be cooked in the same manner as a beefsteak. It is customary to cook them in a very simple manner, either by frying in butter or broiling gently with a little butter added and seasoning to taste. They may also be stewed or baked. The skillful cook will devise many ways of cooking them and various recipes will be found in cook books and in works on edible fungi. Too much cooking may spoil a mushroom as well as an oyster or a tender beefsteak. My efforts to make a tough mushroom tender by steaming have been successful, but the experiments have not been numerous nor long continued. Species too tough to be eaten with pleasure or digested with comfort have sometimes been utilized by making of them a kind of soup or broth which could be eaten with relish and comfort. Sometimes mushrooms are used in small quantity to give flavor to meats and other dishes. Those of inferior flavor are sometimes made more agreeable by cooking with them a few specimens of some more highly flavored species. The same species may vary in flavor according to the method of cooking and the kind of seasoning used as well as by reason of the circumstances previously mentioned.

Mushrooms may be dried and kept for future use. The best method of drying them is to place them in a current of warm air. Dry them as quickly as possible without burning them, and keep the drying process in operation till completed. A common fruit evaporator would doubtless be a good instrument for drying them. The drying of thick and moist ones would be facilitated by cutting them in slices. Like other vegetables, they are largely composed of water, which is from eighty to ninety per cent of the whole. In consequence of this they shrink greatly in drying and lose much weight. The presence of so much nitrogenous material induces rapid decay and loathsome decomposition in them. It should also teach moderation in their use as food. A hearty meal on mushrooms alone would be about as reasonable as a dinner or nothing but beefsteak, and might be expected to be followed by similar ill consequences. Gormandizing is not commendable under any circumstances nor with any kind of food. But especially should it be avoided in mushroom eating, for the human system demands but small quantities of the nitrogenous elements which enter into its composition. An excessive amount is sure to be hurtful, but eaten in moderate quantity it is easily digestible, acceptable and beneficial. The digestive organs of the writer are not strong by nature and are easily affected by unfavorable treatment or indigestible substances, yet he has never experienced any discomfort from eating mushrooms. He has eaten them frequently, partaken of many different species, and experimented with a considerable number of species not classified as edible. The explanation is simple. They have always been eaten in moderate quantity. In my opinion, cases of sickness and digestive derangement that have been attributed to poisonous properties of mushrooms are sometimes really due to the excessive use of species that otherwise are perfectly harmless.

In some countries where edible fungi are commonly and extensively employed as food, even species which we regard as unwholesome are utilized. They are soaked in vinegar or in salt water for the purpose of destroying or rendering inert their noxious properties. They are then carefully washed and thrown into hot water for a short time, after which they are treated in the usual way. This practice is not recommended. Aside from the danger arising from the inefficiency of the treatment in some cases, it is very improbable that any mushrooms so treated would still retain a very agreeable fiavor. There is, besides, no need of running any risks with doubtful or suspected species, for the number of those known to be good and safe is sufficiently great to satisfy all reasonable demands. Possibly the time may yet come when the noxious properties of poisonous mushrooms may be utilized with advantage in medicine, but such species should not be used as food. He who is too ignorant to recognize with confidence the species known to be good, would better abstain from such food entirely unless he can avail himself of the knowledge of some one who can recognize them.

A few edible fungi appear early in the season, but with us July, August and September are the months when the greatest variety is to be found. The fairy-ring mushroom and the glistening coprinus sometimes appear in June, and successive crops follow from time to time whenever the weather is favorable.

A few of the species continue in September. The latter part of August and the first half of September will bring the common mushroom and the horse mushroom, the weather conditions being right. Excessively dry weather and prevailing cold weather are unfavorable to mushroom growth. Heat and moisture combined are favorable. It sometimes happens when the fields and open country are too dry for mushroom growth, a scanty supply may be found in deep woods and shady swamps. It would be useless to look in such places for the common mushroom and the fairy-ring mushroom, for they do not grow in woods; but the delicious lactarius, the Involute paxillus and the Chantarelle may be found there. The oyster pleurotus and the sapid pleurotus may be found in woods or clearings at any time between June and October, provided there is sufficient rain to induce growth, but the honey-colored armillaria, the imbricated tricholoma, the masked tricholoma and the elm pleurotus will rarely be found before the last week in August or the first of September. These hints may be something of a guide to the inexperienced mushroom hunter. The dates and habitat given under the description of each species will furnish more full and definite information on this subject.

CHAPTER VIII

MUSHROOMS AS FOOD

CHAPTER VIII

MUSHROOMS AS FOOD

GENERAL DIRECTIONS FOR PREPARING AND COOKING THEM

A generation ago edible mushrooms were believed to possess high nutritive value on account of the nitrogen contained in them. Authorities in dietetics considered them to be of service as substitutes for meat. Later investigations have seemed to show that, in the cases of several of the commonly eaten species, a part of the nitrogenous element is present in a form that is not available for alimentary use in the human body. Starch and other substances useful as food are present in the fleshy fungi in such small quantities as to add but little to their nutritive value. Their vitamin content is apparently high however, and this fact, together with what fuel value they do possess and that of the materials in company with which they are usually cooked, give ample reason for their employment as food. Moreover, mushrooms have great value as condiments or food accessories and "their value as such is beyond the computation of the chemist or physiologist. They are among the most appetizing of table delicacies and they add greatly to the palatability of many foods when cooked with them." It is not always possible by laboratory analysis to duplicate conditions that exist in natural digestion and assimilation of foods. Statements as to the food value of mushrooms, commonly met with in books on dietetics are based upon incomplete investigations. There is need of careful research in this direction. Lastly, their savory taste and the age-long custom of using mushrooms as food, insure a continued demand for them as articles of human diet.

Preparation of Mushrooms for Eating

The characters of the various kinds of mushrooms determine what is the best way in which each of them should be cooked. Tough species require long, slow boiling, while fragile, tender sorts are quickly cooked. Some kinds are strong in taste and others mild. The preference of the eater is quite as important a guide in cooking mushrooms as are their qualities. One person prefers fried dishes, another wishes his mushrooms stewed, another would select them prepared in some other way.

The following recipes are compiled from the writings of many authorities and are supplemented by some based on my own experience of twenty years.

Some General Recipes

In the following recipes one may use Agaricus campestris, silvicola, arvensis, or Pleurotus ostreatus, or sapidus, or Coprinus comatus, or any kindred mushrooms. The Agaricus campestris, however, are to be preferred.

To Serve Mushrooms with a Boiled Leg of Mutton

Wash and dry the mushrooms. Dip each one into flour, being careful not to get too much of it on the gill side. In a saucepan have ready a little hot butter or olive oil; drop the mushrooms into this, with their skin sides down; dust them lightly with salt and pepper. After they have browned on one side, turn them quickly and brown the gills; add a half-pint of soup stock and let all simmer for fifteen minutes. Take them up with a skimmer and put them on the platter around the mutton. Boil the sauce down until it is of the proper consistency; pour it over the meat and serve at once. Mushrooms prepared in this manner are also good to serve with roast beef.

MUSHROOMS AS FOOD

Mushroom Sauce for Game

Wash well one pound of fresh mushrooms; dry and chop them very fine. Put them into a saucepan with one and a half tablespoonfuls of butter; cover and cook slowly for eight minutes. Then add a half-cup of freshly rubbed bread-crumbs, a half teaspoonful of salt, a salt-spoonful of white pepper; cover and cook again for five minutes; stir and add a tablespoonful of chopped parsley, and, if you like, two table-spoonfuls of sherry; turn out into a sauceboat.

Mushrooms with Fricassee of Chicken

Wash and dry the mushrooms and sprinkle them with salt and pepper. Put some oil or butter into a shallow pan; when hot, throw in the mushrooms, skin side down; cover the pan and put it in the oven for fifteen minutes; baste them once during the baking. Lift them carefully and put them on a heated dish. Add to the fat in the pan two tablespoonfuls of finely chopped mushrooms and a half-cup of soup stock. This is boiled for five minutes to make a separate sauce. Have ready pieces of bread toasted and dish the mushrooms on to these. Put on top a good-sized piece of carefully boiled marrow; season the sauce with salt and pour it (strained) over the mushroom-covered bread. Use these pieces of toast with the mushrooms on them as a garnish around the platter of chicken, or you may simply dish and serve them separately.

Oysters and Mushrooms

Wash and remove the stems from a half pound of fresh mushrooms; chop them finely; put them into a saucepan with a tablespoonful of butter, a half-teaspoonful of salt and a little pepper; cover closely and cook over a slow fire for ten minutes. Have ready twenty-five oysters and put them, perfectly dry, into this mushroom mixture. Cook over a bright fire and boil, stirring carefully, for about five minutes. Serve on squares of toasted bread.

Tomatoes Stuffed with Mushrooms

Wash the tomatoes, cut a slice from the stem end and remove carefully the seeds and core. To each tomato allow three good sized mushrooms; wash, dry and chop them fine, and stuff them into the tomatoes. Put half a saltspoon of salt and a dusting of pepper on the top of each. Put a cupful of breadcrumbs into a bowl, season them with salt and pepper and pour upon it a tablespoonful of melted butter. Heap the breadcrumbs, thus treated, over the top of each tomato, forming a pyramid, and packing it in with the mushrooms. Stand the tomatoes in a baking pan and bake in a moderate oven for one hour. Serve at once, lifting the tomatoes carefully to prevent their breaking.

Another way. The mushrooms may be chopped fine, put into a saucepan with a tablespoonful of butter and cooked for five minutes before they are put into the tomatoes; then the breadcrumbs are packed over the top and the whole is baked for twenty minutes. Each of the above recipes gives a distinct flavor.

Beefsteak Smothered with Mushrooms

Wash a dozen good-sized mushrooms, either Lactarii or Agarici, and put them into a baking pan. Sprinkle salt over them, add a tablespoonful of butter and bake in a moderately hot oven for three-quarters of an hour. Broil the steak until it is nearly done, then put it into the pan with the mushrooms, allowing some of them to remain under the steak and cover it with the remaining portion. Return the whole dish to the oven for ten minutes; dish and serve at once.

MUSHROOMS AS FOOD

Mushroom Pie

Cut fresh mushrooms into small pieces; cover the bottom of a pie dish with small, thin fragments of sliced bacon and place the mushrooms upon them adding salt and pepper. Over these place a layer of mashed potatoes following again with other similar layers of bacon, mushrooms and potatoes, until the dish is filled, the last layer of potato serving as a crust. Bake in the oven for half an hour and brown before a brisk fire.

Fried Mushrooms on Toast

Place a pint of mushrooms in a pan with a piece of butter about the size of an egg; sprinkle in a teaspoonful of salt and half as much pepper. When the butter is nearly absorbed by the cooking thicken with fresh butter and flour and pour the whole upon hot toast, which should be served upon hot plates.

Mushrooms with Bacon

Fry slices of bacon in the usual manner and when nearly done add a dozen or so of mushrooms and fry them slowly until they are cooked. In this process they absorb the bacon fat and, when seasoned, form an appetizing breakfast relish.

Mushrooms En Caisse

Cut the mushrooms into small pieces; put them into cases of buttered paper, each with a bit of butter, parsley and green onions, and enough salt and pepper to season. Cook them on a gridiron over a gentle fire and serve in the cases. The cases may be made of pastry if desired.

Pickled Mushrooms

Use mushrooms in the round or button stage, before they expand; immerse them in cold water for a few moments and drain them. Remove the stems. Boil vinegar, adding to each quart of it two ounces of salt, half a grated nutmeg, a dram of mace and an ounce of white pepper corns. Put the mushrooms into the vinegar and cook for ten minutes, then pour the whole into small jars, taking care that the spices are equally divided between them. Let them stand for a day and seal.

Mushroom Catsup

Place large mushrooms, layer by layer, in a deep pan; sprinkle each layer with a little salt. A day later stir well so as to mash them and extract their juice. On the third day strain off the liquor and boil for ten minutes. To every pint of liquor, add half an ounce of black pepper, a quarter-ounce of bruised ginger root, a blade of mace, a clove or two and a teaspoonful of mustard seed. Boil again for half an hour, add two or three bay leaves and set aside until cold. Pass the liquor through a strainer and bottle it. Cork well and dip the ends of the bottles into melted rosin or beeswax or paraffine.

Care should be taken that the spices are not so abundant as to overpower the true flavor of the mushrooms.

CHAPTER IX

SPECIAL RECIPES FOR PREPARING VARIOUS
SPECIES OF EDIBLE GILLED MUSHROOMS
FOR THE TABLE

CHAPTER IX

METHODS OF PREPARING THE VARIOUS SPECIES OF EDIBLE
GILLED MUSHROOMS FOR EATING

Agaricus

The wild or uncultivated Agaricus campestris or field mushroom which is gathered in the open fields, will cook in less
time than it takes to cook the cultivated variety (Agaricus
campestris hortensis) which is to be had in the markets. The
stems, cut off close to the gills may be put aside and used as
flavoring for sauces or soups. Wash the mushrooms carefully, keeping the gills down; throw them into a colander until
the water has drained off from them.

Stewed Field Mushrooms

Allow two ounces of butter to each pound of mushrooms.
Put the butter into a saucepan and when melted, but not
brown, throw in the mushrooms, either whole or cut into
slices; sprinkle over them a teaspoonful of salt; cover the
saucepan in order to keep in the flavor and cook slowly for
twenty minutes or until they are tender. Moisten a round-
ing tablespoonful of flour with a little cold milk; when mixed
perfectly smooth add a little white pepper; stir carefully
until boiling. Then take off of the stove and serve at once.
Less flour is required when the mushrooms are to be served as
a sauce over chicken, steak or other made dishes.

Broiled Mushrooms

Select those mushrooms that are spread open, keeping the
unopened ones for other styles of cooking. Cut off the stems

close to the tops. Baste well with melted butter and sprinkle lightly with salt and pepper. Heat a broiler very hot, lay the caps upon it with the gills uppermost and broil over a clear fire, turning the broiler over frequently. As soon as the mushrooms are tender, which will be in about five minutes, open the broiler, remove the caps with care and place them on slices of previously prepared, well-buttered toast. Pour over the whole a sauce made of drawn butter, or hot water thickened with flour to the consistency of cream.

Mushrooms Creamed on Toast

Cut off the stems and wash and dry the caps. Put them into a pan and pour over them a little melted butter, dust them with salt and pepper and cook them in a hot oven for twenty minutes. While they are cooking, toast sufficient bread to hold them; put it on a hot platter and, as soon as the mushrooms are done, cover the bread with hot milk, being careful not to use too much, as it would make the bread pasty and too soft. Dish the mushrooms on the toast, putting each of them with the skin side uppermost; pour over them the juice from the pan and serve at once.

Mushrooms in the Chafing Dish

Wash and dry the mushrooms, and cut them into slices. Allow two ounces of butter for each pound of mushrooms. Put the butter into the chafing dish and when it is hot, add the mushrooms and sprinkle over them a teaspoonful of salt. Cook slowly for five minutes, stirring the mushrooms frequently; then add one gill of milk. Cover the dish, cook for three minutes longer; add the beaten yolks of two eggs and a dash of pepper and serve at once. The yolk of eggs is the most convenient form of thickening when mushrooms are cooked in the chafing dish, but they must not be cooked too hard.

SPECIAL RECIPES

Mushrooms Under the Glass Cover or "Bell" with Cream

With a small biscuit cutter, cut round pieces from slices of bread. They should be about two and a half inches in diameter and about half an inch thick. Cut the stems of fresh mushrooms close to the caps; wash them and allow them to drain. Put a tablespoonful of butter into a saucepan. When hot, throw in the mushrooms, gills uppermost and cook them for a minute or two and sprinkle them with salt and pepper. Arrange the round pieces of bread, which have been slightly toasted, in the bottom of the bell-dish. Heap the mushrooms on these; put a little piece of butter in the center of each; cover over the bell, which may be either of glass, china or silver, stand them in a baking pan and then cook in an oven for twenty minutes. While these are cooking, mix a tablespoonful of butter and one of flour in a saucepan; add a half pint of milk (or a gill of milk and a gill of chicken stock) and stir until the mixture boils; then add a teaspoonful of salt and a dash of pepper. When the mushrooms have baked for twenty minutes, remove them, lift the cover, pour a little of the sauce over them, cover them again and send them at once to the table.

Cream of Mushroom Soup

Wash and chop finely a half pound of mushrooms and put them into a saucepan with a tablespoonful of butter and, if you have it, a cup of chicken stock; if not, use a cupful of water. Cover the vessel and cook slowly for thirty minutes. Next, put a quart of milk into a double boiler and add to it a tablespoonful of butter and two tablespoonfuls of flour rubbed together until smooth. Stir all and cook until thick; then add the mushrooms and season to taste with salt and pepper.

Agaricus arvensis may be cooked like its close ally the common mushroom. English epicures shun it but the French people prefer it to that species as a dish.

Amanita cæsarea is edible but the reader is advised not to eat it on account of the danger of confusing other kinds that are poisonous, with it.

Amanitopsis vaginata, though edible, is very likely to be confused with poisonous Amanitæ as the resemblance is close. Dr. Murrill's dictum should be followed in this case. He says, "edible, but eat not!"

Armillaria mellea. Authorities differ as to the edible qualities of this species. Peck considered it "a perfectly safe species, but not of the best quality." I have eaten it but do not care for it. Young and small specimens should be selected for the table. It is best when fried after having been boiled for five minutes in salted water.

Kate Sargeant gives the following directions for stewing the honey-colored mushroom: Soak the caps for half an hour in water to which vinegar has been added in the proportion of one tablespoon to the quart. Roll a tablespoonful of butter in some flour and put it in a saucepan; add the mushrooms and sufficient water to cover them; stew until the caps are tender. Season with salt and pepper and serve while hot.

Cantharellus cibarius; the chantarelle. Light and soft specimens should be discarded as they become leathery when cooked; crisp and heavy plants should be chosen for the table. All those that have been partly eaten by slugs or worms should also be rejected. If, when the chantarelles are brought into the kitchen, they are scalded in milk and are left to soak in it until the next day, they will be very tender.

Cut the chantarelles across into slices and remove the stems; put the caps into a covered saucepan with a little fresh butter and sweat them; then stew in gravy or fricassee until they are tender, at the lowest possible cooking temperature; a great heat destroys their flavor.

SPECIAL RECIPES

Another recipe. Put the prepared chantarelles into boiling water for a few minutes; then stew them in fresh butter to which has been added a little olive oil, chopped tarragon, pepper, salt and lemon peel. Allow them to simmer gently over a slow fire for twenty minutes, moistening them from time to time with a little beef gravy or cream. When about to be served, thicken the stew with yolk of egg.

A more simple dish may be made by frying the chantarelles in butter or olive oil and laying them on toasted bread, adding pepper and salt as required or they may be minced and stewed alone or with minced meat.

N.B.—The chantarelle may be prepared like the common mushroom if care is taken not to cook it too hot. If boiled too violently it will become as tough as leather.

Cantharellus aurantiacus; orange chantarelle; false chantarelle.

Contradictory statements exist as to the edibility of this mushroom. I have eaten it with enjoyment and with no ill effects. Since it is under suspicion, the reader is advised to let it alone as far as eating is concerned.

Cantharellus cinnabarinus is a desirable edible species which, although of small size, often occurs in abundance. It is good either stewed or fried. The stems should be removed before cooking.

Cantharellus umbonatus. As an edible mushroom this species is not as tender as some others nor is it as highly flavored but it is satisfactory and agreeable.

Cantharellus floccosus, although often growing to a rather large size, is not tough but, when cut into small pieces is easily cooked in any of the usual methods. Its quality is good.

Cantharellus minor, although not considered as equal in quality to the best mushrooms, may be cooked with other species and will help to eke out what would be a scanty mess without it.

Clitocybe dealbata. The best mode of cooking this species is stewing. Care must be taken to select young plants as old ones become tough and leathery when heated. Young specimens are quickly cooked, are of a firmer texture than that of the popular common mushroom. This species closely resembles a poisonous Clitocybe (sudorifica) and hence should not be eaten unless positively identified.

Clitocybe multiceps, according to McIlvaine, should be well cooked. The addition of a little lemon juice or sherry conceals a slight raw taste that is sometimes present.

Clitocybe odora is said to be exceedingly spicy. The flavor is pleasant but rather strong. A few specimens mixed with other species of like texture but with less flavor make a tasty dish. McIlvaine.

Clitopilus abortivus is edible in either its undeveloped (abortive) condition or in the perfect form but is of inferior quality. I prefer it when fried, with onion.

Clitopilus prunulus is highly praised as food by some writers. Dr. Badham recommended it stewed or fricasseed, with a sauce made as follows:

Bruise in a mortar some almonds with a little water; add salt and pepper and some lemon juice; rub the whole together until it is of the consistency of table mustard.

Collybia acervata is said to be tender, delicate and of fine flavor. It should not be cooked too long.

Collybia confluens is of good substance and flavor.

Collybia platyphylla. Although edible, its taste is not especially attractive. It is a good plan to mix it with other more savory species when the collected mess happens to be scanty. Then it absorbs the taste of its companions in the dish and supplies bulk.

Collybia radicata is one of the best tasting of mushrooms. The caps should be broiled or fried.

Collybia velutipes. A valuable species because of its extended season and good eating quality.

Coprinus atramentarius

Coprinus comatus

Coprinus micaceus

As these species are not dissimilar in texture, recipes for cooking them are alike. Being soft and juicy, they must be handled with care and are better when cooked with dry heat.

To bake: Remove the stems, wash and drain in a colander; arrange the caps in a baking pan; dot here and there with small bits of butter, allowing a tablespoonful to each half-pound of mushrooms. Dust them with salt and pepper, put them into a very hot oven and bake them for thirty minutes. Serve in a heated vegetable dish, pouring over them the sauce from the pan.

To cook Coprinus. (Mrs. Rorer.) Wash and drain in a colander. Spread out in a long baking pan; dust lightly with salt and pepper and put on them a few bits of butter. Cover with another pan and bake in a moderate oven for twenty-five minutes. Add four tablespoonfuls of cream, bring to the boiling point and dish on toast.

Coprinus micaceus; another method. Wash and dry the mushrooms; put them into a deep saucepan with a tablespoonful of butter to each quart. Hold them over a quick fire, keeping the saucepan in motion but not stirring with a spoon for fear of breaking the caps. As soon as they have reached the boiling point, push them to the back part of the stove for five minutes and then serve on toast. They will be dark in color but are very palatable and are, perhaps, the most easily digested of all fleshy fungi.

Cortinarius. The caps of most of the species of this genus are edible. While they may not be of the very best, young specimens are of good texture and they stew and dry well. No poisonous variety is known to exist among them but several are strong and uninviting.

Cortinarius cinnamomeus. The German people are said to be fond of this species and usually stew it in butter and serve it with a sauce upon vegetables. McIlvaine.

Cortinarius collinitus. The caps should be peeled if necessary, before cooking, in order to remove any dirt that may adhere.

Cortinarius violaceus

Cortinarius alboviolaceus

These are perfectly wholesome and may be stewed in gravy or prepared like sweetbreads with a white sauce. They are, perhaps, the best-tasting of the Cortinarii.

Flammula flavida is good in texture and substance, according to McIlvaine. Its slightly bitter taste when raw is removed by cooking. The stems are too tough to be eaten.

Hygrophorus cantharellus requires long cooking. Its peculiar taste is acceptable to some persons.

Hygrophorus miniatus, in Dr. Peck's opionion, is scarcely surpassed by any mushroom in tenderness and agreeableness of flavor.

Hygrophorus pratensis requires careful cooking as it is liable to be condemned as tough unless treated slowly, but it is a great favorite, says M. C. Cooke.

Hypholoma appendiculatum is one of the best tasting of mushrooms when stewed or fried. The tough stems must be removed.

Hypholoma incertum is a well-flavored and tender-capped species, quite similar in quality to H. appendiculatum.

Hypholoma sublateritium

Hypholoma perplexum. These two species are practically identical. The occasional bitter taste encountered in them is believed to be due to the larvæ with which they are apt to be infested. Great care is necessary in selecting uncontaminated specimens. Considerable cooking is required for these species. Their abundance late in the autumn makes them an important species to the mycophagist.

To stew them, put a tablespoonful of vinegar into a quart of water and soak the caps in this mixture for twenty minutes. Take them out, add water sufficient to cover them and stew for half an hour or until they are tender, in a covered vessel, adding butter, pepper and salt to taste. A small quantity of onion is thought by some to improve their flavor and a thickening of cornstarch and milk added just before serving is an improvement.

Laccaria laccata, while edible, is not especially well-flavored.

Laccaria ochropurpurea is said to lose its toughness when cooked and to make a good dish.

Lactarii. In McIlvaine's opinion the juice of the milky mushrooms and their flavor are best retained when they are baked. They become hard and granular if cooked at too high a temperature. The edible species are good eating when carefully cooked in any manner.

Lactarius camphoratus has a strong taste that may be improved by the addition to it of some specimens of other milder species.

Lactarius deliciosus. The flesh of this mushroom is firm, juicy and nutritious. It may be cooked in the following manner: Take sound, young specimens and cut them to a uniform size; place them in a pie dish, with salt, pepper and a little butter; tie a paper over the dish and bake gently for three-quarters of an hour. Serve them in the same hot dish.

This mushroom requires to be stewed for about forty minutes. It may be fried in considerably less time.

Lentinus cochleatus must be eaten when young as old specimens are tough and dry. It has a peculiar spicy taste that is agreeable to some palates. Soup may be made of it. McIlvaine recommends that the caps be grated before they are cooked.

Lentinus lepideus. A tough species, but when the stem has been removed, the caps finely sliced and fried in butter, or stewed for thirty minutes, it is good eating. Young specimens are equal to the oyster mushroom. A good soup can be made from older specimens.

Lepiota americana. In flavor this species is not much inferior to the parasol mushroom (Lepiota procera) but when cooked in milk it imparts its own reddish color to the material in which it is cooked. Nevertheless it is a fine addition to the list of edible species. Peck.

Lepiota procera; parasol mushroom.

This is one of the best of mushrooms for preservation by drying. In this condition it is easily preserved and will add much flavor to an ordinary meat sauce.

The parasol mushroom, having thin flesh and broad gills, must be cooked quickly. Remove the stems, take the caps in your hand, gill side down, and with a soft rag wash the tops, removing the brown scales. Put them into a baking pan or on a broiler. Lightly baste them with melted butter as they lie with their gills uppermost and dust them with salt and pepper. Place the serving dish to heat. Put the mushrooms over a quick fire, skin sides down for just a moment, then turn them and broil them for an instant on the gill sides and serve them at once on the heated plate.

When cooked in this way Lepiota procera is one of the most delicious of all mushrooms but if cooked in moist heat it becomes tough and unpalatable. If baked too long, it becomes dry and leathery. It must be cooked quickly and eaten at once. All the edible lepiota may be cooked in this manner.

Lepiota procera omelette. Mince some young, fresh caps; season them with pepper and salt, add butter and set them in the oven while you beat well the whites and yolks of six eggs. Then put two ounces of butter into the frying pan and heat it until it begins to turn brown. Having again beaten the eggs, add three tablespoonfuls of the mushrooms and a little milk. Pour all into the boiling butter; stir in one direction and fry on one side for only five or six minutes; drain the fat off, fold the omelette on itself and serve quickly on a hot, covered dish. Kate Sargeant.

Marasmius oreades has long been esteemed as edible but owing to its small size and somewhat tough substance it has not gained the general popularity that it deserves. The following recorded opinions of it may be of interest:

It is very good and may be eaten in an omelette.

It has a very agreeable taste and odor and gives a delicious flavor to sauces but it needs long cooking.

It is delicious when broiled with butter.

It may be pickled or dried for future use.

Its tendency to toughness may be overcome by proper cooking.

An esteemed correspondent gives the following method of cooking this mushroom:

Throw the clean caps into sufficient boiling water to make a nice gravy when done and cook them for half an hour. Then rub together a small quantity of butter, flour and water with salt and pepper and add them to the mushrooms, stirring for a moment. Pour on hot toast and serve on a hot dish.

Another method is to put the caps in water with butter and seasoning and let them simmer slowly for ten or fifteen minutes. Then thicken with flour and serve alone or pour over cooked meat.

As a condiment, chop the caps into small pieces and add them to cooking hash, stews, broths or meats just before the time of serving them. Peck.

Marasmius oreades pickles. Collect fresh young caps of the fairy-ring mushroom and cut the stems quite close and throw the caps into a basin of salted water. Drain them and lay them on a soft cloth to dry. For each quart of mushrooms take nearly a quart of pale white wine vinegar and add to it a heaping teaspoonful of salt, half an ounce of whole peppers, an ounce of bruised ginger, two large blades of mace and one-quarter of a teaspoonful of cayenne pepper tied in a piece of muslin. When this liquid is boiling, throw in the mushrooms and boil them in it for from six to nine minutes. When the caps have become tolerably tender put them into warm, wide-mouthed bottles, dividing the spices equally among them. When cold cork well and stand in a dry place where they will not freeze.

Mycena galericulata, although a small mushroom, often is found in quantity sufficient to make a meal. The flavor of the caps, when stewed, is good.

Omphalia campanella is so small that it is not often eaten, although large clusters of it are often found. Its flavor is fair.

Panus strigosus, when mature, is of woody texture but when specimens are young, they may be used for making soup.

SPECIAL RECIPES

Pholiota adiposa is not classed as edible by European authorities but Dr. Peck found its flavor agreeable and its substance digestible and harmless. It is well to peel the caps before cooking them.

Pleurotus ostreatus

Pleurotus sapidus

Pleurotus ulmarius

To make soup, clean the caps, cut them into small pieces and stew them until they are tender, seasoning with butter, salt and pepper; then strain. Mushrooms that are too tough to be eaten may be used in this way. The clear broth is delicious; but if one prefers, milk or still better, cream may be added.

Pleurotus sauce. A desirable addition to any meat stew may be made by chopping up young, tender caps of the oyster mushroom and stewing them in the meat stock with salt and pepper. This is poured over the veal or other meat.

Stewed. Wash and dry the Pleuroti and cut them into strips crosswise with the gills, trimming off all the tough portion near the stems. Put the mushrooms into a saucepan, adding a tablespoonful of butter to each pint of them. Sprinkle lightly with salt, cover and cook slowly for twenty minutes. Moisten a tablespoonful of flour in a half-cup of milk and when this is smooth, add another half-cup; pour this into the mushroom mixture; add a little grated nutmeg, a few drops of onion juice and a dash of pepper as it comes to the boiling point. Remove the pan from the fire and serve as you would if the dish were of stewed oysters.

Mock oysters. Cut the caps into pieces of the size and shape of oysters. Dip each into the beaten yolk of an egg to which a tablespoonful of water has been added; roll them in cracker crumbs or corn-meal; season with salt and pepper and fry in smoking hot fat, butter or olive oil, as oysters are treated, and serve at once.

Oyster mushrooms with cheese—au gratin. Cut the washed caps into medium-sized pieces. Stew slowly, rather dry, for fifteen minutes. Pour off the liquor and save it for use later. Place the caps in a baking dish (or in individual dishes or clam-shells) in a layer, buttering and seasoning it. Sprinkle this layer with breadcrumbs and grated cheese. On this layer place another similar one and repeat until the dish is filled and has a layer of grated cheese on its top. Pour the saved liquor over the whole. Place the dish in a slow oven and bake until the top is well browned.

This manner of cooking is a favorite. Any mushroom may be cooked in this manner. McIlvaine.

Pluteus cervinus. The caps only, are tender. The stems are much tougher than the caps and hence they should not be cooked together. The caps may be cooked as described under "General recipes." The stems, when fried in butter or broiled, are very good eating. McIlvaine.

Psathyrella disseminata. These fragile little plants cook away to almost nothing but they are of fine flavor and impart this flavor to any medium with which they are cooked. McIlvaine.

Russula. The edible members of this genus may all be cooked after the same recipes. After removing the stems and washing and draining them, they may be broiled or baked. They are also attractive when chopped into small pieces and served with mayonnaise dressing or stuffed into peeled tomatoes or with the same dressing on lettuce leaves.

While russulas apparently do not contain less water than do other species, their flesh is rather dense and they do not so quickly melt upon being exposed to heat.

The green russula (Russula virescens) may be cut into

thin slices, mixed with the leaves of water cress, covered with French dressing and served on slices of tomato. It is well to peel mushrooms when they are to be served raw.

Russula fried with bacon. Fry crisp four thin slices of bacon and lay them on a platter, then fry in the bacon fat a quart of russulas, carefully selected; salt and pepper them and fry them until they are tender. Serve on the platter with bacon.

Russula delica. Peck remarks that this species is excellent when fried in butter.

Tricholoma equestre. This species is excellent when fried; also when creamed and served as patties. When cooked as a soup with water, pepper and salt, it resembles turkey broth. After straining—the soup should be clear—a small amount of butter should be added.

Tricholoma personatum

To bake. Cleanse and peel the caps, cut off the stems and lay the mushrooms, gills up, upon a baking dish; prepare a stuffing of chicken, veal or beef, fill the caps with this, cover the dish and bake for twenty minutes.

To broil. Clean and remove the stems and broil over a clear fire on both sides for a few minutes; arrange the caps on a dish over freshly made toast; sprinkle with salt and pepper, put a small piece of butter on each and set in the oven to melt the butter. Then serve quickly. Bacon cooked over the mushrooms in place of butter is thought by some to improve their flavor.

To stew. Wash the caps and cut them into small pieces. Stew them in water for thirty minutes. Pour off the water and add milk, slightly thickened with flour, seasoning with pepper, salt and a little chopped parsley. Heat and serve.

CHAPTER X

GLOSSARY

CHAPTER X

GLOSSARY

Abortive, imperfect or wanting.

Acrid, sharp or biting to the tongue.

Adnate, growing into or fast to; said of gills that are attached broadly to the stem.

Adnexed, said of gills which are adjacent to the stem but not broadly attached to it.

Agaric, a mushroom having a fleshy cap, on the under side of which are gills.

Alutaceous, of the color of tanned leather; brownish-yellow.

Annulus, the collar or ring on the stem of a mushroom formed by the separation of the veil from the margin of the cap.

Appendiculate, hanging in small fragments.

Appressed, applied closely to the surface; said of the margin of a cap which lies closely against the stem.

Arcuate, arched; shaped like a bow.

Argillaceous, see Clay-colored.

Astringent, puckery to the taste.

Aurantiaceous, orange-colored.

Basidia, mother cells on the spore-bearing surface of agarics and certain other fungi, from which the spores are cast off.

Bay, a rich dark-reddish chestnut color; badious.

Buff, a light, dull, brownish yellow, like the color of chamois skin.

Bulbous, said of the stem of a mushroom when it has a bulb-like swelling at the base.

Cæspitose, growing in tufts or clumps.

Campanulate, bell-shaped.

Cap, pileus; the expanded, umbrella-like top portion of a common gilled mushroom.

Cartilaginous, firm and tough; gristly.

Cell, (a) a small cavity; (b) a mass of protoplasm, generally microscopic in size; the fundamental form element of every organized body.

Centimeter, a measure of length; the one-hundredth part of a meter, equal to 0.3937 of an inch.

Cinnabarine, cinnabar-colored; bright red; vermilion.

Clay-color, a dull, light brownish-yellow, intermediate between yellow ochre and Isabelle-color; argillaceous.

Close, packed closely, side by side; said of gills when they are close together; crowded.

Comate, hairy.

Context, texture; substance.

Convex, elevated and regularly rounded; forming the segment of a sphere or nearly so.

Coriaceous, of leathery texture.

Corrugated, puckered; wrinkled.

Cortina, a web-like veil; the partial veil under the gills of mushrooms of the genus Cortinarius.

Cryptogam, a plant having an obscure method of fertilization; in botany, in the Linnean system of classification, the great series and final class, including all plants having no stamens and pistils, and therefore no proper flowers.

Cyathiform, cup-shaped.

Decurrent, said of gills which extend down the stem of a mushroom.

Deliquescent, said of mushrooms that liquefy or melt when old.

Dichotomous, dividing in two; said of gills that are regularly forked.

Dimidiate, said of gills that extend half way from the edge of the cap to the stem, also of caps that are more or less semicircular in outline.

GLOSSARY

Disc, the central portion of the upper surface of a mushroom's cap.

Distant, said of gills that are far apart.

Eccentric, away from the center; between the center and the edge of a cap.

Elliptical, parallel-sided and rounded at the ends.

Emarginate, notched at the end; said of gills whose lower edge is scooped out at a point near the inner end.

Epidermis, the peel or skin.

Farinaceous, mealy; bran-like; said of taste or odor.

Fibrous, provided with fibers.

Flesh, the inner substance of the cap or body of a fungus.

Flesh-color, a color like that of healthy human skin.

Floccose, downy; woolly; flaky.

Free, said of gills that do not reach the stem.

Fulvous, a yellowish-brown tint like that of tanned leather; tawny.

Fungus, a cryptogamous plant characterized by absence of chlorophyl and getting its nourishment from organic matter.

Gelatinous, jelly-like.

Genus, a group of species that possess characteristics in common.

Gills, the plates attached to the lower surface of an agaric, and on which the spores are formed.

Glabrous, smooth; without down or hairs.

Glaucous, dull-green, passing to grayish-blue.

Globular, globose, nearly spherical.

Gregarious, in groups (not tufts).

Habitat, natural abode.

Hyaline, transparent; clear, like glass.

Hygrophanous, of a water-soaked appearance when moist but opaque when dry.

Hymenium, the spore-bearing surface covering each side of the gills of a mushroom.

Hymenomycetes, mushrooms that have an exposed spore bearing surface and in which the spores are borne on basidia.

Hymenophore, the under surface of the cap, to which the gills are attached.

Hypha (pl. **hyphæ**), a cylindrical thread of the mycelium. Branched threads from the spawn from which mushrooms grow.

Infundibuliform, funnel-shaped.

Isabelline, a light buff-brown color.

Involute, rolled inwards.

Laccate, appearing as if lacquered or varnished.

Lamella, a gill.

Leucosporæ, a group of mushrooms having white spores.

Lignatile, growing on wood.

Lobed, having rounded divisions.

Micron, a unit of measure; the one-thousandth part of a millimeter; .000039 inch. To convert microns to inches, multiply them by (approximately) .00004.

Mold, Mould, (1) fine, soft earth rich in organic matter; (2) a kind of minute fungus.

Mushroom, a cryptogamic plant of the class fungi; applied in a general sense to almost any of the larger, conspicuous fungi, such as toadstools, puff balls, hydnei, etc., but more particularly to the agaricoid fungi and especially to the edible forms.

Mycelium, the spawn of fungi; rootlike threads resulting from the germination of spores, from the masses of which the mushroom arises.

Mycology, the science of fungi.

Mycophagist, one who eats fungi.

Ochraceous, color of ochre, a natural earth used as pigment, commonly understood to mean the color of iron-rust.

Olivaceous, a greenish-brown color like that of olives.

Pallid, pale, deficient in color.

Papilionaceous, resembling the butterfly; mottled, as the gills of some species of Panæolus that are mottled with black spots.

Parasite, a plant growing on or in another living body from which it derives nourishment.

Partial, said of a veil that surrounds the stem of a mushroom and extends to the edge of the cap.

Peronate, said of the stem of a mushroom when it has a boot-like or stocking-like covering.

Personate, masked or disguised.

Pileus, cap; the head of a mushroom.

Porphyrosporæ, a group of mushrooms that have purple or purplish-brown spores.

Pruinate, covered with a frost-like bloom.

Radiate, Radiating, arranged like the spokes of a wheel.

Resupinate, said of a mushroom that is attached to the wood on which it grows by its back and without a stem.

Revolute, turned upwards or backwards; the opposite of involute.

Rhodosporæ, a group of mushrooms that have pink or rosy spores.

Rimose, cracked.

Ring, a part of the partial veil adhering to the stem of a mushroom like a collar; annulus.

Rubescent, blushing; reddish.

Rufus, a brownish-red color.

Sapid, savory; agreeable to the taste.

Separable, capable of being detached.

Sessile, seated; attached by the base and without a stem.

Sinuate, waved; said of the edge of gills that are notched near the stem.

Species, an individual or individuals that differ from all other members of a genus and that propagate others of their own kind.

Spore, a minute cell that is the reproductive body of cryptogams.

Squamose, scaly; scale-like.

Stipe, stem of a mushroom.

Striate, having parallel or radiating lines or furrows.

Sub, as a prefix signifies slightly, almost or somewhat.

Tawny, color of tanned leather.

Toadstool, any umbrella-shaped fungus. The name is usually restricted to gilled fungi but is also applied to almost any fungus that is large enough to attract general attention such as boleti, hydnei, morels, etc. Popularly, the name *toadstool* is applied only to those fungi that are supposed to be poisonous, as distinguished from mushrooms or edible forms. As a matter of fact all true toadstools are really mushrooms, and may or may not be poisonous.

Tomentose, covered with dense wool or hair.

Umbilicate, provided with a pit or central depression; having a navel-like depression at the center.

Umbo, the central elevation or knob of some mushrooms.

Umbonate, with a central knob or boss-like elevation.

Universal veil, the outer wrapper or membrane (volva) which envelops a mushroom in its youngest stage.

Vaginate, contained within a sheath or volva.

Veil, a covering or membrane enveloping a fungus, occurring chiefly among the agarics. See partial veil and universal veil.

Veins, swollen wrinkles on the sides of gills and on the under surface of a cap of a mushroom between the gills, often connected and forming cross partitions.

Ventricose, bellied; swollen in the middle.

Villose, downy; with soft hairs.

Viscid, moist and sticky; glutinous.

Volva, the universal veil (q.v.); sometimes applied to that portion remaining in the form of warts on the surface of the cap (as in Amanita muscaria) or in the form of a cap at the base of the stem.

Wart, a scale on the surface of the cap of a mushroom, the remains of the volva.

Zones, circular zones of color on the surface of the cap of a mushroom, as seen in Lactarius deliciosus.

CHAPTER XI

NAMES OF GILLED MUSHROOMS IN THE KEY;
TRANSLATIONS OF THEIR BOTANICAL NAMES,
THEIR DERIVATION AND PRONUNCIATION

CHAPTER XI

Botanical Name	Translation	Common Name
Agăr'icus	Gr. Fungus	
arvĕn'sis	Lat. Of cultivated ground	Horse mushroom
campĕs'tris	Lat. Of the field	Field mushroom; common mushroom
silvĭc'ola	Lat. An inhabitant of woods	Forest mushroom
Amăn'ita	Gr. A fungus	
cæsa'rea	Lat. Belonging to Cæsar; royal mushroom	Orange amanita
muscăr'ia	Lat. Relating to flies	Fly amanita
phalloi'des	Gr. Phallus-like	Poison amanita; destroying angel
rubĕs'cens	Lat. Becoming red	Blushing amanita; reddish amanita
Amanitŏp'sis	Gr. Resembling an amanita	
vaginā'ta	Lat. Sheathed or encased. (Referring to sheath at base of stem)	Sheathed amanitopsis
volvā'ta	Lat. Sheathed or encased. (Referring to sheath at base of stem)	
Armillā'ria	Lat. A bracelet. (Referring to ring about stem)	
mĕl'lea	Lat. Honey-like. (Color)	Honey-colored mushroom
Cantharĕl'lus	Lat. A small goblet.	
auranti'acus	Lat. Orange-like. (Color)	Orange chantarelle false chantarelle
ciba'rius	Lat. Edible	Chantarelle
cinnabari'nus	Lat. Vermilion	Cinnabar chantarelle
crĭs'pus	Lat. Curly; crinkled	
umbonatus	**Lat.** Knobbed	
floccōs'us	Lat. Flaky; floccose	Floccose chantarelle
infundibulifōrm'is	Lat. Funnel-shaped	Funnel-shaped chantarelle
mī'nor	Lat. Lesser; smaller	Small chantarelle

Botanical Name		Translation	Common Name
Clĭtŏ′cybe	Gr.	Sloping head	
albĭd′ula	Lat.	Whitish	Whitish clitocybe
albĭs′sima	Lat.	Very white; whitest	
cǎn′dicans	Lat.	Whitish	Shining white clitocybe
clǎv′ĭpēs	Lat.	Club-footed	Club-stem clitocybe
cyǎth′ĭfŏr′mis	Lat.	Cup-shaped	Cup-shaped clitocybe
deǎl′bata	Lat.	White-washed	Ivory clitocybe
illū′dens	Lat.	Deceiving	Deceiving clitocybe; Jack-o-lantern
infundibulifōrm′is	Lat.	Funnel-shaped	Funnel-shaped clitocybe
mŭl′ticeps	Lat.	Many-headed	Many-cap clitocybe
odōra	Lat.	Fragrant	Sweet clitocybe
Clĭtŏp′ilus	Gr.	Sloping hat	
abortī′vus	Lat.	Abortive; undeveloped	Abortive clitocybe
prū′nulus	Lat.	Plum-like	Plum clitocybe
Collyb′ia	Gr.	A small coin	
acervā′ta	Lat.	Crowded	Tufted collybia
cŏnfluens	Lat.	Flocking together	
drўŏph′ila	Gr.	Oak-loving	Oak-loving collybia
platyphyl′la	Gr.	Broad-leafed	Broad-gilled collybia
radicā′ta	Lat.	Rooted	Rooted collybia
velū′tipes	Lat.	Velvet foot	Velvet-stemmed collybia
Coprī′nus	Gr.	Filthy (Liddell & Scott; Gr. Lexicon). Probably refers to the inky deliquescence rather than to the place of growth as commonly stated.	
atramentā′rius	Lat.	Inky	Inky cap
comā′tus	Lat.	Hairy; shaggy	Shaggy mane mushroom
mica′ceus	Lat.	Granular	Glistening inky cap
Cortinā′rius	Lat.	Curtain. (Refers to veil between edge of cap and stem)	
alboviolāceus	Lat.	White-violet	
cinnamomē′us	Lat.	Cinnamon (colored)	Cinnamon cortinarius
collinī′tus	Lat.	Besmeared	Smeared cortinarius
violā′ceus	Lat.	Violet (colored)	Violet cortinarius
corrugā′tus	Lat.	Wrinkled-corrugated	Corrugated cortinarius
Crepidō′tus	Lat.	A slipper or sandal	
applanā′tus	Lat.	Flattened	Flattened crepidotus
calolepis	Gr.	Beautiful scale	
malach ius	Lat.	Soft	Soft-skinned crepidotus
versū′tus	Lat.	Inverted	

NAMES OF **GILLED** MUSHROOMS IN THE **KEY**—(*Continued*)

Botanical Name	Translation	Common Name
Entolō'ma	Gr. Enclosed within a fringe	
commū'ne	Lat. Common	Common entoloma
grayăn'um	Lat. Of Gray (a botanist)	Gray's entoloma
stric'tius	Lat. Close; drawn together	Strict entoloma
Flăm'mula	Lat. A little flame	
flăv'ida	Lat. Yellow	
polychrō'a	Gr. Many colored	
Găl'era	Lat. A peaked cap	
hypnō'rum	Lat. Relating to hypnum, a kind of moss; referring to its place of growth	Hypnum galera
těn'era	Lat. Tender	Slender galera; Brownie cap
Hebelō'ma	Gr. Hebe, Youth and Loma, a fringe	
præcox	Lat. Early	
Hygrŏph'orus	Gr. Water carrier	
cantharĕl'lus	Lat. A small vase or goblet	Chantarelle hygrophorus
chlorŏph'anus	Gr. Greenish-yellow	Sulphur hygrophorus
cŏn'icus	Lat. Conical	Conic hygrophorus
miniā'tus	Lat. Red lead	Vermilion hygrophorus
pratěn'sis	Lat. Of the meadow	Meadow or pasture hygrophorus; buff-cap
punĭc'eus	Lat. Purple red (a misnomer)	Red hygrophorus
Hypholō'ma	Gr. A web-like fringe	
appendiculā'tum	Lat. A small appendage. (Refers to fragments of veil hanging from edge of cap)	
incěr'tum	Lat. Uncertain. (Refers to difficulty in identification)	Uncertain hypholoma
perplěx'um	Lat. Perplexing	Perplexing hypholoma
sublaterĭt'ium	Lat. Nearly brick-like (in color)	Brick-top
Inŏc'ybe	Gr. Sinewy, fibrous and head (cap)	
abŭn'dans	Lat. Abundant	Abundant inocybe
Laccăr'ia	Lat. Lacquered	
laccā'ta	Lat. Lacquer; waxy	Waxy mushroom
ochropurpurē'a	Gr. Ochre and purple	Purplish-ochre laccaria

Botanical Name	Translation	Common Name
Lactā′rius	Lat. Milky	
camphorā′tus	Lat. Camphoraceous (odor). A misnomer	Camphory lactarius
corrŭg′is	Lat. Corrugated	Wrinkled lactarius
deliciō′sus	Lat. Delicious	Delicious lactarius
lignyō′tus	Gr. Smoky; sooty (color)	Sooty lactarius
piperā′tus	Lat. Peppery	Peppery lactarius
subdul′cis	Lat. Slightly sweet	Sweetish lactarius
theiŏg′alus	Gr. Sulphur-colored milk	Sulphur-milk lactarius
vellĕr′eus	Lat. Fleecy	Fleecy lactarius
vō′lemus	Lat. (Doubtful. May refer to voluminous quantity of milk)	Orange-brown lactarius
Lentī′nus	Lat. Tough; pliant; flexible	
cochleā′tus	Gr. Resembling a snail shell	Shell lentinus
lepĭd′eus	Lat. Scaly	Scaly lentinus
Lepiō′ta	Lat. Scaly	
americā′na	Lat. American	American or blushing lepiota
molybdites	Lat. Lead	Lead lepiota
naucinoi′des	No translation applicable	Smooth lepiota
prō′cera	Lat. Tall	Tall lepiota; parasol lepiota
Marăs′mius	Gr. Wasting; withering; shriveling	
siccus	Lat. Dry	
orē′ades	Gr. Mountain nymphs	Fairy-ring mushroom; Scotch bonnets; champignon
peronā′tus	Lat. Booted (refers to hairy base of stem)	
plăn′cus	Lat. Flat; plane	
rō′tula	Lat. A little wheel	
Mycĕn′a	Gr. A mushroom	
galericulā′ta	Lat. Resembling a small peaked cap	
pū′ra	Lat. Pure	
Naucō′ria	Lat. A nutshell	
semiorbiculā′ris	Lat. A half sphere	Common naucoria
Omphăl′ia	Gr. Navel; umbilicus	
campanĕl′la	Lat. A small bell	
fĭb′ula	Lat. A clasp or buckle	

NAMES OF **GILLED** MUSHROOMS IN THE **KEY**—(*Continued*)

Botanical Name	Translation	Common Name
Panæ'olus	Gr. Variegated; sparkling	
campanulā'tus	Lat. Resembling a small bell	
papilionā'ceus	Lat. Resembling a butterfly	
retirū'gis	Lat. A network of wrinkles	Wrinkled panæolus
Păn'us	Lat. A name given by Pliny to a tree-growing fungus	
strigō'sus	Lat. Covered with stiff hairs	
styp'ticus	Lat. Astringent; puckery	Astringent panus
Paxĭl'lus	Lat. A small stake	
involū'tus	Lat. Rolled inward (Refers to margin of cap)	Involute paxillus
Pholiō'ta	Gr. Scaly	
adipō'sa	Lat. Fat.	Fat pholiota
caperā'ta	Lat. Wrinkled	Wrinkled pholiota; the gypsy
dĭs'color	Lat. Of different color; changing color	Fading pholiota
præ'cox	Lat. Early	Early pholiota
squarrō'sa	Lat. Scurfy; scaly	Scaly pholiota
Pleurō'tus	Lat. Side. (Refers to the marginal insertion of stem)	
ostreā'tus	Lat. Oyster-like	Oyster mushroom
să'pidus	Lat. Sapid; savory	Sapid mushroom
ulmăr'ius	Lat. Relating to the elm.	Elm pleurotus
Plū'teus	Lat. A shed. (Refers to shape of cap)	
admirăb'ilis	Lat. Admirable	
cervi'nus	Lat. A deer. (Refers to color. A misnomer)	Fawn-colored pluteus
Psathyrĕl'la	Gr. Fragile	
disseminā'ta	Lat. Scattered or spread	
grăc'ilis	Lat. Slender	
Psilō'cybe	Gr. A naked head	
fœnisĕc'ii	Lat. Of the mower	Mower's or harvest mushroom
spadicē'a	Lat. Date-brown	Bay psilocybe
Rŭs'sula	Lat. Red	
alutā'cea	Lat. Like tanned leather (color)	Tan colored russula
emĕt'ica	Lat. Emetic; nauseating	Emetic russula
fœ'tens	Lat. Fetid; evil-smelling	Fetid russula

Rŭs′sula *(cont.)*			
mariæ	Lat.	Mary's	Mary's russula
purpurī′na	Lat.	Purple	Purpurine russula
virĕs′cens	Lat.	Becoming green-greenish	Greenish russula
Schīzophyl′lum	Gr.	Split leaf (or gill)	
commū′ne	Lat.	Common	
Strophăr′ia	Lat.	A chaplet or wreath (Refers to ring on stem)	
semiglobā′ta	Lat.	Hemisphere	Hemispheric stropharia
Tricholō′ma	Gr.	A hairy fringe	
ăl′bum	Lat.	White	White tricholoma
equĕs′tre	Lat.	A horseman	Equestriantricholoma
personā′tum	Lat.	Masked	Masked tricholoma; blewits
rŭs′sula	Lat.	Red	Red tricholoma
sejŭn′ctum	Lat.	Separated	
transmū′tans	Lat.	Changing	Changing tricholoma
Volvăr′ia	Lat.	With a sheath or wrapper	
bombycī′na	Lat.	Silky	

BOTANICAL NAMES OF NON-GILLED MUSHROOMS WITH TRANSLATION, DERIVATION AND PRONUNCIATION

Botanical Name Pronunciation	*Translation*		*Common Name*
Ganodĕr′ma applanā′tum	Gr.	Varnished skin	Common shelf fungus
	Lat.	Flattened	
Poly′porus sulphurĕ′us	Gr.	Many pored	Sulphur mushroom
	Lat.	Sulphur (color)	
betuli′nus	Lat.	birch (tree)	Birch polypore
Polystĭc′tus	Gr.	Many-pitted ((microscopic pores?)	
versĭ′color	Lat.	Varied color	
Daedā′lia	Lat.	Labyrinth (of spore-holes)	
quercī′na	Lat.	Of the oak	Oak bracket fungus
Bolē′tus	Gr.	A kind of mushroom	
fĕl′leus	Lat.	Gall-like (bitter)	Bitter boletus
scā′ber	Lat.	Rough	Rough-stemmed boletus
granulā′tus	Lat.	Granular	Granular boletus
Boletī′nus	Lat.	Modified boletus	
pĭc′tus	Lat.	Painted	Painted boletinus
Strobilomy′ces floccopus	Gr.	Cone-like fungus	Pine cone mushroom
	Lat.	Tufted foot	
Fistuli′na hepăt′ica	Lat.	Small pipe	
	Gr.	Liver-like (flesh)	Beefsteak fungus
Sparăs′sis crī′spa	Gr.	Torn	
	Lat.	Curly	
Clavā′ria	Lat.	Club. (Shape of stem of some species)	
fūsifŏr′mis	Lat.	Spindle-shaped	Spindle coral mushroom
strĭc′ta	Lat.	Straight	Straight coral mushroom
flā′va	Lat.	Yellow	Yellow coral mushroom
pistillā′ris	Lat.	Pestle-shaped	
Auricularia auricularis	Lat.	Cup or jug	
	Lat.	Little ear	Jew's ear mushroom
Craterĕl′lus cornucopioi′des	Lat.	Little cup	
	Lat.	Resembling a horn of plenty	

BOTANICAL NAMES OF NON-GILLED MUSHROOMS—*continued*

Botanical Name Pronunciation	Translation	Common Name
Hyd′num	Gr. A truffle	
că′put ŭr′si	Lat. Bear's head	Bear's head fungi
repăn′dum	Lat. Wavy edge	
coralloid′es	Lat. Resembling coral	
Crucī′bulum	Lat. Crucible	
vulgā′re	Lat. Common	Bird's nest fungus
Calvā′tia	Lat. Bald head	
cyathifor′mis	Lat. Cup-shaped	Common puffball
Lycoper′don (Michaux)	Gr. Not explained. The meaning may be surmised after consulting Gr. lexicon under λυκος and περΔομαι	
gemmā′tum	Lat. Budding	
Geă′ster	Gr. Earth-star	Water measuring earth star
hygromě′tricus	Gr. Water-measuring	
Scleroder′ma	Gr. Tough-skinned	
vulgā′re	Lat. Common	
Pezī′za	Lat. A rootless, stemless mushroom, mentioned by Pliny	
bă′dia	Lat. Bay (brown)	Brown Peziza
repan′da	Lat. Wavy	
Phăl′lus	Gr. Penis	
impū′dicus	Lat. Immodest	Common stinkhorn
Mutī′nus		
canī′nus	Lat. Pertaining to a dog	
Morchěl′la	Gr. Morel	
esculěn′ta	Lat. Edible	Common morel
Gyromī′tra	Gr. Twisted turban	Brown gyromitra
brūn′nea	Lat. Brown	
Helvěl′la	Lat. A fungus referred to by Cicero	
lacunō′sa	Lat. Full of hollows	
Cord′yceps	Lat. Heart-shaped head	
militā′ris	Lat. Of a soldier	
Leō′tia	Unknown	
lū′brica	Lat. slippery	

GENERAL INDEX

GENERAL INDEX

GENERAL INDEX

GENERAL INDEX

361

GENERAL INDEX

GENERAL INDEX

363

INDEX TO BOTANICAL NAMES OF GENERA AND SPECIES OF FLESHY FUNGI

INDEX OF BOTANICAL NAMES

INDEX OF BOTANICAL NAMES